The Resigned

Lieutenant

The eyewitness account of Artillery "friendly fire" in Vietnam that ended a promising career

Jeffrey Lumbert

**ISBN-10: 1984954210
ISBN-13: 978-1984954213**

Dedicated to

The many Vietnam veterans
who did not tell their story

TABLE OF CONTENTS

INTRODUCTION

Based on events at Fire Support Base Diamond II in April of 1969 near the Cambodian Border of the Republic of South Vietnam.

This book is dedicated to the men of the Second Battalion, 27th Infantry Regiment, 25th Infantry Division (Wolfhounds) who fought with me during the massive ground attack April 16, 1969. My account of the battle is written from an eyewitness viewpoint because I was there and was wounded by beehive fleshettes fired point blank from 105mm howitzers within our own perimeter. I was wounded by "friendly fire." The incident was covered up at the time and no information can be found to this day. I was awarded a Purple Heart and Bronze Star with "V" for my actions that night and was hospitalized for ten days after the wounding. My records are blank regarding my medical treatment and hospitalization. I am covered with a service-connected disability for facial scars and loss of teeth but there is no information available regarding how I was scarred nor how I lost six teeth.

I served as an Infantry Platoon Leader during the summer of 1969 and met a fine group of young men who accepted me as their leader. I came under suspicion of dereliction of duty and rebelled. The remainder of my second tour in Vietnam was as described, although I admit to embellishing certain areas of this narrative where my memory was not explicitly clear. I did become a larcenous disrespectful misfit and briefly served as the Officer-in-Charge of half the perimeter of Cu Chi Base Camp late in 1969.

I was sent to a fire base near the city of Tay Ninh after punching out a Korean civilian and was reprimanded by the Commanding General of the 25th Infantry Division for being a discipline problem and conducting myself in a manner unfitting for an Officer. I painted a room in a newly constructed Bachelor Officers Quarters flat black as a token of my disrespect and rebellion.

I resigned my commission as an Officer in the United States Army on February 7, 1970, while in Vietnam, and received an honorable discharge. I received another honorable discharge certificate in Oakland three days later. If I am not the only one, I speculate I am among a very small group of combat Officers who have resigned while serving in a combat zone. The clause read, in effect, that I resigned my commission "for the good of the service." I was an unacceptable officer but the Army had no definite reason to court martial me. My decisions were clear at the time and my position remains the same to this day: given the circumstances, I sometimes put the welfare of my men above the accomplishment of the mission. I believed the justification, the stated purpose and the general conduct of the war was futile. History has shown this belief to have been correct.

I fought the war when I could find it. My men fought the war whenever possible. When the enemy was not visible and men were being shredded and killed by booby traps, alternative plans became necessary for simple survival. There was a morale problem and I was not part of the solution.

The characters presented here are based on actual soldiers. I have altered their names when I could remember them. This is not an autobiography, though written in the first person point of view. This work is an explanation of the effects of the war in Vietnam and the life changes engendered by individual experiences in that war. This is an attempt to elucidate inner dialogues and emotional responses during wartime and during the first several years after returning home. This book is a naked attempt to answer the question: "what happened to you guys?" (That we seemed so disturbed when we returned).

I have no intention of portraying any man in uniform in a negative manner and this is not a condemnation of the US Army or the efforts in Vietnam. Very little research was done in the preparation of this manuscript so technical or descriptive errors are acknowledged at the outset. The principle story is true. Some aspects are inserted as hyperbole for effect. Portions of this manuscript are fiction. No further explanation is offered so as to not nullify the effect on the reader. Other combat veterans can understand. Truth is stranger than fiction and poetic license is my inspiration and my justification. This is my truth. It is not the whole truth and it is damn sure not nothing but the truth. It is just my story.

TO THE UNITED STATES ARMY RANGERS WHO TRULY ARE ALL THAT THEY CAN BE

CHAPTER I

The Ranger

First tour of Vietnam

I felt a vague sense of unease as I stomped my brand new Harley-Davidson to life. Maybe whatever thrills might happen on this long-coveted machine would not match the intense experiences I had just been through in Vietnam. Pausing for a moment as the Sportster rumbled between my thighs, I wondered about a heavy feeling in my chest – a feeling of emptiness, of nothing being important or even interesting. I Cranked the throttle a couple of times to focus on the matter at hand, indifferent to any neighbors who might still be asleep at six in the morning, then headed north out of San Antonio on highway 281. At the edge of town I leaned over to grasp the throttle-grip firmly at the base of my palm then slammed the shifter down into third and rolled that throttle wide open and held it there. Reaching 90mph I power-shifted to fourth gear and lay on the gas tank trying to focus on the vibrating needle as it passed 110. The speedometer needle never quite touched 120.

Easing back down to 60mph, I felt deeply disappointed in realizing the bike had a top speed of only about 117mph. There had always seemed something special about that 120 mark – the highest speedometer reading in most vehicles at the time, and I really expected the Sportster to make it. I could not understand why I felt so unfairly cheated and was uncomfortably resigned to owning a bike that did not go as fast as expected.

I had returned from Vietnam about a month previous, in the fall of 1968, indecorously sent all the way back to Ft. Sam Houston Army Medical Center in my home town of San Antonio for minor knee surgery. The injury had been lightly referred to as a "football knee"- a tear in the medial meniscus cartilage due to extreme flexion with outward rotation of the foot. The orthopedic Doctor said it would be almost as good as new in a few weeks. I was released from the hospital about a week later by performing a deep knee bend without much stiffness or pain. Though carrying ten stitches along a two inch incision on the inside of my left knee, I was not proud of my scar from the war; but felt cheated out of my job as an Infantry soldier and depressed at the fact of having failed as a tough combat-ready Ranger.

During the stay at the hospital I had isolated myself as I had during the three weeks of waiting and shuttling from Vietnam to Japan to the US. Isolation seemed natural since Officers generally did not associate with Enlisted men and most of the other patients were from the Enlisted ranks. My acute sense of failure was the deeper reason for isolating myself. I felt embarrassed when among the men recovering from what presumably were real combat wounds. Isolated, nobody seemed to notice my depression nor my self-critical internal conversation: *I don't even belong on the "walking-wounded" list with these guys...what am I?...the walking-injured?"* Struggling against disappointment or regaining self-esteem never occurred to me at that time. I thought a new motorcycle might help me feel better.

When I could walk well enough to swing my good leg over it I paid $1725 cash for the motorcycle I wanted ever since owning my first Honda 50 at age 14. I bought a Harley-Davidson Sportster XLCH, black in color. It suited my mood exactly. It was the last model made in the "old" way with the magneto advance on the left grip, no electric starter, and no frills whatsoever. An XLCH was an 883cc engine, a gas tank, two wheels, and the barest of necessary controls. I loved that bike from day one.

On day two a careless idiot pulled out of a side street right in front of me and I slammed into the side of the car, a VW squareback. I struck my chin on the roof, somersaulted over the car and landed on my sacrum on the asphalt. My immediate concern, after pressing my lacerated chin together, was for my bike that was still chugging away laying on its side with the front end crushed, 236 miles on the odometer.

My younger brother riding on the back of the bike had been thrown clear of the car and landed unhurt on a grassy lawn. We had only been going about 20mph after just leaving a stop light and had almost stopped after jamming on both brakes. "Are you hurt man," he asked.

"Yeah. Turn off the bike Phil and help me up. I'm going to punch this moron before the cops get here," I answered, fully intending to do just that. *This son-of-a-bitch doesn't know who he just messed with,* I thought. *I'm a Ranger goddamnit, I'll kick your ass.* My association with the Rangers, though brief, had left an indelible influence on me. Impressed with their toughness and combat readiness, I was prone to overcompensate back in the civilian world due to having failed to live up to the Ranger ideal.

The driver of the VW was a really upset young college student though, and he started profusely apologizing, saying the sun was in his eyes and he was at fault. I could not bring myself to just sucker punch the poor guy. The police soon arrived at the scene and expressed appropriate grief over the motorcycle as we waited for an ambulance to arrive. I was not seriously hurt. I was fortunate to have been wearing a helmet at the time and it was deeply scraped and scratched. One of the cops told the ambulance attendant I was in the Army so they transported me back to Ft. Sam Hospital at no charge. After a set of X-rays and a benevolent "tsk-tsk" at possible damage to the knee, the Doctors pulled my chin together with ten stitches and sent me home. *That makes twenty-two stitches in two locations...a new personal record* I thought sardonically when leaving the hospital. I was still on my 30 day leave after returning from an overseas duty station. The motorcycle was taken back to the dealer for repairs thanks to my brother who had stayed at the scene.

My "home" was not the last of the many houses we had lived in when I was growing up. My Father had died suddenly of a first-time heart attack which was misdiagnosed by the family Doctor when I was in training at Ft. Sill only five months into my enlistment. Since that surprising and catastrophic event my Mother had closed a very successful real estate business she had spent ten years developing. She was unable to cope with the shock of the sudden loss of her husband of thirty years. My older sister had moved to Dallas and my younger brother had become a daily marijuana smoker and was in constant danger of being sent to prison. There was nothing familiar for me to come home to. My Mother and brother now lived in a small apartment near the high school. We had always lived in houses that my Mom had bought and sold after my Dad and I had painted and repaired them. Now all that was gone. I felt lost and completely out of touch in my own hometown. Everything seemed so different than it was in 1966 when I had enlisted almost two years before.

My brother had been driving and maintaining my '65 Ford Fairlane for about ten months while I was in Officers' Candidate School, Airborne training and Ranger school. The car showed the ravages of teenage driving and stoned mishaps on almost every fender and door panel. "What the hell have you been doing to my car, Phil," I asked when he showed up at the hospital to take me home after the surgery. I had the tolerance to have not mentioned anything upon arrival several days previous.

"Just driving around getting stoned, man," came the unabashed reply.

And soon we two brothers were doing exactly that – driving around smoking pot. I had never smoked cigarettes while growing up and had never even seen marijuana, though I traveled with a rowdy crowd in high school. I never liked being drunk and had been sick on a few occasions after drinking too much alcohol and feeling tipsy or dizzy. Being an athlete, I had generally been the most sober of whatever group I hung out with. Being stoned on marijuana was different though because it helped me relax, relate, laugh, and have fun; very unlike a military life devoted to serious training and accomplishment of goals and objectives.

My brother enjoyed knowing about something big brother did not, so I allowed for the introduction into the "head scene" and the music and beads and bangles of hippydom. It was an interesting and amusing diversion from military life at the time. Always conscious of the fact of being a soldier on leave, however, I was proud to be in the Army and very proud to be an Officer in the Airborne Rangers. There were no second thoughts about having served in Vietnam, however briefly.

There were no encounters with any strong antiwar sentiments from anyone during that 30 day leave after my brief first tour; but there was an awkward pause when it was revealed I was just back from Vietnam.

"Oh wow, man...what was it like?" some long-haired freak would ask, just as bleary-eyed serious as he could be. There was no comprehensible answer. I did not know how to respond to such questions on the rare occasions they came up. So the hippy did not find out what it was like. A minor knee injury had ended a brief experience in Vietnam. I could not tell these young kids that, so the answer was usually something like, "oh bad, man. I'm glad to be back.

But I was not glad to be back. There was only acute disappointment; and due to familial changes, deep feelings of being rootless and homeless. It was impossible to sort out these vague sentiments. Undoubtedly the loss of my father had something to do with my current discomfort...the overall sense of failure and confusion. I had not done very much in the war and there was nobody to talk to about what little I had done. My dad would have understood and probably offered some consolation and appreciation. When, as a young volunteer soldier, I had called home to report my acceptance to Officers Candidate School (OCS) my Father had expressed so much pride and confidence in me that there was never a moment of doubt about my future in the Army. Now for the first time serious doubts had arisen as to whether I was suited for the military and the one person whose opinion was needed was no longer available.

The city of San Antonio was home to three Air Force bases and Ft. Sam Houston Army Base so I had many friends throughout my youth whose fathers were career military men. I enlisted with a good friend from high school whose father was an E8 First Sergeant in the Army. My enlistment in 1966 was driven more by a thirst for adventure than a pure patriotic duty to my country. Restless and undecided regarding college or work, I had joined the Army. The main enlistment "guarantee" was to be considered for Airborne training and I had a definite interest in the newly created Special Forces. I approached a three - year enlistment with all the personal zeal and trust in institutions that most college freshmen probably had towards a university degree program.

I had been very serious and committed during all the initial tests the Army had required and was completely enmeshed in the military buildup of the time. No serious thought occurred regarding the possibility of being sent to defend a tiny Asian nation. If asked about my political views I would have been hard-pressed to make a definitive statement. I believed in my country. My Father had fought in WWII and one of my Mother's brothers had been killed in 1944 while bombing Nazi Germany. As a soldier, I had felt increasing levels of self-esteem in my attainments and experiences. But sustaining such a minor injury had opened a window of doubt.

I excelled in Basic Training by scoring a perfect 500 on the physical conditioning test – no small athletic feat and seldom accomplished on the first try in Basic. My self-imposed exercise regimen started when I was seven years old learning Judo at the

YMCA and later included every muscle building course from George F. Jowette and Charles Atlas materials ordered from the back pages of Superman Comics to serious weight training during my high school years. I had been a regular daily exerciser for most of my life and was gifted with fast reflexes and a healthy metabolism. However, to the chagrin of the coaches in high school, I had disdained team sports after Little League baseball at age 12, preferring my own exercise program to being prodded by a coach and evidently lacking in "school spirit."

I was somewhat surprised at the scores on aptitude and intelligence tests administered prior to my enlistment. Just drifting through school making A's and B's by just glancing at the books and showing up for classes, I knew I was blessed with above average intelligence; but had never seen explicit test scores before. There were very high aptitudes in many areas and an overall IQ of 128, creating an opportunity by default... intelligent but not well educated, from a small city where there was no strong antiwar sentiment, and physically fit and willing.

The unfit and the unwilling would easily avoid the military altogether and the well-educated would often encourage them to do so in that particular war. Those who lived in large metropolitan areas had already been influenced by war protests at major universities; but in 1966 most of middle-class America held the some political views as their parents. I fit into a chute of rapid advancement along with other naive small-town boys at the time –

looking for action, numb and unsuspecting, unaware of personal mortality, and automatically loyal to country.

Once my Sportster was repaired I spent the remainder of my leave time driving around San Antonio feeling disconnected and wondering how everything could have changed so much in just a little over two years. I began to look forward to reporting in at my next duty station, Ft. Hood Texas, but felt more and more uncomfortable about my brief first tour in Vietnam. What justification could there be for wearing an overseas stripe having only been in-country for less that a month? How would I tell my story? What would others think of my being in charge, not having seen any form of real combat? What would experienced combat soldiers think of me? I was disappointed in myself since failing to be tough enough to serve with the Rangers...since being sent home with a minor injury. The fact that I could wear a Ranger tab on my uniform was no consolation for missing out on what I knew was the major defining event of my generation – the war in Vietnam. I did not wish to be excused for an injury.

I remember driving along at a steady 60mph after the obligatory high-speed test and thinking about the Rangers, wondering who in my prior outfit was out in the bush on a mission right then...that very minute. On the way at last to report in at Ft. Hood Texas, my next duty station, I fell into a reverie while following the turns of the highway and imagined flying in a helicopter again. I remembered swooping down a valley, the foliage rushing by, and when zooming over a rise in the highway I imagined popping over a hillock in a chopper and seeing upturned peasant faces in conical hats. I got a chill remembering the chopper flaring out to land and leave me and five other men alone in the jungle...a long-range recon patrol. My imagination substituted the rumble of the Harley for the chattering an M-60 machine gun. My mind to drifted back to the time I had flown in to extract a team that had a man killed by sniper fire and had to wait all night with their dead buddy until they could be extracted. The door gunner had opened up with a burst of 100 rounds – about 10 seconds worth – just to make sure the Vietcong or NVA (North Vietnam Army) would keep their heads down if they were still in the vicinity. It was a powerful memory for a 20 year-old to have. It had only been about eight weeks earlier when I was a Ranger in Vietnam, one of the Army's finest.

The realization suddenly hit me to return to Vietnam. I could not stand the thought of someone replacing me over there. I had learned to handle the job and wanted to fulfill my obligation. It was a decision based as much on personal pride as on a possible career in the military. Even at that young age I was conscious of the fact that the Army had instilled a high level of personal pride in me. There was no recognition of how vulnerable I had become by tying my self-worth – my name – with my rank and service number. Perhaps that is part of what made me a good soldier at that stage of my development. And I was a good soldier.

Approaching my post as one of the youngest Company Commanders in the Army – a First Lieutenant only twenty years and six months of age – I was mentally composing a letter to resign from that post and volunteer to serve another tour in Vietnam. A thrill hit me leaning into a 40mph curve at 60mph, confident that the signs had been designed for 1950's automobiles, and accelerating through the bend in the highway my mind raced ahead. *Oh yeah...I can go back. They are using up infantry lieutenants pretty fast over there.* The memories of my brief tour with the Rangers flooded in so vividly that, though riding a motorcycle in Texas, I was mentally reliving each day with the Rangers.

My tour of duty with the Rangers of F Company, 50th Infantry, 25th Infantry Division had lasted only 29 days and had been the most exciting and memorable weeks of my life. I was a young man who had had my share of excitement growing up. I had flown around the Southwest in small airplanes with my Father since infancy and had illegally soloed at only fifteen years old, too young for even a student ticket – the first step in licensing as a private pilot. I had been an accomplished swimmer, scuba diver, and acrobatic high diver able to perform assorted feats off 40ft. cliffs, 10 meter platforms, or 3 meter springboards. I once ran a hundred yard dash in 9.8 seconds. I had been involved in numerous high-speed auto and motorcycle escapades while growing up half wild in San Antonio and had loved jumping out of perfectly good airplanes during Airborne School – something most pilots would insist was the height of stupidity. And I had enjoyed the added tension of using a standard Army parachute casually tossed from a pile in a warehouse ten minutes before takeoff. But the assignment with the Long-Range-Reconnaissance-Patrol Rangers had been the ultimate – a whole different category of thrill.

Remembering first entering the compound of F Company, 50[h] Infantry, I could recall the 30ft. rappelling tower that demarcated the Rangers' territory. They were off to themselves within the sprawling Cu Chi Base Camp and they had a very specialized mission to perform. They functioned as "LURPS" - Long-Range Reconnaissance Patrols, sending out six-man teams into remote areas where there were no other US or South Vietnamese forces. The teams concealed themselves in dense thickets and remained silent and watchful day and night for several days at a time. It was the only way to gain information about the movements and regular activities of the local peasants and it was one reliable way to observe the movements of enemy troops and supplies. It was also a very dangerous method of information gathering; but the Rangers did not mind danger – it was their middle name.

As an idealistic green Second Lieutenant I found the 18-20 men who comprised my Platoon to be quietly confident in themselves, as well they should be. They had already survived missions requiring the avoidance of booby-traps, snakes, and all manner of nightly jungle horrors, while observing the enemy from a concealed position. They had successfully operated as guerrilla forces harassing a larger enemy force in an arena the enemy knew intimately but in which they were total strangers. At first glimpse, these men looked like some very serious soldiers. On closer inspection they looked even more serious and decidedly dangerous. They carried conspicuous personal knives and other weaponry at all times as they sauntered about the base camp wearing jaunty black berets and they carried some very advanced armaments and equipment into the field. They were the Elite of the US Army and they well knew it. I was mildly intimidated, felt unsure of myself and overwhelmed by the idea of being assigned as the leader of these seasoned serious soldiers.

After meeting these men, I found myself uncomfortably struck by one of the many peculiarities of the Vietnam War. Being the "newby", the "cherry" - the most recent arrival, I was supposedly in charge. Obviously these men had already been performing their job before my arrival and as a perceptive young Platoon Leader I was in full and uncomfortable realization of the fact of not having any idea what the hell was going on. So there commenced a week of humbly acquainting myself with my surroundings and earnestly seeking my role - my job. I felt unprepared on many levels because most of the training had presupposed leading men I had already trained with on a mission that was understood beforehand. Here, I did not know the men and uncomfortably realized a complete lack in understanding the mission. It was a very humbling experience with the Rangers from the start.

I tried to look calm and strong during introductions during the next several days; but was inwardly awestruck by the scent of war on these men. I was dazed by the reality of actually being there in Vietnam and that these were "my" men. The training was over and this was the War. *Holy shit, what do I do?* A mere two years training was insufficient. I was probably too young to be in such a position of authority and leadership and ardently hoped these men realized how incapable I might be. I was surprised to be assigned to a Ranger unit since I had sprained my ankle and knee in the fifth week of training and could not continue. I did not graduate from Ranger School. Perhaps the assignment clerk overlooked this fact and just saw the word "Ranger" on the list of schools attended.

I had been prepared to start the Training all over again; but instead had been sent to Vietnam. Hopefully these experienced soldiers would not rely on me for anything important right away. I did not know that most of these men already doubted my capabilities and newby lieutenants were the subject of jokes and derision as a matter of course. I had no real idea of the enormous and difficult mountain to be climbed before gaining even a modicum of respect. I had to trust in guidance by the experienced NCO's (non-commissioned officers - Sergeants) though, knowing that they had already seen many green Second Lieutenants trip, stumble, bumble and fall through their area of operation in the past. OCS did not prepare me for the amount of automatic distrust and derision I faced when assigned to a combat unit.

I was assigned to the 82nd Airborne at Ft. Bragg after graduating from Jump School but was the assistant S-4 Officer instead of a Platoon Leader because they were going through a period of intensive inventory and requisitioning prior to being shipped out to Vietnam. There was little contact with the combat soldiers during that period so I was not aware of the disrespect and suspicions of incompetence that were directed towards new Lieutenants. From this assignment I went to Ranger School and the 82nd Airborne went to Vietnam.

I received guidance from Captain Richards, the Company Commander, who told me to trust in my NCO's; and the E8 First Sergeant. "Top", as First Sergeants were generally referred to, was about as tough a man as I had ever met. His face was like chiseled granite, his eyes the color of a gun barrel. His thin smile betrayed no humor. Top Sergeant E8 Reynolds had been engaged in serious ground combat in Korea when I was a three year old pedaling a tricycle down the sidewalk. We got along well from the start though, because we both acknowledged the above facts – a Lieutenant showing respect and awe and a "top" Sergeant showing a paternal interest in all his troops, even newby Lieutenants. In the course of my orientation I would become acquainted with the Supply Sergeant, the Company Clerk, and the RTO's (radio telephone operators). I immediately felt immense respect for every one of them. They were Rangers.

After a week or so I began to understand my duties and responsibilities. It was disappointing to realize that my main jobs involved planning, training and logistics. A Platoon Leader in the LURPs did not normally go out on the missions. He studied the AO (area of operation) and sometimes accompanied the Captain to meetings with Division level officers. A Platoon Leader merely conveyed directives back to the Platoon level then coordinated with the Artillery and helicopter support units while his men were "out in the bush". He was also responsible for conducting a continuous training program within the Company, facilitating improvements based on each prior mission. A Lieutenant sat in the radio room when one of his teams was out on a mission, listening to cryptic clickings of handsets and whispered reports. I observed my Platoon Sergeant, E6 Beeson supervise several missions from the commo room and became more familiar with that aspect of the job.

Sgt. E6 Clyde Beeson was from a small town in Indiana and grew up in a farming family. He was quiet and serious and almost always had his nose in some type of technical manual. He liked to ask obscure questions like, "do you know how many foot pounds of torque you should use to tighten the lug nuts on the wheels of a deuce and a half?" or "do you know which car had the first automatic transmission?" He knew. He would ask and answer these questions with a look of boyish wonderment on his face. When it came to the missions though, he was serious, precise, and did not allow for any small talk or bullshit. He had total respect from the men. They would follow his orders and recommendations to the letter. Every time.

I was in the radio room one evening with Beeson at dusk waiting for the SITREP (situation report) from a team inserted that morning. The team leader reported on schedule, just before dark, and requested to coordinate a move to a prearranged alternate location. "Probably thinks they might have been spotted going in," Beeson reasoned. The exact location of a team was carefully planned and coordinated with other units – the artillery for instance – so a change entailed more than just "getting permission." It had to be coordinated. Beeson remarked it was too late in the day for this shit because an unscheduled move or possible extraction was damn near impossible. He instructed the RTO to give them a "proceed" message, which was transmitted by prearranged clicks of the microphone button.

About half an hour later as the team was carefully packing and preparing to move, they came under sporadic small-arms fire and one man was immediately hit. The team leader called in, no whispering this time, "we're taking fire...need dust-off, over!" I cringed inwardly at hearing the intense firing over the radio. I could barely understand what was said. I was supposedly "in charge" of this mission and Sgt. Beeson was present to observe the new Lieutenant in his first official supervision of a patrol in the bush.

I took the handset from the RTO and replied to the team leader, "roger on the dust-off. Stand by for possible extraction, over." I glanced at the dubious look on Beeson's face as I called the First Air Cavalry for a Medivac chopper and to attempt to get an unscheduled immediate extraction of the team. Much to my chagrin, annoyance and vexation, I was told that "things were awful busy" at the moment but maybe a chopper could be dispatched later when the area was secured – in other words, when the shooting stopped. They would not usually fly into a "hot LZ (landing zone)" especially when it was almost dark. There was no sense risking a valuable helicopter with its crew of three or four to pick up one wounded guy in a hot LZ at night...sorry.

I saw the look of acceptance on Sgt. Beeson's face regarding the Medivac, so immediately called the Artillery to order a prearranged bombardment around the team. I called the Air Cav again and requested a cobra gunship to the area but got a "wait one" message, so I had to just sit there with a feeling of horrific uselessness after doing everything I could think of. I looked at my experienced Platoon Sergeant and made a gesture of questioning, wondering if there was something else to do. Beeson said nothing and his look of grim acceptance was answer enough. There was nothing else to do as a dismayed Lieutenant and a gritty Sergeant sat there thinking about their men being shot up. The Sergeant probably mentally reliving a dozen firefights he had survived during 20 months of deployment and the Lieutenant imagining possibly equally chilling spectacles.

We sat there smoking cigarettes and slurping oily military-strength coffee while looking at the radio steadily as if we could create the next transmission by our undivided attention. The team was fighting for their lives. Every minute of waiting to hear from them was excruciatingly slow in passing. Finally the team leader reported the firing had ceased; the Artillery had done an excellent job walking the rounds right up to the team without hitting them and a Cobra gunship had shown up and fired several rockets into a nearby treeline with accuracy. He further reported that the wounded man had died, so there was no need for a Medivac. It was strange to feel relieved and kicked in the gut at the same time, but that about summed up the internal state of this young Lieutenant at that moment. I felt a confusing combination of emotions: relief, dread, shock, dismay, and a mild personal pride, to name just a few. I coordinated the extraction flight at dawn, then the good Sergeant invited me to his quarters for a drink. The time was 0130.

Later that night I sat alone in my quarters as an initiated combat Platoon Leader, speculating on war and philosophizing on the history of warfare as I imagined other young and inexperienced officers in the past might have done, sadly reflecting on war as they awaited the dawn of yet another day of it...as they awaited meeting their troops coming in from the real fighting. I felt for the first time the great sorrow of war. I felt pure undiluted grief over the sad and relentless loss of life and limb. The plain fact that men die in a war was now clearly realized. Gazing out the window at the familiar military environs: the trucks and jeeps, the exercise fields and buildings, I realized another chilling fact. These familiar sights were set in a most unfamiliar setting. It was a hot, hostile, deadly, inscrutable land where legs and lives were lost and Lieutenants wrote letters to parents explaining that Johnnie was coming home in a box. I sipped a single shot of scotch at about 0200, wondering what it felt like to be sitting out there in the jungle with your dead buddy lying there, not even knowing for certain the location or extent of his wounds until daylight came hours later.

I reflected on the value of the helicopter as an advantage in Vietnam. I knew, from flying around in small airplanes with my father, that there was no way anyone could safely fly into a dense jungle at night. "Charlie" owned the jungle at night and all we could do was hunker down, bunker in, and wait. But the Vietcong and the North Vietnamese Regulars could move at night. They would move men and equipment quietly through the jungle guided by local peasants who knew every footpath and trail. And furthermore Charles usually knew where we were, but we seldom knew where he was. It was frustrating at times, just trying to locate the enemy. It was even more frustrating when Charlie located the Rangers, an essential part of whose mission was stealth and concealment. It was more that just a little embarrassing when a team of six lost their advantage, such as it was, over numerically superior forces. The helicopter then became the means of escape; the alternative being called "escape and evasion" - fleeing through the jungle on foot.

Despite the recent loss of a good man, I could not help feeling a sense of accomplishment at having played my part to the maximum. I had personally given orders in wartime. I had responded with appropriate decisions on behalf of my Rangers and felt proud to be a part of the elite brotherhood. I finally felt like a real Ranger and that was very satisfying.

The sorrow of war, though, the human loss and suffering, was an experience that would be with me for the rest of my life. I had a disturbing image of a life unfolding in a series of instances in which I sat sorrowfully awaiting an outcome, resigned to acceptance of losses even though I had done everything that could be done. But I shook off the feeling of "being resigned to losses" - it was a disgusting and erroneous military expression. I vowed to do everything possible to execute every plan and procedure with serious precision. The least I could do was to insure that no mistakes were made due to ignorance, laziness or indecision. Naiveté allowed me to feel temporarily comfortable with this mindset.

I had already heard about some missions gone awry because the Officer(s) in charge did not know what they were doing or made a bad decision. There were also stories of such incompetence leading to those officers being "fragged" during a mortar or rocket attack – a disgusted errant soldier tossing a fragmentation grenade in the wrong direction. I thought at the time that such stories were extremely rare if they occurred at all. Sometimes there were causalities in a war, no getting around that, but allowing for causalities due to mistakes or laziness? *No way! Not on my shift.*

In the gray light of early dawn I maintained radio communication with the team as we flew out in the extraction chopper. After a minute of high circling the pilot spotted a yellow smoke grenade thrown out by the team and correctly identified the color to the Team leader, thus negating the possibility that sneaky

Charlie was monitoring the radio and had thrown out his own smoke grenade to lure the helicopter in for an ambushed landing. The pilot swooped down to land in a small clearing. The five Rangers hoisted their dead buddy out of the bushes and hustled over to board. As they neared the Huey the door-gunner opened up with his M-60 spraying the nearby treeline in case any VC remained. The team quickly scrambled aboard and I helped pull the dreadfully heavy – surprisingly heavy – body across the corrugated floor of the Huey and pile packs and gear around it.

The team leader shouted over the engine noise, "they saw us when we came in, sir, the fuckin' pilot put us in without any evasion!" He was flamingly angry...furiously mad as he continued, "why didn't we get a Medivac? It was still light enough when we called in and Charlie split when the artillery started coming in...aw fuck!" He put his crimson face in his trembling hands and took some deep breaths. He knew the score. He knew they might not fly into a hot LZ when it was almost dark for one wounded man...even a Ranger.

The distraught team leader, Sgt. E5 Marquez, disgustedly half-listened as an embarrassed Lieutenant tried to answer his rhetorical question. Marquez was not known to be easy-going. He was tough, rough, and ready for a fight or an argument anytime, anyplace. You definitely wanted him on your side in any confrontation. "The Medivacs were busy...lots of contact yesterday...then it was too late...too dark, "came the paltry reply from the remorseful Lieutenant. Sgt. Marquez grunted and glared at the young officer, knowing it was probably true. There was nobody to blame. Shit happens and one of his team members died. Fuck. He watched the new Lieutenant turn aside, probably to hide his own confusion and anger. He realized this Officer was still totally inexperienced though, and he could not help wondering whether there <u>had</u> been a way some other Officer could have <u>ordered</u> a chopper to respond and pick up the wounded man or evacuate the whole team. Lt. Lumbert quelled an impulse to explain he had done all he could. He wisely said nothing more. The Lieutenant was fighting a feeling of physical nausea in addition to the mental and emotional strife of the moment.

They flew back to Cu Chi with the bloody shitty-smelling corpse laying there on the floor of the Huey wedged in place by their boots and gear. Lt. Lumbert could not stop himself from watching in morbid fascination as one of the boots with a dead foot in it flopped one way, then the other, as the chopper banked and turned during the flight. It was the first dead man he had seen. The body was a former member of his Platoon – one of <u>his</u> men. He could not even remember for certain what the man's name was. It was a decidedly inauspicious beginning to his supervision of the Rangers.

When we arrived at the Company HQ, Buck Sergeant Marquez was still flaming mad as he demanded of the Company Commander, the First Sergeant, and anybody else within earshot, "why didn't we get a Medivac last night goddamnit?...the fuckin' insertion pilot didn't do any pop-ups at all...just sailed right into the middle of a clearing and yelled for us to exit...we weren't even in the right field...he put down almost right beside the fuckin' village!" And as he ranted on and on and his Officers listened, one of those Officers decided then and there to go have a talk with these chopper pilots and tell them a thing or two. Their new Lieutenant decided to march right into their territory and tell them what's what when they are flying for the Rangers. *Damn!*

The pilots were supposed to make several apparent landings and swoop around a bit to disguise where the team got out. I rehearsed my diatribe to myself and my jeep driver as we proceeded over to the First Air Cav. "When you fly a mission for the Rangers, you do it <u>our</u> way!" My driver nodded his assent at this obvious assertion. Oh I was going to tell them all right.

My little speech was immediately squashed by the First Sergeant over at the airfield, who broke right in, interrupting me. "Well lieutenant, I tell ya, I would let you in to see the old man (the Colonel) but I have to warn you he doesn't listen to any happy horseshit from the Infantry – even Rangers...and anyway he's out on the flight line kicking ass and preparing to fly a mission his own damn self 'cause we're awful busy right now, sir. Is there anything else Lieutenant?" And without waiting for a response after saying the word "Lieutenant" like he was hawking up a gob of phlegm, he executed the vaguest suggestion of a salute and promptly turned and walked into an inner office and closed the door, leaving me and my complaints hanging in midair. The First Air Calvary definitely thought they were top-notch...hot shit...number one.

I was somewhat taken aback by his abrupt and sarcastic manner, so I sought counsel with my own First Sergeant, the steely-eyed E8 Reynolds. "Well L T," he replied, initiating a familiarity by using the common nickname for Lieutenants, "I tell ya...there've been some liaison problems between us and the Cav, especially since Tet." (Chinese New Year celebration)

"But what's the sense of us practicing and rehearsing a maneuver when the pilots won't do it?" I persisted.

"Well some of them do and some of them don't. That's about all I can tell you, sir. There's not much I can do about it," Top said with a shrug.

The First Sergeant looked at the Lieutenant and thought that Lumbert might be inexperienced in some respects, but one thing he should have learned during his two years of training was that the day-to-day Army was run by the Sergeants – not the Colonels, not the Generals. And furthermore, he hoped Lumbert knew that a green Second Lieutenant was no more than a bothersome gnat to a seasoned First Sergeant. And if a young Officer had any sense at all he would accord any First Sergeant the utmost of respect and courtesy even though the Top saluted him and called him "sir" occasionally as per military etiquette. *I certainly hope Lumbert gives some serious thought to what I just said and doesn't go back to the Cav and get himself into any trouble.*

To my chagrin, I began to realize the realities of this war were much different than anything that had been taught in training.

I once again faced the uncomfortable realization that I was still wondering about my role in this unfamiliar milieu.

I had only been in-country for about three weeks and already had heard about the Tet offensive the previous spring when the "gooks" had overrun most of the base camps in the whole country, including popping out of tunnels and trapdoors all over Cu Chi Base Camp. And I had heard reports of teams attacked and wiped out completely by large forces of NVA Regulars that the Rangers had "discovered" sneaking through the jungle. Then in one case the local villagers had mutilated the bodies beyond recognition and left them in plain sight to be discovered by rescue personnel. There was a report of a team inserted near the Cambodian border – a team of six experienced men – and never heard from again. I wondered what one of my predecessors might have written to the families of the men who were gone without a trace. I hoped that situation would never arise. There were also instances of a team being hit by our own artillery with random interdictory fire at night because the OIC (Officer-in-Charge) had not clearly indicated or communicated the exact position of all the ambush sites and recon patrols to the Artillery. And to me, meticulous by nature, the whole affair seemed terribly uncoordinated, even chaotic. I had a lot to learn, some of which would undoubtedly be unsettling and unpleasant. And I knew that what I knew was a mere fraction of all the unknown possibilities. I felt very inadequate...small, ignorant and untrained. I resolved to keep my eyes open, my head up, and my listening keenly alert. I demanded of myself the utmost of my learning capabilities. I would survive.

I began to listen more closely at planning sessions between the Captain and the Division level Officers and was appalled at how little was actually known regarding the location and strength of the enemy forces; how they moved so much equipment through the jungle; or even, for instance, how many Divisions of NVA Regulars were out there right that very minute within a few miles of Cu Chi Base Camp. Not to mention the incredibly vast underground as yet unexplored city of tunnels right under our feet. Vast areas on the map were completely blank regarding these and other relevant questions and the prevailing attitude and tactical plan was to send out enough men into the jungle and the villages to eventually bump into the enemy forces then blast the hell out of them with all the technology and weaponry in the most advanced and devastating arsenal in the world. I thought this seemed a rather haphazard game plan, if it could be called a plan at all. After further consideration I felt justified concern that some of the "players" in this obscure game plan were my men and the "game" was a real war where men were being killed and mutilated. Even the non-wounded were being changed forever in what I now considered to be a possibly unwinnable fiasco.

It was more than a little disconcerting to realize that the other Officers at these meetings seemed to consider men as being expendable as long as the war was being won – as long as somehow at the end of the week the body-count statistics contained more of "them" than "us." Then I was struck by the fact of being not only one of the commanders who attended meetings, but was also one of the men who were expendable. This realization evoked the question of whether or not we were actually winning the war in Vietnam – a question that, oddly enough, in all my months of training I had never seriously considered. Now I pondered: are we winning the war?...what exactly are we winning, if anything...should we even be here at all? These musings brought up another obvious question that slid obliquely into my mind: what happened to the guy I replaced, by the way? I also wondered why that particular personal question had not occurred previously. There were more and more questions and fewer answers.

I felt the need to know more about the conduct of the war and with this objective in mind decided to go out on a mission with the men as soon as possible...as soon as they think I am ready. This decision stemmed purely from the "need to know" level of military jargon and was in no way due to bravado on my part. I felt the need to know what was happening out in the bush when I was back at HQ on the radio or flying around in the insertion or extraction helicopters. I was once again awake deep into the night thinking about these and other issues. My training did not cover the heretical questioning of superior officers nor these personal doubts as to the advisability of invading this country to begin with. Evidently I had not been thoroughly indoctrinated into military thinking.

The next day I asked Top casually, "Hey First Sergeant, what happened to the Platoon Leader before me? What kind of job did he do?"

"He was a fine young officer, L T, just like yourself...did a good job here. He went out on three or four missions, stayed up all night listening to SITREPS...he was here about six months then rotated to Division. I heard he made "first louie" and he just signs papers now," said the Top Sergeant with a sly grin and a good-natured chuckle. "You're about due for your first mission sometime soon aren't you Lieutenant Lumbert?"

"Yeah, I think so. I need to know more about what actually goes on out there," I said casually. "I'm sure this next mission could use an extra man since it's so far out in the boonies. The rumor is we might even put in with eight men."

"That's what we were thinking, the squad leaders and myself...to maybe put in with eight and for you to be one of them, sir. It'll probably mean two choppers so I will have to arrange that if possible," Top said with an encouraging wink.

So, I've been voted in by the guys...wow...I'm about to go on a mission out by the Cambodian border! I tried to mask my excitement from Top's knowing look as he continued, "Better get with the Supply Sarn't, sir, make sure your shit's together."

The Supply "Sarn't" had a crafty look to him, as most Supply Sergeants seemed to have. They know they are in a position to grant special favors at times and they are also in the position that sooner or later they might have you by the balls. *It always pays to get along with your Supply Sergeant,* I reflected when entering his Supply Room. He looked up and immediately said, "hey there, Lieutenant Lumbert, I was just gettin' your gear together, sir. You got your choice of rations here...what little you might be allowed to eat out there...hee hee...how many canteens you want to carry?" Staff Sergeant E6 McGinty had been with the Rangers long enough to know that the new Lieutenant was probably the last one to find out he was going on a mission. After 15 years in the Army he treated newby Lieutenants like a benevolent uncle might treat a young nephew.

Sgt. McGinty looked around with justified pride at all the arms and equipment he could issue to these LURPS. Most of the men of F Co. 50th Inf. had been through Ranger Training; but others had been trained in specialties such as Sniper and Pathfinder schools. They were all elite soldiers and he had access to some armament and equipment not normally found in regular Infantry outfits. He had been trained far beyond the Supply Sergeants in regular Infantry Companies as well. Also, being a good Supply Sergeant, he could trade for just about anything since he had quality, hard-to-find items on hand.

In weapons, for instance, he had the standard M16 and also the new CAR15 which was a commando version of an M16 with a folding stock and other possible attachments. Also available was the M14 with bipod legs, sniper scope, and full-auto selector switch, along with a variety of pistols besides the old standard .45 caliber semi-automatic. There were M79 grenade launchers, sawed-off Remington 12 gauge shotguns, claymore mines, trip flares, fragmentation grenades, smoke grenades, and a nice assortment of bayonets and survival knives he could issue. The LURPS seldom carried an M60 machine gun because their tactical mission involved stealth and concealment, not serious firefights. They did sometimes carry one LAW (light anti-tank weapon) – a disposable, collapsible bazooka that was compact and fairly reliable in the jungle. It was an exciting and impressive array of destructive devices. "You want it...I got it," McGinty said with a grin. "If I don't, I can damn sure trade for it somewhere. It's all gov'ment equipment, sir, and we're all gov'ment employees. Inventory lists can be juggled every which 'a way, believe me." I believed him.

"Take a gander at this Air Force survival rifle issued to pilots, especially Search and Rescue personnel." My well-supplied Supply Sergeant proceeded to show me an amazing rifle in a compact case. The stock contained a compass, fire-starter, saw-toothed wire with finger rings for cutting almost anything, extra .22 caliber long rifle ammo and magazine, waterproof map case, and other extras. Very impressive. Extremely difficult for the Army to obtain. My admiration for this Supply Sergeant increased with every item.

There were also high-quality binoculars, 60x spotter scopes, compasses, map cases, and starlight scopes that enabled clear vision at night. The Rangers had the best of the new compact radios equipped with special "squelch signal" relay lights so you could tell when someone was trying to call you even when the volume knob was turned off and signals could be sent and received by just keying the handset on and off. This invention enabled avoidance of the sound of a voice on the radio that could be heard far into the jungle. The Rangers understandably liked total stillness and quietude. I selected exactly what I thought would be needed, savoring the moment, proud to be among the Elite.

Later that day Sgt. Beeson called the men together for a briefing. He would be the Team Leader on the mission. "You gather a whole bunch of quiet, startin' right now," he said quietly, "and you carry that quiet with you like it's your precious family jewels (military euphemism for testicles)." All five of us nodded our assent as our Team Leader continued. "Because believe me gentlemen we are going to see Charlie out there and we better be damn sure he don't see or hear us." After consulting with the helicopter units it was determined that eight men would require two choppers and only one could be allocated, so the mission would proceed with the standard six men. Beeson looked directly at each man, his penetrating steely eyes moving slowly around the group. *I wonder how many missions this man has been on* I thought as the Sergeant's eyes bored into mine, lingering for several seconds before moving around the circle of men. This novice Lieutenant could not yet understand how a mistake by a newby could endanger the whole team. I trusted them to guide me and was proud they had enough confidence in me to believe I was not going to commit a major error in a crucial situation. Mutual trust and respect is an absolute necessity at such a time.

"Now the Lieutenant here is going to carry his load and take guard duty just like everyone else...and we're going to show him clearly how the Rangers operate...show him how much we like our quiet, right boys?" Then came the obligatory end-remark to every military lecture, class or briefing: "Are there any questions?" After a slight pause Sgt. Beeson added, "you have anything to add, sir?" he asked with standard military deference to this intense Lieutenant.

"Not a thing Sergeant," I quietly replied. That night, reflecting on my training, recalling the practice missions conducted in Ranger School, I wondered whether the next day would prove to be anything like the training. So far it seemed the tactics here in Vietnam were similar to some of the training exercises; but I felt a justified anxiety concerning what I knew I did not know. This anxiety was compounded by the fact of having been injured in the fifth week of Ranger School and being set back to start the nine week program all over again once a sprained ankle and knee had healed. However, I was sent to Vietnam instead of finishing Ranger School. I would rely on my men and ardently hoped I did not make a fool of myself. I resolved once again to keep my humility intact and learn from each experience. This resolution helped me to relax into a light military form of sleep.

The next morning long before dawn the team gathered our gear and weapons and rode over to the airfield. There was no conversation. As the heavily laden chopper lifted off, the sky was just beginning to lighten in the east. The pilot banked and headed west towards Cambodia. I calmly reflected...*this is the single most important event of my life.* There have been many attempts at explanations of emotions when heading into a possible combat situation, but there is no sports analogy, social event, or conceivable human endeavor that can compare to the intense, serious, and overwhelming feelings that occur at such a time. The training and camaraderie of the military allows a man – demands of him – to remain calm, alert, and seemingly confident regardless of his inner conversations. I hoped I appeared to be holding up to the initial strain and excitement.

It wasn't long before the trees and vegetation became vaguely discernible in the growing light as the pilot swooped down abruptly and hovered briefly a few feet off the ground. The co-pilot turned and shouted, "next stop boys." The chopper zoomed across a clearing, leaped over a treeline, and descended rapidly to flare out and bump the earth. We needed no coaxing as we scrambled out and headed into the nearest brush line, our sixty pounds of gear not slowing us in the least. Seconds later the Huey lifted off, roared over another treeline then touched down again briefly as per instructions, I noted with some gratification. Then it faded out to the east leaving a team of Rangers in the preternatural stillness of the early morning countryside.

This almost looks like certain parts of south Texas, I thought, automatically arranging myself into the characteristic tight defensive circle. There was absolutely no movement for at least fifteen long minutes as we silently scanned our surroundings in every direction. There was no noise whatsoever – not a cough, not a rustle of clothing nor a clank of equipment as we watched and waited. Finally Sgt. Beeson was convinced we had not been observed and indicated through a hand signal that we would set up right there. No sense in moving because the cover was good and the field of vision was excellent. We began slowly slipping out of our packs and arranging ourselves for the day...and the night...and the next day and night...and possibly longer. The mission was scheduled for two or three days depending on what we saw and what transpired.

The rucksacks and gear were placed in the center of the position and we would lie facing outward like spokes in a wheel, feet almost touching the packs. Each pair of men was responsible for one third of the perimeter and one man would always be watching and listening in each direction day and night, day and night. My partner was PFC Ralph Morgan who had been trained as a sniper and carried an M14 with a scope and bipod legs. Morgan was from Tulsa, Oklahoma and as we got acquainted before takeoff I asked him about his choice of weapons. He had piercing light blue eagle eyes and a slow manner of speaking as he related growing up hunting and target shooting with his family. He said he could hit a prairie dog at 50 yards with a BB gun when he was six years old. Claimed he could make a kill at 1000 yards with his rifle. I didn't doubt it. This was his third mission. He admitted he had not made a kill yet and seemed disappointed.

Vigilance was the name of the game - silent alertness. One man from each pair slowly and noiselessly crawled out about ten meters and carefully set up the claymore mines and trip flares while the other meticulously manicured the grass and shrubbery to allow for a modicum of comfort and maximum vision. There was no conversation, not even whispering. There was no unnecessary movement of the bushes. We moved with stealth and in slow motion, our eyes and ears as alert as those of tiny field mice negotiating a barnyard, watching for the owl, the fox, the enemy – aware that death could be just seconds away...acutely aware that any movement can be detected by keen eyes from afar.

I gladly accepted the task of setting the trip flares and claymores in my sector of the perimeter. It was a tricky business. A trip flare is a small cylinder about an inch in diameter and three inches long with a tiny pin at the top holding the firing mechanism open. I wired several to the stalks of plants and carefully connected another wire to the straightened pin of each one, creating a web of thin wires that hopefully would give us early warning if anyone was crawling up on our position. The claymore mines were set just inside the web of trip flares. A claymore antipersonnel mine is a piece of C-4 plastique explosive shaped into a bent rectangle, about an inch thick and 10X4 inches in size containing about 600 steel balls. Each mine has little folding legs to hold it upright and a squeeze-type detonator on the end of about 50 feet of wire. The detonator blew the charge outward due to the shape of the weapon, shredding everything within several meters. That is, if Charlie had not crept up somehow and reversed them to blow back at you. Sneaky guy, that Charles – quietly courageous too. Due to our extremely slow movements, these activities required several hours to complete.

After settling in, we six Rangers are locked and loaded, our own booby-traps all around us, nearly invisible from even a few meters away. If anyone were to approach close enough to see us they would undoubtedly trip a flare by moving one wrong twig then be instantly pulverized by a claymore detonation. That was the theory. The most important elements were concealment and silent watchfulness from that concealment.

I was looking south, Cambodia about one "click" (one thousand meters) to my right. I glanced to my left and was surprised to see my buddy Ralph already taking a nap during my mid-afternoon watch. *He's storing up his quiet* I thought with some amusement, looking out through about four feet of bushes onto a vast open area running east to west all the way into Cambodia. It was about 200 meters across the clearing to a treeline and beyond that was the low rise we had popped over in the chopper that morning. It was the dry season, with sparse bushes and grasslands interspersed between rolling wooded hills. That particular area resembled certain familiar parts of south Texas where I had grown up. I did not see or hear a living thing all day except for the various insects that kept me entertained. I counted each "plop" as the sweat rolled off the end of my nose and dropped onto a leaf. The Sarge and his buddy were silently pegging little chess pieces around on a tiny board, poking each other for "check" and communicating with smirks and frowns, each looking outward when it was not his turn to move.

So far so good I thought as I ground up a pasty C-ration cracker between my teeth. The Rangers' diet in the field was sparse and simple. The sound of a can opener was muffled with a towel and crinkling of wrappers was frowned on. We lived on Kool-Aid, crackers, chocolate, and maybe a little tin of "mystery meat" (the Army version of Spam) or a can of beans-and-franks. There were no fires, of course, not even with the little cans of Sterno that came in some cases of rations. After a man emptied a canteen of water he filled it with urine. Shitting was highly discouraged. It is surprising to the average person what men can be trained to do for a few days at a time – the apparent hardships they can undertake without complaint because the guy next to them is in the same situation and sometimes their commanders are also right there living the same stark reality. The day before a mission we would not shower so there would be no odor of soap on our person.

I recalled with some amusement one of the training Sergeants in Ranger school telling us, as he squished a sun-dried grasshopper between two crackers and took a big bite, "a Ranger doesn't start fires...a Ranger doesn't mind the weather...a Ranger eats whatever crawls by, ha-ha," and we had all eaten our grasshopper canapés while growling "RANGER!" When it rained one of us would suddenly shout, "the rain god eats shit!" and we would slog happily onward. The Rangers were the toughest men I would ever know, and now I was one of them. My chest expanded with pride, lying there in the silence dripping sweat and smiling at my predicament, actually glad to be there.

Now I understood the importance of the rigors of training and discipline. I more fully understood the necessity of learning to depend on your team and being utterly dependable yourself. I appreciated the testing of extreme limits during training and realized there was no such thing as over-training for this type of operation. Two men in my class at Ranger school had died during training – one of heat stroke and another who fell to his death while rappelling off a 200 ft. cliff in northern Georgia. I had felt at the time that something should be done to prevent such catastrophes during a mere training exercise; but now realized all those months of training and exercises had maybe, just barely, prepared me to be accepted as a beginner in the real arena of combat operations. I remained firm in my resolve to observe the other members of the team and was keenly alert while on watch. *Now I am finally learning how to be a Ranger* I thought with pride, stretching out on my back, confident that my buddy was now on guard. I watched the sky fade and rested, preparing for the first night in the bush.

It looked to be a clear dark night with a sliver of new moon sinking in the west at twilight. Rangers knew the phase of the moon. Such details could be extremely important. We busied ourselves checking the starlight scope, straightening out poncho liners, and placing each item exactly so it could be instantly found in the dark. The claymore detonators were placed precisely and whispered orders and signals were passed around the circle as a last confirmation of the prearranged plans. A single firm nudge meant, "I think I heard something." Two distinct taps on the arm meant, "I have spotted enemy troops." We alternated guard every two hours after dark, with one of each pair always looking and listening in the designated direction while the other rested quietly or napped. Usually everyone was awake all night on the first night.

Even when we were asleep we were somehow still conscious of maintaining silence. A Ranger did not roll over or groan in his sleep. To do so would result in a sharp jab in the ribs from your buddy. To change positions we would wake up, slowly readjust ourselves, take a quiet breath, then drift back off to sleep. Such patterns of sleep when learned under severe conditions of life or death would stay with many of us for the rest of our lives. This hyper-vigilance was later recognized as an aspect of Post-Traumatic-Stress-Disorder (PTSD) by psychologists and would not serve us well back in civilian life.

On my first two shifts I peered into the night, looked through the starlight scope, counted trees and bushes in the distant treeline, and listened to the various sounds of the insects. I did not feel in the least bit inclined towards sleep and was surprised to have drifted off during my buddy's second watch. I was instantly awakened by a grasp on my arm, then two sharp taps. Easing over to my right, I felt out to the man there, and gave him two taps on the arm. The whole group was immediately aware of the situation even though not a sound had been made. My buddy Ralph was gesturing toward the south as he handed over the starlight scope. The time was 0340. Sgt. Beeson slithered noiselessly over and trained the scope across the clearing, confirming the sighting. He handed the scope back to me and in focusing the greenish images I began to see movements. Then I clearly saw a man walk between two trees, moving from right to left and carrying something on his shoulders. *Holy shit...there they are...humping in supplies from Cambodia...there's another one!*

These were not local villagers – Vietcong. These were trained experienced soldiers of the North Vietnamese Regular Army. They were soldiers in the Army that had kicked the French out of Vietnam the previous decade. Some of them might have been fighting the Japanese the decade before that. I remembered to count and picked up the tally estimating eight or ten men had passed while I was gaping in astonishment. *Twenty-five, twenty six...hundred and one, hundred and two...whoa! we're watching a whole damn battalion move quietly through the woods only 200 meters away...holy shit!*

We waited intently for about thirty minutes, counting and trying to discern what type of supplies were being carried. *There must be a path or a trail for them to be moving along like that in the dark,* I thought, having stopped counting at two hundred. We waited in complete silence after the last man had passed from sight. When nothing was seen for several minutes, we risked a whispered conversation. "I figure well over two hundred – a whole damn battalion," Beeson said, confirming my estimate. We waited, thinking things over. Charlie would probably not be moving in the daylight which would be coming soon, therefore that whole battalion of NVA could be settling down into concealment just a short distance away to await the next night.

It was time to call in the dawn SITREP so Beeson keyed the radio handset to break squelch three times, then whispered into the mike, "eagle base, bravo one, over." A tiny red light blinked twice indicating acknowledgment - they were listening back at Cu Chi. "SITREP...two five zero november victor alphas...two zero zero south...moving east, over." The light blinked twice. About three minutes later the artillery shells began sailing in and crunching resoundingly off to the south and slightly east of our position, about a half mile away. It was possible that was about where the NVA might have stopped for the day. It was also possible they had not gone that far and were just a few hundred meters away out of sight in the trees, settling down for a day of concealment just on the other side of the clearing. Having a whole battalion very close by was a dangerous situation for the Rangers; but exactly what we were out there to find. It was exactly what we were trained to deal with. It was also what each of us, deep inside, perhaps did not want to experience at close range. But we were professionals and we never hesitated doing our job of observing the enemy and reporting their location and activities.

About an hour later as the sky began to lighten Sgt. Beeson called in for the orders of the day. There were normally only two possibilities: remain in position or prepare for extraction – both of which could be transmitted by coded clicks of the handset. "Eagle base, bravo six, over," he whispered into the microphone. I could imagine them back in Cu Chi, no doubt drinking strong morning coffee and listening – the First Sergeant, the RTO, maybe the Captain, and probably some other team leaders. Beeson had the volume control knob barely cracked open in case there was an order not previously arranged with signals. The RTO responded immediately, "eagle base, over."

"Bravo six...what's the plan, over?"

Headquarters ordered clearly, "good job...inbound ETA six zero...pop smoke, over." We could expect a Huey to extract us in one hour and we were to pop a smoke grenade to indicate our position when the chopper approached.

On hearing and understanding the message, I simultaneously felt relieved, tired, and satisfied. Then came a feeling of mild disappointment because the mission had seemed so easy and unspectacular. I did not know how lucky we were because it was my first mission. Having begun to enjoy myself in an odd way, I did not want it to end so soon, so quietly and uneventfully. I liked being a Ranger out in the bush spying on Charlie and calling the Artillery down on his ass. It was thrilling to nap like a cat, eat like a bird, and piss in a canteen. This had been the culmination of all my training...my graduation as a combat soldier...a fulfillment of a dream.

As we were packing the gear and retrieving the claymores and trip flares one of the men suddenly froze and placed a fist over his chest. The signal meant "stop everything...I think I saw movement...possible enemy forces nearby." We all instantly crouched, weapons at the ready, and looked in the direction indicated – to the south in the treeline where the battalion of NVA had passed less than an hour before. Binoculars were focused and breath was held as we intently watched the distant treeline for any sign of life or movement. After a long silence, Beeson quietly asked, "what" with a gesture and Ranger Boyd whispered close to his ear, "I definitely saw movement Sarge...not sure what though."

We did not have much time to decide our course of action. The extraction chopper was due within minutes and it would be nice to leave without any fireworks. There might be a full platoon of 25 or 30 seasoned NVA soldiers hiding in the treeline watching for any movement from us. It was not a pleasant prospect. Sgt. Beeson quickly decided we would move to the north a couple hundred meters and try to find a small clearing for the Huey to land safely. We quickly gathered our gear and started moving out.

As I duck-walked backwards, shuffling around a bush while still looking to the south, I momentarily lost my balance and sat down on my left foot with the toe turned out to the side. There was a sickening "pop" and a searing hot pain in my knee; but I could not pause to think about it because the team was moving out through the woods and I had to keep up. I struggled along, unable to straighten the leg and nauseous with the pain, until the team finally stopped by a small clearing.

"Bingo," Beeson said, then noticing his Lieutenant struggling asked, "what's up L T?"

"I don't know sarge, something popped in my knee," I replied. It was the same type of injury that had set me back in Ranger school. Then I remembered injuring the same knee in a similar way in the eighth grade in P.E. class trying to do a forward hand-spring and landing wrong. At the time, I had forced the leg out straight and popped it again and in a few days it was fine. This time I could not make it pop again. There was no way to force the leg out straight. It was too painful. *Shit! I hate being the injured man on the team, goddamnit.* I was accustomed to being fast, and agile, and strong and had never before been seriously injured.

We heard the chopper coming in from the south. Then we heard several short bursts of AK-47's from the treeline. Charlie had left a rear guard directly across the clearing from our position and for some reason they had not attacked during the night. Now we were about 300 meters farther north and we could reasonably expect the NVA to head straight over towards us when they realized the chopper was going to land. Beeson tossed a smoke grenade into the clearing identifying our position to the Huey and the enemy as a purple cloud of smoke began boiling upward.

The helicopter machine-gunner cranked up his M-60 to its full 600 rounds per minute as the Huey descended and we clambered aboard before it even touched down. I had a tough time climbing in and one of the men calmly chuckled as he grabbed me by my pack straps and hauled me in. The pilot did not hesitate for a second before he began moving, tilting forward then roaring out to the north. The gunner was still firing off bursts of twenty rounds until we were too far away for accuracy. It was a close call.

When we had gained some altitude, Sgt. Beeson cracked a big grin, lit a cigarette and shouted over the noise of the Huey, "congratulations, sir. You have just completed your first successful mission and you have been under enemy fire." I had not noticed the several spots of sunlight that had appeared on the floor and walls of the chopper – evidence of bullets having passed through our transportation. Then the other team members all smiled, gave me a thumbs-up, a slap on the back, a tip of the canteen...whatever, to show their approval of my conduct. I had done well and felt great even though the knee was throbbing like hell. I figured the doctors could fix me right up and it would be fine after a week of rest. It did not seem to be a serious injury.

As we flew back to Cu Chi I recounted the valuable lessons learned during the past 28 hours, preparing myself for the next mission. By the time we landed I was deep into my reverie...out on my tenth mission...extending for a second tour because the men needed my experience...training some newby Lieutenant when I became Company Commander. I wanted the full experience of the assignment. I absolutely loved being a Ranger-Long-Range-Reconnaissance-Patrol Officer.

We landed without incident and the pilot began pointing out the holes in his aircraft and cursing Charlie. "Look at this shit, man, they thoroughly perforated my helicopter. This kind of thing really pisses me off fellas," he said to the team in a joking manner, as if we were fault. Beeson responded quickly, "oh gee, sir, I'll send some men over in the morning to patch it up for ya." We all had a few laughs as we counted the bullet holes and tried to picture the trajectories. It was hard to understand why nobody was hit and the chopper still flew. There were three or four observable bullet pathways through the helicopter, none of which destroyed a major component or hit any of the men aboard. We Rangers were in high spirits by the time our truck arrived, laughing and discussing the air holes. "Quit complaining, sir, you got air conditioning now, ha-ha," someone quipped.

Back at the compound the Company Medic took one look at my knee and said, "that there is a million dollar injury you got there, sir. You're going back to the world."

"No way!" I responded indignantly. "I just got here." But to my astonishment, the Medic was correct. A doctor at the hospital took one look at the knee, poked around on it a bit, glanced at the X-rays and said curtly, "Medivac to Japan, Lieutenant. Your tour is over." The hurried Doctor then immediately turned and walked away, unaware that he had not given good news. The injury was too minor to be attended to there in Vietnam.

That was it...my whole tour was over and done...just like that. I was stunned. There was no way to argue about it though.

When the Army tells you to go to Japan, you ask what time the flight leaves. Actually an Officer does not even have to do that. The orderly summoned a jeep and I was driven back to the Ranger HQ to gather up "bag and baggage." I paused to say good-bye to the First Sergeant; but the men were all in the mess hall and it was too humiliating to go in and face them. I felt like a wimp. It was embarrassing to be going to Japan for an injury suffered when we were not engaged in a sustained firefight. None of us had returned fire from the chopper because the sound of the engine made it impossible to even hear whether we were under fire from the ground. Being unqualified to receive a Purple Heart medal made the minor injury all the more disgusting.

The driver headed over to the airfield and pulled right up to a Caribou aircraft sitting by the terminal. Within minutes I limped aboard with the real wounded, feeling like a turd in a punch bowl. As the Caribou took off for Tan Son Nhut Air Base, I wondered sardonically, *what kind of dipshit newby will get my job?"* I had been working twenty hours a day for almost a month and had experienced a lifetime of excitement during my brief tour with the Rangers. It just did not seem right to be leaving after putting in all that time to learn my role. I was just beginning to feel a glimmer of confidence. *First mission, last mission.* I was disappointed in the extreme, pissed off to the maximum, and frustrated at the undignified end of a brief tour in a combat zone.

We landed at Tan Son Nhut and the wounded and injured were immediately taken aboard a hospital-equipped C-141. Within an hour or so, we rolled down the runway and I felt the wheels lift off. I was out of Vietnam. I could not even look out a window as the aircraft began a steep ascent. Late that evening – the same day that began at 0340 when we counted over two hundred NVA – I disgustedly found myself safely ensconced in a pristine orthopedic ward in a sparkling clean US Army Hospital in Japan. I did not even know which city. I sat feeling numb, dumb, and awestruck. I just sat on my bunk and looked intently...at nothing.

I had been totally committed to a larger cause for the first time in my life. Now I felt a crushing sense of defeat and humiliation. I withdrew into myself during the week of waiting in the hospital in Japan, spoke to no one and made no friends. My isolation led to speechless depression and the depression led to a sense of loneliness. It was a very long time before I learned how to break this downward spiral of despair and depression.

When I finally reached my hometown of San Antonio, I procrastinated for several days before trying to call my Mother. To my surprise and concern, she had moved and I did not even know the telephone number. After another day in mute depression I summoned the energy to call information and learn my "home" phone number. Despite my protests, my Mother came to the hospital. I was shocked watching an old woman approaching from a distance, walking slowly down a long hallway – a woman I did not recognize until she was twenty feet away – my Mother. Evidently she had gone through quite an extended ordeal over the death of my Father and been engaged in her own depression and isolation for, by then, over two years.

My Brother had sprouted from being a fifteen-year-old who was small for his age to being an inch taller than myself. I found out my best friend from high school had been killed in a shootout with the police during a drug raid. My former girlfriend had entered a convent and was writing a book denouncing all men and me in particular, to whom she had sacrificed her blessed virginity on her living room sofa about a month before my enlistment. My high school looked drab and small. San Antonio seemed dirty and boring. My only surcease from suffering and ennui was in blasting around on my Harley-Davidson Sportster.

CHAPTER II
The Executive Officer
Second tour of Vietnam   March 1969

At Ft. Hood, Texas this recently promoted First Lieutenant had the assignment of a lifetime had I been on a career track in the Army. I was not yet 21 years old, had graduated in the top fourth of my class in Officers Candidate School; had successfully completed Airborne School; and had served with the elite LURPs in Vietnam even though it had only been for a month. I was a volunteer all the way and had undertaken every school and job the Army had demanded. Excellent efficiency reports from all my Commanding Officers so far in my career would possibly lead to a promotion to Captain at just 22 years of age. A career was definitely an option being considered.

I had a beautiful motorcycle, a trusty '65 Ford Fairlane, and as easy job as Company Executive Officer in a mechanized Infantry Battalion, waiting for the Captain to be reassigned when I would take over as Company Commander. It was unlikely that this unit would be sent to Vietnam. Knowing all this, anyone would wonder why I could not just kick back and enjoy life. There were only about ten months left in a two year commitment after being commissioned in September of 1967. Whether it was clear at the time or not, the tide of good luck had cast me up onto a pleasant sunny beach.

I gunned my Harley east out of Killeen from a small apartment off base, and headed over to Temple with my Company Clerk, E4 Corporal Quarles. We had started hanging out together in off-duty hours, drinking beer and shooting pool at several bars in Temple and Waco, which everybody pronounced "wacko" because it was such a crazy town.

Corporal Quarles was a smart-ass tough guy from New York who was a known discipline problem, but he was likable in his own way. We got along fine after an initial confrontation. The Captain informed his new Executive Officer that Quarles was an excellent clerk; but he had a shitty attitude, especially towards Officers. The Corporal had several reprimands in his records and two Article 15's (the military equivalent of a misdemeanor) for lack of proper respect. He had a smirky look to him and when he spoke he pressed his mouth forward, enunciating a typical Brooklyn accent.

When we had the office to ourselves on my second day there, I said, "Hey, Corporal Quarles, the word to me is you aren't exactly cooperative at times..."

"Sir," Quarles interrupted, "I do my job and I do it right."

"Yeah, okay," I continued, "well I just want to do my job too, and part of the job entails asking you questions concerning the procedures around here...know what I mean?"

"Yeah, yes sir, a'course," Quarles replied with a grimace.

I paused for a moment and fixed the Corporal with a steady stare. "You look to me like a pretty tough guy...probably did some boxing when you were growing up, right?...one of the roughest guys in your high school, I bet."

"Yeah, probably..."

"Well I was a pretty rough guy in my high school too and now that I have been in a combat zone I don't feel like fucking around with you so I'll just say this once, straight out. If you start screwing around here and messing up my day I am going to invite you somewhere off base, someplace private, and I am going to kick your ass or give it my fucking best effort, Corporal. And if you have any doubt about it you follow me today after work and we'll find out in about three seconds," I said with very unofficer-like bluntness while staring intently into his eyes,

"Oh jeez, sir, hell no. I ain't going to give you no problems, Lieutenant Lumbert. I mean we're both pretty tough guys, we both got motorcycles...we got no reason to have any problems." He arose from his desk and stuck out his hand which his new Lieutenant gripped very firmly. Then he executed a theatrically precise salute and his Lieutenant flipped off a return salute that resembled the rude Italian gesture of brushing the fingers out from under the chin. We both laughed and became riding buddies that night. Viewed from proper military standards by a straight-laced West Point Officer, my response was an obvious lapse in proper decorum expected from a commissioned officer when relating with an Enlisted man. It would not be the last time I acted in such a manner.

I felt completely invincible roaring around on my Sportster with my buddy Quarles. The Corporal had a radical hard-tail chopper that always drew looks and knew his way around the local bars and hangouts. Quarles had a way of getting himself in some shit, though, that much was obvious from the start. It did not take a deep investigation to find plenty of trouble in the wild and woolly Texas bars the two of us frequented. It was humorous at times seeing the drunken barroom scenarios where guys were reeling drunk yet still walking, talking, shooting pool, and having fistfights over practically anything. Besotted combatants engaged in pushing, glaring, and cussing matches where both drunks would usually end up on the floor flopping around like a couple of walruses, trying to bash each other's head with little or no effect. I had been in a few bars in Fayetteville, N.C. when assigned to the 82nd Airborne Division before the first brief tour in Vietnam and had been in a few bars around San Antonio while still underage; but never in my life had I seen such a level of drunken revelry and sloppy fisticuffs on a regular and predictable basis. It was highly entertaining.

One night we had to make a hasty exit out a side door because Quarles punched some cowboy during a dispute over the jukebox. The Corporal knocked the guy flat with a clean straight right; but then three of the slob's friends all grabbed Quarles and were starting to work him over. I stepped in without hesitation delivering a stiff forearm smash to a jaw; a heavy two-handed shove to a chest; and a quick side-kick to a bloated midsection. Then we immediately burst out the side exit, laughing like maniacs, hopped on our bikes, and hauled ass. We were doing over 100mph just a few seconds later, wailing like banshees and shouting to each other over the roar of our engines, "way to go...did you see me punch that fucker?..." along with similar banalities.

Sometimes we would just ride and glide, mile after mile, smiling grimly, looking good. I would crank that Harley and lie flat on the gas tank with my feet on the rear foot pegs and hold that throttle wide open for ten miles at time. And once it was broken in that Sportster would do 120mph and I never once felt even a faint gap in my imagined shield of invincibility. There was simply no expectation whatsoever of anything happening at that speed except the sheer thrill of the wind and the unbelievable blast and vibration that only a Harley Davidson can provide. There truly was nothing to fear. We had some roaring good times together, a rambunctious Lieutenant and his smart-ass Corporal, and we got away scot-free with every episode.

My buddy the Corporal was really the only person who could even faintly understand my volunteering for a second tour in Vietnam. As Company clerk Quarles had to do the paperwork to extend my enlistment for another two years in order to have a full year in Vietnam possible. Upon signing those papers I had an idea to possibly stay in the Army, put in twenty years and retire as a Lieutenant Colonel at age 38. It seemed entirely possible. Knowing it was a monumental decision when signing those forms, I had no hesitation and thought only of duty and service and of making up for having failed, in my mind, to live up to the ideal of Ranger toughness. There was no thought regarding how soon and to what extent I would regret that decision and how unlikely was the possibility of a career in the Army.

It did not take long for the Army to accept the application and within a month I had orders to return to Vietnam. I had been experiencing occasional boredom and depression, but these feelings lifted like a morning fog under a bright Texas sun once I had orders to return to the 'Nam. I put my motorcycle in storage, briefly tried to explain to my completely bewildered Mother, and then caught a flight to Oakland, Ca. There was simply no way I was going to miss out on the intense excitement and fulfillment of purpose briefly experienced with the LURP Rangers.

When processing out-of-country at Oakland I felt like an experienced longtime soldier, patiently enduring the momentary tedium of taxis, boarding passes, etc., in order to return to the war...to get back to the job I was trained for – Infantry Lieutenant in the United States Army. I proudly wore my class A uniform that clearly showed rank, schools and attainments, and which unit I had already served with in combat – all conveyed to every passing soldier and civilian. Some of the civilians looked askance at me and there was more than an occasional frown of disapproval but I took no offense and did not understand the level of anti-war sentiment that was prevalent among the young hippy-types and the general populace of California. I felt proud to be an Airborne Soldier returning voluntarily for a second tour in Vietnam.

As I sat talking to the bartender at the Officers' Club awaiting the flight, I picked up a cup of dice nonchalantly, shook it once while looking at the bartender and tossed, on my one and only throw, five sixes. Barkeep said, "Whoa! Never seen that before, Lieutenant."

"Yeah, well no sense throwing again is there?" I replied casually, feeling the double scotch I had just put down. Then my stomach did a weird little flip as the thought occurred, *I'm throwing the dice again by going over to the 'Nam again.* And for the first time I seriously pondered what sort of hand might be dealt in the game this time. No feelings of apprehension or nervousness had occurred until that minute, sitting there looking at those five dice laying on the bar – five sixes – every dot on the matrix. "Looks like good luck to me," I lied, realizing that maybe I was facing all the possibilities this tour. All possibilities meant what? I could not imagine and knew it was beyond imagining what was in store for me. Leaving a $20 tip, I exited the bar and headed out to catch the flight to the land of all possibilities – The Republic of South Vietnam in 1969.

Processing into the Country was even easier than leaving the States and in no time at all I found myself assigned, once again, to the 25th Infantry Division. Boarding an ugly green bus with screens on the windows and sandbags on the floor, I joined twenty soldiers headed northwest out of the Saigon area towards Cu Chi Base Camp, some 40 miles away. At Cu Chi the assignments clerk told me that, regrettably, there were no openings with the Rangers but he had the next best thing. "The Wolfhounds, sir, the Second of the 27th." I could see by his badges and patches that he had served his time in the field. "I'll give them a call, Lieutenant. I'm sure they'll be glad to send a jeep over for you," he said, handing the packet of orders and records back to me.

Thirty minutes later a smiling, round-faced, pudgy driver pulled up in a jeep, his hair much longer than military regulations, and asked with a sloppy salute, "You the replacement XO for the Second of the Twenty-seventh, sir?"

"Yes, I'm going to the Wolfhounds but I imagine I'll be a Platoon Leader," said the experienced not-so-new newby. "What makes you think I will be an Executive Officer?"

"Well sir, I'm PFC Phil McPhaille, the Headquarters Company clerk and the Colonel's driver and I already heard 'em talking about how they need some experienced administrative Officers back here at the Base Camp."

I looked at the red, slightly puffy eyes of the PFC as we drove off and was reminded of my brother Phil. Realizing this guy was totally stoned on pot, I leaned over and said, confidential like, "you know who you remind me of? My brother Phil who is a stoned hippy and you look like a fuckin' nut so I am going to call you Filbert. What do you think of that?"

McPhaille burst into a fit of laughter and barely negotiated a turn while pounding on the wheel of the jeep and said, "Well sir, you know what they say...you don't have to be a nut to work here...but it helps...ha-ha hee." I found myself liking this evidently intelligent good-natured guy and could not help laughing too.

McPhaille knew what he was talking about, though. I was ushered into the Battalion Commander's office and met Lt. Col. George Branson, a big man with a ready smile and a warm handshake. "We're glad to have you aboard, Lieutenant Lumbert," the Colonel said, taking the packet of records and quickly leafing through them, "I see here that you were an assistant S-4 Officer with the 82nd Airborne when they were still back at Bragg...and most recently you were a Company XO...then Commanding Officer of a mechanized Company at Ft. Hood. What brings you back to Vietnam, Lieutenant?" he asked with a level look of appraisal.

"Well, sir, I was only here for a month and felt that, after all the training...well I didn't even find out what the war is all about, sir."

"Very commendable Lieutenant. I am assigning you as Executive Officer of Alpha Company which means you play a double role as Battalion S-4 Officer in charge of convoys. How does that suit you?"

"Fine, sir. I'll do the best job I can," replied the new XO earnestly.

"You'll find out what the war is all about with the Wolfhounds, Lieutenant...we kick ass out there," Colonel Branson said as he led this earnest Lieutenant back into the outer office. "My driver will show you over to your Company Headquarters."

At the headquarters of Alpha Company this proud new Executive Officer met my Company clerk, a thin nervous-looking young man from down south somewhere who drawled, "ten hut," as Filbert and I entered the office.

"As you were," I said casually to the men who had assumed a mild version of the stance of attention when I had entered. Ceremony here in a combat zone and many standard rules and procedures were ignored or treated lightly.

"Morning, sir, I'm Spec. four Marcus and this here is Tom Bartlett, your driver. We're mighty glad to have an Officer around here because the Captain has been out in the field a lot lately."

"Uh, in fact sir, the convoy hasn't left yet, so if you want to you can ride out to the fire base and meet the CO," said Bartlett, a grinning, blond-haired, California surfer type of guy about eighteen years old. "Here comes your Supply Sergeant now, Lieutenant, he can issue you your weapon and everything."

"Let's go Tom," a big E6 Sergeant was saying as he entered the office, then as he saw his new Lieutenant he saluted and stuck out a big round hand. "Sarn't Mac, sir, you the new XO?" Staff Sergeant E6 Gene "Mac" MacAnally was a career Army man from Bozeman, Montana, with a big laugh and a bigger belly. He had an amusing habit of taking a deep breath and rubbing both hands down his ample midsection when he was thinking.

"That's right, Sarge," I replied, offering my hand to be crushed and enthusiastically pumped by my Supply Sergeant. *It always pays to get along with your Supply Sergeant.*

"The convoy's just fixin' to leave...you want to go out and meet the Captain?"

"I guess so...you got a weapon for me?"

"Sure thing, sir...won't take but a minute," he said as he turned and hustled towards the motor pool and supply area.

Filbert and my driver Tom seemed to be good friends, as evidenced by their familiar jocularity. They helped carry my bags over to a hooch while engaged in brotherly teasing of each other, then showed me into a nice BOQ with four semi-private rooms and a bunker right outside the door. There were fans, mosquito nets over the bunks, and even a small desk in one corner. It felt like a familiar home and I felt proud and confident while stowing a few personal belongings quickly. Then Tom and I walked over to the supply room.

We found Mac recording the serial number of an M-16 laying on the counter. "You want to carry a forty-five (standard-issue pistol for Officers), sir?"

"Naw. Sarge, just an M-16 will be fine...and give me a bandolier of magazines (eight magazines of 18-20 rounds each) would you?"

Mac grinned and said, "You got an M-60 mounted on your jeep, L T...you can fire that if we're ambushed, ha-ha." We all laughed.

Tom said, "We don't worry too much about ambushes L T...just land mines and booby-traps...ha-ha." It felt great to be back among the kind of men who could take such possibilities so lightly.

So within an hour of my arrival at the Wolfhounds I found myself in the lead jeep apparently in charge of a re-supply convoy of two deuce and a halfs (Army trucks with a 5000lb. capacity) with Mac in a three quarter ton Army pick-up truck bringing up the rear. We left Cu Chi Base Camp and passed the dilapidated, aggregated, confused clusters of shacks and hovels that had sprung up outside that gate and headed west on increasingly bad roads.

We passed Vietnamese people riding every conceivable type of motorcycle and bicycle-driven vehicle imaginable. I marveled at seeing a whole family riding a Honda 50 exactly like the one I had at age fourteen...papasan driving, two toddlers straddling the gas tank, and mamasan on the back with an infant on her lap. They probably weighed a total of less than two hundred pounds. *What an amazing people,* I thought as we drove past cultivated fields, little hamlets with a few stucco buildings, and neat little roadside food stalls built entirely of bamboo, rattan, and palm fronds.

I admired the lush countryside and appreciated the tenacity and ingenuity of this ancient culture. The Vietnamese people could build an entire village and all the required furniture out of the simple materials they had amply at hand and they had been successfully cultivating the same fields for centuries. The question of whether the US Military would preserve this marvelous culture or trample and destroy it somehow slipped into my consciousness. It would not be long before the answer became obvious. Once again, I had evidently avoided the thorough indoctrination of the military. The question was of no relevance to a combat Infantryman.

As we passed through a hamlet with a half-demolished yet still stately French Colonial mansion off the road by a dense forest, Tom informed me, "That's the old Michelin rubber plantation, sir...or part of it anyway. We pulled some mighty spooky missions in there when I was out in the field. They're supposed to defoliate the whole thing and drive Charlie out of there. It's full of Vietcong and NVA Regulars." It did look like an awesome dark woods to investigate all right...deep, dark, and dangerous.

The Fire Support Base – called Diamond – was close to the Cambodian border, not far from where I had been on my one and only LRRP mission. One could not help noticing a really strange and incongruous mountain standing all by itself in the distance. Tom pulled over by a big mess tent and parked the jeep then led me to the HQ bunker. I entered by ducking down and descending three steps into a cool, well-lit field office. A light-complected "Black" Captain sipped an iced Kool-Aid as I entered, saluted, and said, "Lieutenant Lumbert reporting for duty sir."

The Captain returned the salute, smiled warmly, said, "Hey, good to see you Lieutenant. Welcome to the Wolfhounds." He gave a firm handshake then turned and yelled out one of the firing slits on the upper wall of the bunker, "Hey top!...First Sergeant...we got us a real First Lieutenant Executive Officer here!" Ordinarily the CO and the First Sergeant would not both be out in the field, but this Fire Support Base had just been built in the previous few days and everyone had been working hard out there except the one clerk and the support personnel back at Cu Chi.

First Sergeant Gonzales crouched in the doorway of the bunker and said, "you mean I won't have to forge your signature on all those forms any more, sir?" Then he grinned as he saluted his new XO. First Sergeant E8 Manuel Gonzales was a serious-faced, round-bodied man from Flores, Texas, just south of San Antonio. "Welcome to Vietnam, sir. They'll show you around the bunker line if you want. I'm awful busy right now. Excuse me." Then he disappeared from the doorway and hustled off shouting some instructions to one of the men.

"That is a good First Sergeant, let me tell you," Captain Ashley said. "He cares about the men and he kicks his own ass harder than anyone else's." The man did seem like a hard worker, I thought with admiration. Captain Albert Ashley was a college-educated man who had gone through ROTC (Reserve Officers' Training Corps) to receive his commission as a Second Lieutenant five years previous. He had served in the Reserves for several years before being sent to Vietnam and was only four months into his first combat deployment. At forty years of age, he was considered "old" for a Captain by most wartime standards.

A forward Fire Support Base like Diamond was built very quickly – in a matter of days. First of all, the Engineers would come in and bulldoze a mound of dirt about three feet high into a big circular ring about 100 meters in diameter. Outside of this berm line they would string two or three concentric rings of concertina wire – huge coils of razor sharp barbed wire that they stacked, two on the bottom and one on top, and wired together. Then the Infantrymen came in and wired hundreds of trip flares and claymore mines within the concertina wire enclosures. The Infantry then dug about thirty regularly spaced holes around the donut shaped berm line and put all the dirt in sandbags. The sandbags were stacked in interlocking layers around the holes to form three-foot high walls. Heavy steel planks would form the roofs of the bunkers and several layers of sandbags on top of the steel planks would complete the bunkers.

The resulting bunkers were tall enough to stand up in, about six by eight feet in dimension, and capable of withstanding enemy fire from anything except a direct hit by one of the larger rockets or mortar rounds. There might be six or eight men or more sleeping and keeping watch in these bunkers at night, peering through small firing slits left open in the upper level of the sandbag walls.

At Diamond there were two Companies of Infantry, about 80-100 men each, manning the perimeter, and a battery of six 105mm Howitzers set in a circle in the center and surrounded by sandbags and piles of ammo boxes. Each Company had a command bunker in the middle of its sector, and the Battalion command bunker and communications bunker were in the center of the perimeter. There were also mess tents, makeshift lean-tos and stacks and stacks of ammo boxes piled everywhere. Men were working incredibly hard where ever I looked. *Looks to me like these guys are preparing for a war, all right.*

I stood out by the bunker line gazing off at the mountain looming up so defiantly on an otherwise flat and level terrain. "That's Nui Ba Den, sir, the Black Virgin Mountain. Charlie owns the whole thing except for some Special Forces guys who maintain a communication relay station on the very top," Tom informed me as he approached, having just smoked a reefer from the smell and the look of him.

"Wow...how do they get up there?" I asked, surveying the nearly perpendicular rocky sides of the mountain.

"Choppers are the only way. Whenever the NVA wants to they crawl out of their tunnels and overrun the place, then we bomb the shit out of the whole mountain and start all over again." It was awe-inspiring to think about – a Special Forces Team all alone on top of a tunnel-riddled mountain way the hell out here by the Cambodian border. *This is some very serious shit,* I thought as my stomach tightened at being so hear the enemy – the well-seasoned North Vietnamese Army. There were hundreds of them in tunnels inside Nui Ba Den mountain.

The Fire Support Base would serve as a temporary home to the Infantry. Each Company would send one or more of its three Platoons out each day on "search and destroy" missions. They would explore ever more widening loops of the surrounding countryside, checking houses and villages for anything considered to be possibly Viet Cong weapons or supplies of any type. They would also detain anyone they thought was a "VC sympathizer" and turn them over to Intelligence units for questioning. Sometimes, if they discovered a large weapons cache or simply too much rice stored in one place, they would confiscate or destroy everything, possibly igniting the entire village. It was not a tactic that was winning the hearts and minds of the people; but that is what the Army was doing at the time.

The Wolfhounds were trying to stem the flow of supplies and personnel streaming into that region, sometimes referred to as the "parrot's beak." At this point the border between Cambodia and Vietnam was a river that curved east towards Saigon. From the parrot's beak it was only about fifty miles to Saigon and in early 1969 this southern route of the Ho Chi Minh Trail had become a major avenue for infiltration by the NVA because the northern route had been disrupted by a massive bombing campaign by US B-52 bombers. More bombs were dropped during the Vietnam war than all the bombs dropped in the entire WWII campaign. Yet the North Vietnam Army led by Ho Chi Minh was undeterred. Amazing but true.

When attending meetings and briefings over the course of the next few weeks, the Army began changing the name of some of its tactics, for instance, calling the Infantry operations "sweep and clear" instead of "search and destroy." I wondered about the rationale behind this renaming of tactics, unaware of the influence of the press coverage and its result in the minds of the United States populace. Though the anti-war protests were in full swing in the United States, we soldiers were unaware of the daily news back home in the USA. This lack of information was a deliberate tactic of the Military.

I wandered around the Fire Base while the trucks were unloaded and towards mid-afternoon took charge of the convoy again as we hauled ass back to Cu Chi. It came as a complete surprise to my driver when I leaned over and asked Tom, "so, there any good grass over here Private?"

"Goddamn sir," said a very surprised PFC, then recovered and quickly added, "I thought you'd never ask, ha-ha...me and Filbert figured maybe you turned on." He had already adopted McPhaille's new nickname. Tom immediately produced a half-smoked Have-A-Tampa Jewel cigar – the type with a wooden mouthpiece - from his pocket. He lit it with a Zippo lighter burning aviation fuel, took a big hit, then said in a high-pitched voice while holding in the sweet smoke, "try this Lieutenant."

"No thanks Tom. Just wanted you to know that I know what's going on. Please don't smoke in my presence and don't assume I smoke marijuana, especially while on duty," I replied, not wanting any rumors to float around...not intending to continue the occasional smoking of pot here in Vietnam. Tom accepted this mild admonishment and started talking about the best surfing spots along the coast of California. He was from Ventura and had been surfing since he was four years old. He stowed the half-smoked marijuana cigar in his top pocket as he explained various surfing terminology.

That was one way marijuana was smoked in the 'Nam – in small cigars or cigarettes that had the tobacco carefully rolled out and manicured grass tamped in. There were also pipes of every description passed around in groups of men everywhere you looked if you knew what to look for. Thanks to my younger brother, I knew what to look for. I began to get mildly stoned occasionally with Tom and Filbert in the evenings and became acquainted with aspects of Cu Chi Base Camp and the hamlet outside the gate that I had never discovered during my brief intense tour with the Rangers. For instance, there was a massage and steam-bath establishment outside the gate where cute little Vietnamese girls would wash and massage you for a solid hour for a small fee. A "happy ending" was provided at no extra charge. Filbert was really amused to take his Lieutenant for his first "steam-job and hand-bath."

Filbert knew a lot about the plans and activities in the Battalion, being a Headquarters Company clerk and the Colonel's driver. He was a reluctant draftee with a recent degree in English Literature from somewhere in the Midwest and he casually informed me that he had smoked pot all through college and it had never interfered with his job or his studies. He said all his friends back home were protesting the war and he didn't think we should be in Vietnam at all, especially since we were wrecking the countryside the way we were. "Have you seen parts of the country out by Nui Ba Den, L T? It looks like the friggin' moon it's so pockmarked with craters from all the B-52 bomb runs," he commented sadly one evening as we watched a distant artillery bombardment glow and rumble. "You can feel the ground shake from even five miles away when they drop a load of five hundred pound bombs."

There was a distinct polarization among the troops that was evident during my first several weeks in the country. This separation was especially obvious due to my position as an Executive Officer in a rear area. I could enter the Battalion HQ or radio room and find out what was happening out in the field. Roaming the motor pool and supply room as the S-4 Officer I was certain to get acquainted with the men in those areas. It was plainly evident that there was a vast chasm between the career men and the everyday soldiers and that gap of understanding and agreement on even the simplest matters was nowhere more apparent than in the choice of substance – either alcohol or marijuana – as an occasional indulgence or daily habit.

The job of Executive Officer required contact with lifers like Sergeant MacAnally, who was easily respected as a man and as a good Supply Sergeant. I also had frequent contact with Filbert, a chronic weed smoker who also deserved respect as an excellent Headquarters Company clerk. Furthermore, my occasional indulgence in marijuana along with drinking a beer every now and then, led to frequent contact with both career men and draftees. The polarities and differences were impossible to miss.

Filbert was the first of many war-resisters I encountered during my second tour of duty. These men had their own web of information and connections and were smoking weed and coordinating resistance among themselves while the lifers were drinking beer and discussing the apparent morale problems they could observe. The "hippy soldiers" were protesting the war from close quarters, though, so they had to tread a thin line to avoid becoming enmeshed in the Army's Uniform Code of Military Justice (Presumed Guilt) jurisprudence system. Undoubtedly some of these men did more to stop the war than any thousand protesters back in the US. They were there in the war while protesting in their own way.

The efforts of these soldier protesters would never be recognized by the cowardly, blameful anti-war activists who screamed insults and spit on them when they returned home. For many men, the initial insults they received from the peace-loving, self-righteous activists would be a heavier burden to carry than their experiences during the war. Statistically, only about ten percent of personnel in a combat zone were engaged in actual ground combat; and in Vietnam the real number of atrocities like My Lai was extremely low. Certain events were greatly exaggerated by the American media, which was, and still is, dominated by left-wing liberals who were against the war.

Later, in the 1980's, it was estimated that fifty percent of the combat veterans who returned from the war in relatively one piece would succumb to the onerous burden piled on them by the war protesters and not live to see age forty. Fifty percent of the combat veterans who returned from the war were dead or MIA in their own country within about ten years after the war ended in 1975. There was such a large number of Vietnam Veterans who did not show up in any household for the 1980 census that counseling centers were established, initially called Vietnam Veterans' Readjustment Centers.

If these soldier-resisters had been in the US and still been civilian students, they might have been draft-dodging, long-haired, stoned hippies, many of them. But they were not in the US and they were not civilians anymore. They had screwed up and gotten themselves drafted into the Army and they had fucked up by winding up in the Infantry. And they had further fucked up by being sent to Vietnam. So they saw no reason to not get still further fucked up by smoking another sweet joint. This is probably the reason they referred to getting high as "gettin' fucked up" and damn near everything else, including every fuckin' sentence included the word "fuck" in it. Most would find this coarse language a difficult habit to break. They had to be careful not to ask mother to "pass the fuckin' salt" at the dinner table when they got home.

Lieutenant Lumbert did not yet realize he was fucked. He was still under the illusions of the "war effort" and of fighting off the dread forces of Communism that he had been raised with. He thought he was there to save this little country – these little people – from some big fat Russian or some Chinese Communist. That is what his superiors had told him and he did not have any reason to entertain serious doubts yet.

Many participants did have reservations about the bombing and it did seem that just counting up the bodies at the end of the week was a questionable method of conducting a war – even when the totals reflected more of "them" than "us." I found myself troubled by the suspicion that nobody really knew how to win the war nor even how to conduct it, much less what a certain tactic should be called in press releases. My gloomy introspection was fortunately broken by good old "Sarn't Mac."

"You look like you need to get laid, sir," he said one morning. "I need a Officer-in-charge of a requisition run down to Long Binh and Saigon...probably have to spend the night. Might even find some pussy at the HO-tel too, you never know, hee-hee."

"What sort of requisition run, Mac," his XO asked matter-of-factly.

"Oh some regular stuff you have to sign for and some other stuff we trade for with the Air Force. For the stand-down." One of the Companies would periodically come in from the field for two or three days of in-country R&R (rest and relaxation) in the Base Camp. They would enjoy barbecue, volleyball, movies, and of course beer – lots and lots of beer. The men could take care of minor medical problems and administrative matters as well as shopping at the PX for snack foods, paperback books, magazines, and other personal items. It was usually a good time for everyone involved and I had been seriously and conscientiously preparing for the upcoming stand-down.

"Sounds good to me, sarge. Anything for the troops, you know I'm ready." All we had to do was inform the HQ Company Clerk, my good friend Filbert, and a few minutes later we were out the gate in a ¾ ton pickup headed for Saigon.

The highway to Long Binh was well traveled and generally safe during the day, so we had an uneventful trip. As we approached the gate at Tan Son Nhut Air Base I asked Mac what was in all the ice chests and coolers in the back of the truck.

"Nothing yet, sir," Mac replied with the sly look seen so often in Supply Sergeants. "But there's going to be iced-down steaks in 'em after I see a friend over here about an air conditioner." Mac parked the truck by a small office at the end of a warehouse and went into a side door of the long Quonset-style building. When he returned a few minutes later he pulled the truck around the end of the warehouse and stopped behind a small office, which I could see had just been built.

"You talk to your friend about the air conditioner?" I asked innocently.

"Nossir, nobody around, heh, heh. This here is my friend," Mac said as he pulled a screwdriver from under the seat, "and that there is our air conditioner." He casually indicated a unit installed in the back window of the office.

Having more than a trace of larceny in my heart, this XO caught on quickly. I could not help laughing as I aided and abetted Mac in prying open the window, removing two screws, and within about two minutes flat, lifting the air conditioner and setting it in the back of the truck. Seconds later we were driving away inauspiciously and obeying all the normal traffic laws. "So we're stealing this evidently brand new air conditioner from the Air Force..."

"Requisitioning, sir...it's all guv'ment property and we're all guv'ment employees," Mac said, not wanting the Lieutenant to get the wrong impression.

"Okay then, we're requisitioning this air conditioner from the Air Force and we're going to trade it for steaks?"

"That's affirmative, L T...Navy steaks...prime T-bones."

Now this formerly honest XO laughed out loud. "This is starting to remind me of Milo what's-his-name in <u>Catch 22</u>." I had read the hilarious novel when a senior in high school. "So who's got the Navy steaks? Where is the Navy stationed around here anyway?"

"The Navy's got the best chow, sir," said the Sarge, stating a well accepted fact while he decided how much of his business to reveal to the young Officer. "Our steaks should be waitin' for us at the NCO club supply warehouse over in Long Binh. A buddy of mine is holdin' 'em for me. That's what all those flack jackets are for, L T. Those are a friendly storage fee I'm paying my buddy who, by the way, controls the flow of all the beer and liquor to all the NCO clubs in the whole damn country." I had noticed more than the usual number of flack vests piled around the cab and stuffed behind the seat.

"So we got plenty of flack jackets, huh?"

"Plenty, sir. A lot of the men won't even take 'em out to the field when we issue one. Too hot and too heavy they say."

"Ah-ha, so what does your buddy do with the flack jackets, trade them for something else?" I was thoroughly enjoying the turn of the conversation...the idea of pulling off some minor escapades.

"Gives 'em to his truck drivers. They wear one, sit on one, put one or two against the doors and on the floor...they can't get enough of 'em," the crafty Supply Sergeant explained.

"And so...what happens to the air conditioner...it goes to the Navy?"

"Nossir, they'll probably install it in one of our NCO clubs," Mac said with a giggle. "They ain't so easy to come by, you know.

We already gave the Navy some other stuff for the steaks." Sarn't Mac glanced slyly at me to see how I was reacting.

"Some other stuff?...never mind Mac," this Officer-in Charge of illegal shenanigans said with a grin. "Oh, they ain't so easy to come by, huh Sarge. Haa-ha." Once we were clear of the scene of the crime we both burst out laughing like a couple of schoolboys who had pulled a prank on a teacher. I never was clear on what the air conditioner was payment for...interest maybe, or just plain mischievous opportunism, I supposed. It seemed some part of the explanation was missing or unclear to me...no doubt just what the sneaky Sergeant had intended.

We dropped off the air conditioner and all the coolers and flack vests at a warehouse in Long Binh and I watched as some men unloaded the truck. Mac talked and joked with an E9 Sergeant Major on the loading dock, occasionally glancing in my direction with a nod that everything was proceeding according to plan, then he followed the Sergeant Major inside the warehouse. He returned with a bottle of Johnnie Walker cradled in his arm and a smug smile on his face. "All set, sir. We'll pick up our steaks in the morning. You want to have a drink at the finest HO-tel in Saigon?" he asked as he drove out the gate into the most amazing, confusing mass of cars, trucks, buses, mopeds, and rickshaw-like "cyclos" that I had ever seen or even imagined could exist in all the world. Wartime Saigon just after Tet in 1969 was a very busy and hectic place.

Mac negotiated the truck with scant inches to spare and added his bellicose cussing and honking to a thousand others in every block. I just sat there, clinging to my seat, too stunned to say anything. We parked in an enclosure guarded by American Military Police and ARVN "white mice" - soldiers of the South Vietnamese Army who always seemed to be the smallest of the diminutive race and functioned as the Police of Saigon. They wore stark white helmet liners that looked much too large for them, thus earning the undignified appellation.

We walked the few blocks to the Saigon Hilton, a one-time five-star International Hotel. On the way, cab drivers, money changers, hustlers and beggars accosted us as we passed one sleazy-looking bar after another. Mac stopped to talk to one of the more well-dressed cab drivers and pulled out a twenty dollar bill – an American greenback – and traded it for a pile of piasters from the cabbie. "A little spending money, L T...buy ya a beer?" he asked as he steered me into a garish, noisy bar. On a small stage at one end of the bar a band of four Philippine girls was punishing their guitars and drums playing <u>Satisfaction</u> by the Rolling Stones in the late morning gloom of the poorly-lit dingy interior of a place that looked like the set of a cheap "B" movie. Their rendition seemed somehow appropriate.

This bemused Lieutenant smiled while following Mac over to a table. I looked around, peering through the gloom and thought, *jeez, it would be kind of funny if it weren't so sad.* I glanced again at the rocking Philippine girls as a tired-looking young woman approached and said to me, "ah, tungwee (lieutenant), you buy me drink, okay?"

"Naw, no...no tungwee buy you drink. You bring us beer, okay," Mac broke in, pulling out his roll of bills. He peeled off two fives, enough for two beers and a generous tip then gave her a friendly pat on the ass as she left giggling. "We'll find us some fine-looking women over at the HO-tel, L T. Everybody's got to make a livin', even in a war...right Lieutenant?" The easy-going wheeler dealer winked and seemed to be very much in his element, familiar with the scene.

"That is an obvious fact, Sarge," I readily agreed, sipping tepid beer and listening to the raucous rock & roll that was actually not too bad once you acclimated to their accent. The Asian beauties strolled in and out, giggling and smiling among themselves and eyeing us for a possible lucrative half hour of licentious pleasure. *This is turning to out to be an excellent assignment...excellent indeed.* A fantasy flowed through my mind...a plan to be the best damn S-4 Officer the Battalion ever had...a regular Milo Minderbinder...that was the name of the hustler depicted in the novel Catch-22. I began to imagine being a real slick wheeler-dealer procuring all sorts of goods for the men. When we left the bar a half hour later, the ever-surprising Mac demonstrated some more sidewalk magic.

Mac pulled several blank ration cards out of his wallet and negotiated selling them to a carefully selected cabbie for a sizable wad of bills. "For the girls sir, you know...heh hee." Ration cards are issued to each American soldier, enabling them to buy specific high dollar goods at the Post Exchange at duty free prices. For instance, Seiko watches, Pentax cameras, Sony TV's, and stereo equipment could be bought by GI's and their ration card was punched like a bus ticket for each type of purchase. If a cabbie had his own ration card he could persuade a GI to go into the PX and buy an item that could then be sold on the black market at a huge profit. Therefore ration cards were worth a lot to cab drivers who knew how to use them and the cabbies were worth a lot to Sergeant Mac, who knew how to use <u>them.</u>

"Where did you get the blank ration cards," I asked, just out of curiosity...not for a moment considering the illegality of such a transaction.

"Right out of your safe, sir, you got a whole stack of 'em," Mac replied with an innocent look. "The XO before you, Lieutenant Lumbert...well we did some tradin' and dealin'."

"Oh yeah? Doesn't anyone notice?"

"Well, I don't know...you're the one, the Alpha Company XO, who keeps track of that sort of stuff," Mac responded casually as we strolled up the street to the "<u>HO</u>-tel," as he pronounced it, referring to the likelihood of meeting hookers...women of the night.

The Saigon Hilton was indeed a fine old hotel, only slightly faded from bygone days, and there were certainly some fine-looking women in the bar and ballroom on the top floor, just as Mac had promised. One of the most beautiful women I had ever seen in my life walked right to me and said, "hello Lieutenant," in near perfect English. "Are you staying at the Hilton tonight?" she asked as she leaned forward a bit, exposing some delicious-looking mounds of breast beneath her silk dress.

"Why yes," I replied coolly, ignoring Mac's leering. "Can I buy you a drink?"

Mai explained over drinks that she was half French and half Vietnamese and she worked in some sort of agency, thus the fluency in English. We dined and we drank as I admired her smooth skin and gazed into her fathomless dark eyes. We enjoyed a pleasant evening getting acquainted as if it were an ordinary date. I wanted to draw out the evening while also being increasingly impatient to arrive at the real reason she had approached me in the first place. Mai suddenly leaned across the table and took both my hands in her small, smooth, long-fingered hands and asked me, "so, do you want a woman tonight, tungwee?" She flashed an irresistible coy smile, elevating my blood pressure by twenty points and noticeably increasing the blood flow to certain areas.

"Yes," I responded immediately. I enjoyed a night of sexual pleasures beyond any previous experience, filled with innovations and ministrations by her that went further than my most lurid and lascivious fantasies. *Oh wow...how does she know that about a man's body?* Like most twenty-year old men raised within the morality of the previous decade, I was just plain naive sexually. It was a night to be remembered explicitly for years to come.

Next morning, Mac tapped on the door and peeked in, then entered with two beautiful smiling girls, one quite skinny and the other one slightly fat. "Who you got there Sarge, Laurel and Hardy?" I asked with a relaxed laugh.

"Well sir, I like one to play with and one as a pillow, heh-hee," he replied as he re-wrapped the bath towel around his ample midsection, the only thing he was wearing besides his flip-flops. "You gonna be ready to head out pretty soon, L T?"

"Sure thing, be ready in a few minutes," I replied as I stroked the silky thigh of the woman I would remember for many years. Then I kissed her passionately on the mouth one last time before taking a characteristically quick military shower and shave. After dressing I met Mac out in front of the hotel about ten minutes later and we caught a cyclo back to the parking enclosure instead of walking because we both felt, understandably, just a wee bit tired. Saigon was already hot, noisy, and congested as Mac started the truck and headed back out to Long Binh to pick up the steaks.

And sure enough, the steaks were all iced down and ready. It was no surprise that Mac had arranged for a successful business deal, however complicated and questionably within legal limits. Dealing with a Sergeant Major who controlled all the beer and liquor in the country allowed for some leeway beyond the strict legalities. We connected with a convoy and made the trip back up the highway to Cu Chi without incident. This overwhelmed Lieutenant was glad for an uneventful trip so I could relish the memories of the previous night.

In my role as Battalion S-4 Officer I assumed command of the precious beer and steaks when they were unloaded at the HQ mess area and was engaged in planning with the cooks when the word came in that second Platoon of Bravo Company had made contact and was in a serious firefight out by Diamond Fire Support Base. I spent that late afternoon and early evening in the radio room with Mac, Filbert and several other men from Bravo Company who had come in early for the stand-down. Later that evening, when nobody could think about sleeping anyway, they started a poker game in the back of the commo shack next to the Battalion Command Center.

The game included Staff Sergeant E6 Don Guessler, the Bravo Company Supply/Mess Sergeant, who sat in with weak enthusiasm initially, playing a few hands occasionally during the evening. Guessler felt understandably subdued since his Company had been ambushed that day resulting in three or four wounded, one seriously. Guessler played due to a tradition of throwing a poker party the night before a guy went on R & R out of the country...in this case to Hawaii. Sergeant Mac, Filbert, and a few of the RTO's who were working the radios all night wanted to give Guessler his going-away party where it was assumed the guest could not lose, one way or another. Sergeant Guessler was going to Hawaii to meet his high school sweetheart and get married amidst a huge celebration by both families who had all been friends for many years. The two lucky fathers were partners in a very successful business.

But Guessler was a damn good poker player on any given night, a fact that was well known before the game got serious. On this particular night, however, the man had cards dealt to him that were purely astonishing to everyone present and the losing hands were so good that nobody could fold and had to see each hand through to the end. Guessler himself was embarrassed to have the single wild joker three times in a row and started apologizing...while scooping in the money, of course. There was nobody present who was such an expert card manipulator to have deliberately dealt him such hands.

There was action on the radio for most of the night as a heavy squad from Bravo Company went out on an ambush patrol right back into the same area where their second Platoon had been fired on that afternoon. I thought it was a pretty gutsy thing to do and felt pride at being a member of these Wolfhounds. Most of the clerks, drivers, and supply personnel who knew Sgt. Guessler in the rear area dropped by for a hand or two and when word got out of the kind of cards that were falling, several sat in and really tried to win some money, driving the stakes up, trying to break the flow of cash towards Guessler. But they never did. It was as if he was sitting at the end of a funnel and any money on the table just slid into his pile. No one had ever seen anything like it.

The poker game went late into the night, punctuated by radio transmissions and only momentarily interrupted when three mortar rounds dropped into the Base Camp. Someone remarked, "sounds like that one landed near the airfield," prompting several muted "yeps." They played subdued deliberate poker, inwardly agonizing over what had happened out in the field that day. It was another 24 hour day for many present. It was another day and a night in Vietnam. It was just Vietnam.

The next day, Guessler was due to fly out to Hawaii and he was standing outside the terminal at the airfield showing someone a picture of his sweetheart whom he would be embracing a few hours later that day. He was just standing there in the middle of Cu Chi Base Camp talking and waiting for his flight. Then, in one of those moments that are forever etched into the mind of everyone present, Sgt. Guessler...the luckiest man alive at poker...was struck in the neck by a stray rifle bullet fired from so far away that nobody even heard the shot. He was struck down on the tarmac and dead within minutes. The widespread shock and grief and unbelievable irony of his death definitely put a damper on the poker games for everyone aware of the event. That one night was the only time I played poker in Vietnam and it is a safe bet that I never again played any game of chance without remembering that horrific incident. My attitude towards "luck" changed that day. Maybe a person had only a certain quantity of luck in life and one should not waste it on unimportant endeavors. A guy might need it later for an eventuality of genuine importance. The man Guessler only had about a month left on his tour.

That day I had an uncomfortable revelation as I remembered tossing those five dice just a few weeks back in Oakland, and decided not to be too lucky. Maybe the day after winning the biggest jackpot will be the worst day of your life...or the last. I concluded that I did not want to experience every possible combination of the dice...every dot on the matrix. When the report came that the second Platoon Leader, a Lieutenant I had not even met, had died as a result of wounds suffered the day before, I thought, *there's one of the thirty dots on the five dice...there's one of the possibilities on those five sixes.* And that night I did not sleep well, pondering the other twenty-nine possibilities, knowing they were twenty-nine thousand.

The next day Bravo Company came in for their in-country stand down as scheduled. The men had fun and relaxed despite the recent losses – heavy losses in that their experienced Platoon Sergeant had been seriously wounded and would not be going back out to the field. They had also lost their Lieutenant but he was new in country and nobody seemed to know much about him. The other two casualties were relatively minor and the men would return to duty in a few days.

Unforeseen stress factors were being created by the simple fact that each man came alone to each unit for a set period of time – one year. Usually they had not only left their families, they had left whatever friends they had made during training. Each man came alone. Each man experienced the uncomfortable time of being the "newby." When his year was over, if he survived, he went home alone and once again left any friends he had made in Vietnam. One lasting consequence of these repetitive experiences was the tendency to not make any serious commitments towards lasting friendship because one would always leave later and go somewhere alone. In other wars this was not always the case. Units trained together, fought together, and then went home together. Of course, new recruits would be shipped in as replacements from time to time; but in Vietnam one was a new recruit over and over, always leaving whatever friendships had developed and going on alone.

As a man neared the end of his tour he had known more and more friends along the way who had died or suffered horrendously right in front of his eyes, so he gradually withdrew into himself. He became less interested in meeting anyone new whom he would be leaving soon anyway. He prepared himself to leave everyone he knew and had lived and fought with and go back home alone. The team spirit and unit cohesiveness and many other factors which were heavily emphasized and obviously functioning during all their stateside training were sometimes absent in the small group each man joined in Vietnam.

Another aspect of this replacement procedure was that there was seldom anyone present with a full year of experience doing anything in any type of unit in Vietnam, from front-line troops to the jeep drivers and mail clerks. It was evident to me at the time that this situation was leading to a lot of morale problems. There was no solution to this circumstance; it was just how the Government and the Commanders had decided to fight this particular war. I did not think I was part of the morale problem yet; but I could not imagine a solution either...a way of thinking and acting which would prevent becoming part of the problem. As an Officer, I was automatically separate from my men according to the dictates of Army etiquette. It was a part of military indoctrination.

During the stand-down I met the first Platoon Leader of Bravo Company, the aptly named Lt. Manly. Greg Manly was athletic, gung-ho, and could serve as a handsome clean-cut example of a military man on a recruitment poster. He led a dozen volunteers on a midnight sweep and ambush patrol in retaliation for the firefight earlier that day. Manly described in detail how they had found the Vietcong hiding in a hooch and blasted them with machine guns, hand grenades, and M-16's until there was nothing left but dust and ragged remnants of the bamboo and rattan structure. Then they had confirmed three Vietcong dead without any casualties themselves.

Lieutenant Manly was a career Officer who had already been awarded a Silver Star for bravery and a Purple Heart for minor shrapnel wounds received during the Tet offensive in February. He advised me of some of the realities of leading an Infantry Platoon in Vietnam. "Sometimes the main thing I stay focused on is to try to get the men to move slowly. I have lost more men to booby-traps than anything else. That ambush yesterday...those were local villagers armed with AK-47's who had watched us making sweeps past their village for several days, then bam! They hit 'em with an ambush in broad daylight when the platoon was tired and almost back to the Fire Base. They didn't expect us to pursue them after dark but I was all het up for an ambush patrol anyway so we went out and heard them talking and smoking in a hooch at the edge of the village...and opened up on 'em." The man presented this account without bragging or even thinking he had done anything unusual. Just doing his job. I decided to remember everything this modest hero said. The simple factual presence of Lt. Manly brought out immense respect in everyone. In a lighter moment, he said, "we reduced that hooch to a pile of perforated palm fronds...yes we did. In about ten seconds."

On the third night of the stand-down Diamond Fire Support Base was hit with a full-scale mortar and ground attack that started with dozens of mortar rounds at about 0300 and continued all night. Hundreds of NVA were thrown against the perimeter in a sustained ground assault with sappers getting through the wire and blowing up bunkers with hand-held satchel bombs. With only two Companies of Infantry, minus one Platoon, manning the perimeter, the Wolfhounds survived almost total annihilation because massive Artillery bombardments had been planned in advance and helicopters arrived to deliver accurate fire with rockets and machine guns. Lieutenant Manly had a total shit-fit at being in Cu Chi eating steaks and drinking beer instead of out there in the fighting. He tried to get some choppers to take him and his men out to land outside the Fire Base and attack the attackers from the rear. It was an ill-conceived plan that was nixed by Battalion; but Manly was ready with extreme malice in his heart and not a trace of fear in his electric blue eyes. Lieutenant Greg Manly was an awesome force of nature, ready to lead his men on a path of destruction; but he thought he was just a soldier doing his job.

Our casualties were four dead and twelve wounded during about three hours of fighting. The enemy left eighty dead on the battlefield and it was assumed they dragged an equal number away when they broke off the engagement. I realized the seriousness of the situation when the incident was lauded as a success. Due to the overall body count, the encounter was considered a rout of enemy forces and plans were initiated to dismantle Diamond I and build Diamond II.

As the S-4 Officer I was in the position to listen to the planning sessions in the Battalion HQ. Sometimes, with information from Filbert, I knew more about an operation than the Company Commanders. For instance, there were plans to provide an immense amount of fire power at Diamond II in the form of more M-60 machine guns and claymore mines, and more ammunition of all types for the Infantry. And there was a plan for more Artillery support from distant units and more ammo of various types for the 105mm howitzers within the perimeter. Air support in the form of Cobra gunships, Hueys loaded with rockets, and a C-47 with "miniguns" capable of firing an astonishing 6000 rounds per minute, were all coordinated beforehand. Diamond II was a deadly trap designed to lure the NVA into another full-scale ground attack where we would tally up impressive body count statistics.

A feeling of sadness entered my heart at the thought of all the men who would undoubtedly die at Diamond II and I was surprised to find myself also feeling remorseful over the enemy forces who would die. Live men were the bait and living men would attack. And many soldiers on both sides would die or suffer life-changing wounds and injuries. It was possible that I was the only participant at the planning sessions who questioned the whole premise...who realized the absurdity of such a plan...who wondered about the "why" of the endeavor. There occurred the uncomfortable thought that maybe I was not Officer material to begin with. I was questioning the rationale behind our engagement in Vietnam and the tactics we were using to locate and obliterate the North Vietnamese Army. They were fighting for the unity of their country and we were an alien invading army. These were not appropriate sentiments for an Infantry Officer.

A few days later, and in a single day, the Battalion constructed Diamond II. I flew out on one of the Chinook helicopters – huge two rotor supply craft – and watched the Fire Base being constructed. After supervising the unloading of the choppers and trucks, I met 2nd Lieutenant Charles Bertolcinni, the Artillery Forward Observer attached to the Infantry. "Bert" was from Chicago and had volunteered to serve just as I had. He had attended OCS, then advance training in coordinating and commanding Artillery units that were sometimes miles away from the targets. I had been taught the theory of calling in fire missions in OCS and was interested in knowing more about the actualities here in Vietnam. My sincere questions sparked an instant friendship between us, knowing we were two lowly Lieutenants trying to understand tactics of survival and destruction in a war we were about to experience close at hand. It was a very serious conversation, for sure.

When the last chopper departed late that afternoon, I was supposed to return to Cu Chi Base Camp. I decided to stay and asked my Commanding Officer, Captain Ashley, if I could help "killer" call in the Artillery if we were attacked that night and Bert had to coordinate many different sources of supporting fire. Captain Ashley gave his consent, figuring that since I was on my second tour I must know what might happen. I actually had no idea, never having experienced a full scale ground assault by the well trained and seasoned North Vietnamese Army. Perhaps my recent observation and conversations with Greg Manly had some influence on my nonchalant attitude. I did not consider myself to be brave. I was just going to do one of the jobs I was trained to do.

The Infantry applied the nickname "killer" to the Artillery Forward Observers who were temporarily attached during certain circumstances. The nickname was obviously appropriate once one saw a good Forward Observer adjust the tremendous crunching explosions fired by distant Howitzers, walking the fire right up to your position, wiping out anyone and everything except you and your trembling companions...obliterating the enemy who was trying to creep up and ruin your day. Such an Artillery bombardment was truly a killing phenomenon and the one responsible for calling in and adjusting the explosions was aptly referred to as "killer." An affectionate and respectful nickname.

The rapid construction of Diamond II was an astonishing sight to behold. An extraordinary number of ammo boxes and crates was distributed to the three companies of Infantry that would be manning the perimeter, more that twice the number of men as had been at Diamond I. I had never seen so many men working so hard for an entire day. After most of the supplies were distributed or stored I spent the late afternoon with Bertolcinni, plotting fields of fire and establishing coordinates for planned bombardments.

Early that evening in the Company Command bunker, Captain Ashley was obviously tense as he gave out the watch schedules for the night. "Now when your watch starts, you go out there and you creep around to every bunker on our side of the perimeter, whisper the password, and you make sure two men are awake in every bunker," he directed with military explicitness and automatic repetition. I thought it was unlikely we would be hit with a ground attack on the first night. The NVA probably was not yet ready to duplicate the attack of four nights earlier on Diamond I. Little did I know. The general opinion around the command bunker was that we would be probed with mortars or rockets. Everyone was urged to stay alert and expect anything. The foot patrols and random ambushes would begin the next day. Little did we know.

As everyone got set for the night, Bert and I extended our friendship and talked about home towns, girlfriends, the Army, the war, and the amount of time left in our deployments. "Man,

Lumbert, you volunteered to come back for a second tour when you didn't have to?" Bert asked, not quite masking his amazement.

"Yeah, well I guess it's sort of like training for years for the Olympics then stubbing your toe in the hotel room the day before your event. I was embarrassed to have been sent home for a minor injury."

"Shit man. Well, you served with the "Lurps" and trained with the Rangers, right? How's about you talk to the Cobras if we get in some serious shit tonight?" Referring to the plan for several Cobra gunships that could be dispatched to defend us in case of a major ground assault.

"Oh sure, no problem," I replied. I had requested support from Cobras once from back at the Base Camp during my first tour and I felt confident I could do the job if necessary. I had no doubt I could perform my job out in the field of battle, whatever job might arise. I still did not think we would experience a major attack that night. How little I knew about the field of battle.

I was Officer-of-the-Guard from 0200-0400 and I crept around the bunker line as instructed, whispering the password and finding almost everyone awake at every bunker. The men were tense. Wide awake and alert, everyone of them. At 0300 I froze in my tracks when I heard from the distant treeline, the distinctive sound of a mortar round coming out of the tube "boomph." Before I could yell "incoming" the sound was repeated so many times that it sounded like a movie theater popcorn maker was cooking at full blast in the next room. *HOLY SHIT! This is the real thing.* I ducked into a bunker and quivered and quaked with the cacophony of explosions as the mortar shells rained down on Diamond II like hail stones on a tin roof. Each "stone" exploded and sent shards of screaming hot metal shrapnel through the air. The sense of hearing was overwhelmed...the intensely bright flashes of the explosions blinded the eye...and the whole body vibrated with each crunching flash. The very bones felt melted...the teeth rattled...and one lost consciousness of whether one was awake or not...of whether the eyes were open or not. Then it stopped. Dead silence.

It took a moment to realize I was hearing the "pop" and "crack" of incoming small-arms fire. The "pop" was the sound of a supersonic bullet passing nearby, then the "crack" was the sound of the rifle that was fired. Thus the expression, "you never hear the one that hits you." True. "Here they come! Let's go...on the berm line." I charged out of the bunker with a machine-gunner and helped him get set up on the berm and start firing. When the M-60 momentarily jammed, the entire manual of instruction flashed in my head as I had seen it in OCS and I disengaged the ammo belt and inserted a new one from the can the assistant gunner had just set down. When I saw the M-60 cutting down shadowy figures coming through the wire I realized my place was back at the Company CP so I low-crawled back that way amidst bullets, shrapnel, dust, smoke, and noise beyond description. *Goddamn this is really it!*

Killer was there, crouched behind a semi-circle of sandbags at the entrance to the bunker, shouting into a microphone. I crawled up beside him and surveyed a scene of total bedlam. Our own mortar platoon had fired flares overhead and each intensely bright flare swung and glided beneath its little parachute, casting changeable perspectives. Much of the time the scene was lit as brightly as a lightening strike, every object limned in stark whites and blacks, no shadows anywhere. Then a momentary faltering of light from the flares would allow blackness to crowd in with afterimages of the preceding minutes of splendiferous fireworks still emerging from over-stimulated retinas and it was impossible to tell if one's eyes were open or shut.

As I leaned over to say something to Bert there was a brilliant flash of light and a tremendous thump. We were both thrown backward to the ground by the force of an explosion right in front of us. Reaching for my helmet and replacing it I noticed a trickle of blood on my forehead and had trouble regaining my balance and crawling back behind the sandbag wall which was half demolished and smoking. A rocket propelled grenade (RPG) had hit the sandbag wall. I realized I had seen it streaking towards us for a split second in the corner of my eye. "Are you hit?" Bert yelled as I sat up, surprised by how calm I felt. "Maybe...I don't know. Which mike do I use to talk to some Cobras?" Killer laughed and gave me a handset and we both resumed our positions, crouched between the bunker and the semi-circular wall of half destroyed sandbags at the entrance. For some reason there was also a SP4, one of the regular RTO's out there with us. The Captain and the First Sergeant were down inside the bunker.

Three Cobra Attack Helicopters had been immediately dispatched to the scene and I directed their fire based on what could be seen through all the dust and smoke. Nothing could be seen clearly, so I directed them to fire into the concertina wire surrounding the perimeter. Dizziness and mild nausea distracted me and at times it was impossible to tell whether what I was seeing was just blurred vision or images of distorted men charging back and forth in front of us. I didn't really understand what the hell was happening.

The attack continued for maybe an hour with continuous firing of small arms, machine-guns, exploding RPGs, and artillery shells falling all around the perimeter adding a constant rumble of bursting and screaming of flying shrapnel. There was no way to distinguish one sound from another. The sense of hearing was completely overwhelmed and vision was confusing, distorted, and unreal. Words fail in describing the chaos and cacophony of the scene. The Cobras overhead were sending a constant fire of 20mm grenades and rockets. A C-47 aircraft called "Puff the Magic Dragon" arrived and began firing miniguns at 6000 rounds per minute, seemingly connecting the airplane with the earth with a sweeping solid red line due to every fourth round being a tracer. It was fascinating. At one point, I realized I was just stunned by the fireworks and sat there suddenly proud of not being scared. I was probably just in a state of mild shock.

I was not brave. I was in a state of thoughtless ignorance and shock. There had been a moment of sheer ass-clenching terror when the mortar shells first started raining in; but after that I just performed my duties without a thought of personal survival. Later in my tour of duty I realized that a brave man is one who is scared shitless but still pokes his head up, takes aim, and fires his weapon accurately at an enemy who was firing back. That is bravery.

I was peeking over the sandbag wall to shift the next pass of the Cobras when – BOOM – Bert and I were thrown through the air by a blast. When I managed to connect my brain to my vision I realized I was on the other side of the bunker about ten feet away and there was some trouble with breathing because some sand or dirt was blocking my throat. I sat up feeling dazed and realized Bert was lying nearby twitching spasmodically. I had to keep coughing and spitting and my vision was not clear as I dragged Bert around the side of the bunker and down inside. His legs and arms seemed uncoordinated and his whole body seemed limp yet convulsing automatically. I noticed my right arm was beginning to ache as I dragged the completely limp body of the SP4 RTO down into the bunker. There was no awareness of what else was happening at the time.

Someone was attending to me, trying to determine the extent of my wounds. *I'm hit. I'm wounded in action. What the fuck was that?"* I had to keep spitting as I struggled for each breath and something seemed to be blocking my throat. I sank into a feeling of numb security after the medic gave me a shot of morphine in the thigh. Some level of consciousness remained of the battle raging outside the entryway – outside the haze of pain in my face and throat – and I inwardly congratulated myself on my sense of calm. A realization hit me of the brevity of my second tour – about four weeks again. A strange sort of amusement arose from within at the thought that Infantry Lieutenant really was one of the most dangerous jobs in this war. It had just seemed like a joke bandied about to scare inexperienced young Officers.

In what seemed like an hour later I noticed most of the shooting had stopped and someone, the First Sergeant I thought, was preparing me for a dust-off. I was having trouble focusing my eyes in the half-light of dawn. When I emerged from the bunker into the gray morning light, I was staggered by the sight of the destroyed Fire Base. In three hours of intense combat, everything was blown up, scorched and demolished. There were dead bodies strewn in grotesque juxtapositions: enemy soldiers, unidentifiable body parts and pieces, US soldiers, shredded clothing, boots and equipment, unidentifiable body parts, and uncountable pieces of former human beings. Every bunker was damaged and every square foot of ground had been churned up. Thousands of spent cartridges were piled up, sometimes a foot deep beside machine-gun positions. Chunks of smoking metal emitted noxious gases and the familiar scent of ignited gunpowder hung palpably thick in the still air. And the air was filled with the sounds of suffering, of pain, and of madness, as men begged for help, or provided some, or sat stupefied.

As I lifted off in the Medivac helicopter I surveyed a scene of wreckage, carnage, and strewn bodies that would haunt me for the rest of my life. By official body count, the enemy left over 200 dead on the battlefield and we lost about 50 men dead or wounded. I would remember every body I saw as the chopper rose and crossed the destroyed Fire Base. The combination of shock, morphine, and surprise produced a mental state that captured images like permanent photographs, forever clear when recalled. These images would remain invisibly floating on the outskirts of consciousness, ready to intrude...showing horrific photos at inopportune moments...striking me mute in casual conversation while they paraded through my mind. Some mental photographs last forever and some memories do not fade. Some wartime experiences change a person forever. It is not something you "get over!"

At the hospital in Cu Chi I was fully conscious as doctors examined my head and face, discovering small puncture marks on my cheeks and a piece of metal barely visible beneath the skin behind my left ear. There was a straight laceration in the center of my scalp that was only skin deep. I was also missing the crowns of several molars, both upper and lower, which explained the sensation of "grit or sand" in my mouth after the explosion. I listened as the doctors discussed injecting only light anesthetic due to multiple head and facial wounds. They removed a tiny slightly bent dart from behind the left ear. "I'll keep that, Doctor," I said to a very surprised medical staff. They ware amazed at my awareness of the procedure and surroundings. I was given the dart. Then they extracted the roots of several molars, upper and lower on both sides, that had been pulverized by the passage of tiny darts through my face. It required several surgical personnel to hold me down during the dental procedure, but I did not resent them restraining me and they did not seem to mind my struggles. They were just doing their job. This patient would remember that dental procedure.

Five small darts had passed through my body, one of which had stopped after smashing eight teeth. The wounds were medically classified as "through-and-through" shrapnel penetrations and there were clearly discernible pathways from the entry to the exit scars. It was an amazing incident to the medical staff in that there were no injuries to a major blood vessel or nerve center. However, it was only one case among many that day in the trauma unit. The medical personnel saw mutilated or missing limbs, eviscerated torsos, and bodies so badly damaged that listing the entirety of the injuries in a single case was almost impossible. I was categorized as a post-surgical dental patient with possible complications from swelling and infection, and the doctors, nurses, and technicians turned immediately to the next patient.

Three of the darts had gone through my face from right to left. One had entered about an inch below the right eye, passed behind the nose, and exited at the high point of the left cheek bone. A second had entered the right cheek and exited in front of the left ear, just barely missing the temporo- mandibular joint. Another had entered the right masseter muscle, pulverized some teeth, ripped across the soft palate, shattering several molars on both sides, and lodged beneath and behind the left ear in the neck muscles. The fourth dart had penetrated the right arm just above the elbow and passed clean through without hitting a major tendon, artery, or bone. The fifth dart had lacerated the left shoulder blade, leaving a neat two inch slash as it continued on its flight and probably wounded Lt. Bertollcini next to me.

The laceration of my scalp was caused by a tiny piece of white hot shrapnel from the RPG that had exploded right in front of me. The shrapnel had gone under my helmet as I was thrown backward. The wound was immediately cauterized by the heat of the hot, lacerating shrapnel; but it was extended for cleansing and examination by the doctors. They quickly stapled the skin back together leaving me with a real shocker when I first viewed myself in a mirror. It initially looked like the grotesque remnants of the surgeries of Dr. Frankenstein on his monstrous creation.

Bertollcini also had multiple puncture wounds and unknown spinal injuries as a result of the explosion. The young SP4 RTO had died as a result of his wounds. A few hours or a few days later, time passing incomprehensibly when one is semi-conscious, Bert yelled from across the ward. "Hey Lumbert...did you know we were hit by our own artillery?...fuckin' beehives fired from the Howitzers inside our own perimeter." I knew. I had been lying there thinking about the only known weapon that fired such tiny darts when the round exploded. At Ft. Sill they had given a class on the weapon of last resort that could be fired from 105mm

Howitzers when the entire area was completely overrun by enemy forces.

I surmised that the Artillery Commander, the Captain in charge of the battery of six guns inside our perimeter, had ordered the firing of pointblank beehive rounds because he thought massive enemy forces were overrunning the entire Base Camp. He was probably right, from his perspective. These shells contained 7000 tiny steel darts, packed in such a way as to spray out in all directions when the round exploded. The darts had tiny fins and needle sharp points capable of penetrating the body, as I well knew. The round that had wounded us had exploded right next to us. As I lay there, these deductions were gradually sorted out in a mind dulled by twice daily injections of Demerol.

The Artillery CO was required to inform the nearby Infantry with a code word on all the radios or a special flare triggered before the firing of such a blast, so the Infantry could momentarily duck back down into a bunker. That was the theory anyway. Combat actualities rarely coincide with theoretical speculations by engineers and desk jockeys. I did not recall any warning on any of the radios and was certain no mention had been made at the briefings of the possibility of using such a weapon.

One day, as I was lying there feeling woozy after a shot of Demerol, a Captain from Division came by to present me with a Purple Heart Medal for wounds received and a Bronze Star with "V" device for something I did not hear about because I interrupted the Captain's little speech. "Bhuck your medals...and

BHUCK YOU!" I screamed out of a grotesquely swollen face. I was starting to get pissed about the whole thing.

I did not want a Purple Heart for being shot by our own Artillery and could not understand how they could award me a Bronze Star with "V" device when I had not done anything valorous. That the Army even wanted to do such a thing just reinforced my growing cynicism about the dishonesty and pure bullshit that was happening all around me. It seemed everybody was trying to conceal the fact that they did not know what the hell they were doing, either personally or as a part of the "war effort." I sensed a cover-up in the making.

A day or two later, also just after I had been given a pain shot of Demerol, another Captain from Division came by and said he was part of an investigation and they understood I had one of the darts I had been hit with. I gave him the dart without thinking and never heard from him again. I cursed myself for being so stupid as soon as I could think straight, then I became so angry I could not think straight. I realized I should have kept that dart – not as a souvenir – but as evidence supporting my reporting of the incident. I was going to write my congressman and urge a non-military investigation of not only the firing of point-blank beehive rounds without notifying the nearby Infantry, but the whole premise of deliberately setting up a tempting target so close to a known large concentration of the North Vietnamese Army just over the border in Cambodia.

My normally thin face looked like a blue and purple pumpkin the first time I looked in a mirror and the scar on my forehead looked positively horrendous with the clamps holding together the now four inch incision that the doctors had made to clean and examine what had been a one inch scratch. One of the Doctors, after removing the staples from my head and examining my restriction to jaw mobility said cheerfully, "well no more double-decker hamburgers for you." He meant that would be the worst of my lasting problems – a good outcome. He was suggesting I should consider myself lucky. One should never tell a wounded soldier he was lucky. The lucky ones were never wounded or saw any real combat. They were not in the Infantry to begin with or had a desk job in a rear area.

You're wrong there, Doc. I'll eat a triple-decker cheeseburger some day. I began a regular program of forcing my jaw open more and more each day by jamming two, then three, fingers into my mouth and twisting them sideways. I was an intelligent young man with quite a wide vocabulary; but I was reduced to muttering three words over and over while practicing my self-imposed jaw mobility exercises: "OH HELL NO!" My latent rebellion had definitely been aroused.

Lt. Bertollcini was shipped out to Japan in a wheelchair, not expecting to ever walk again. I was released after ten days antibiotic treatment and bed rest. It was actually due to the fact that my wounds were more serious than the knee injury that I was kept in Vietnam and shipped back to the Wolfhounds pronounced "fit for duty." I was not fit for duty and never again felt fit to even be in the Army, let alone as an Infantry Officer in Vietnam. I was "fit to be tied" is about what I was fit for.

The firing of the beehive rounds had pissed off almost everybody in the Battalion. The investigative Captain from Division had already made the rounds of witnesses and survivors taking note of injuries and collecting evidence. Filbert told me the rumor around the Battalion was that the firing was ordered by Major Stinson, the Battalion Executive Officer who was present at Diamond II and was the overall commander of the Base. The Battalion Commander, LTC Branson flew out from Cu Chi after the attack ended.

In my rage and disappointment I began committing acts of gross disrespect towards authorities and superior officers as I prowled the Base Camp muttering the three word exclamation that had become my mantra of maniacal negativity. "Oh HELL no!" I never again addressed any superior officer as "sir" and I canceled all pledges of allegiance or duty to the organization responsible for shooting me in the face with a 105mm Howitzer, then not even admitting it...wanting to give me a medal for it. I felt tremendously disgusted and penultimately pissed off.

At the first opportunity I went over to Major Stinson's hooch and started venting my anger over the incident. The Major was a big, solidly built, very tough-looking, very black "Black" man who was mature for his rank due to having spent many years as an Enlisted man before being commissioned. He had served in an

Infantry outfit in Korea and had seen serious ground warfare. It was very doubtful he had ever taken any shit off anyone and he did not listen very long to me before pulling a .45 cal. pistol out of a drawer of his desk, chambering a round, and breaking into my tirade. "You listen to me young fella, we were being overrun! And the Artillery Officer gave that order to fire the beehives...you understand me?"And without pausing for an answer, eyes glaring and right hand flexing on the pistol grip, he continued, "And rather than even think you are going to track him down and issue him veiled threats like you just did to me, I'd rather arrest you or just SHOOT your ass right now!" He really looked about to do it, I realized without a doubt...shoot me that is.

So I backed off and cooled down. "Well it didn't look like we were being overrun on our side of the perimeter, Major, and anyway there was no warning given..." My point of argument faded under the implacable gaze of the Major, however, and I began excusing myself and my behavior. Then I stopped, stood there insolently, and was curtly dismissed. I did not clearly know to what extent we were being overrun and the total destruction of the Fire Base indicated that a lot of NVA soldiers had been inside the wire and done a whole lot of damage and inflicted many injuries and deaths. So I had no point.

I really started flying off the handle again when I found out I was being sent out to the field as a Platoon Leader in Bravo Company. It seemed they were short of personnel for some reason. No more "Executive" for this Officer. In fact, there were no

Executive Officers in any of the three Companies. The job was given to me initially because all the Platoons had a Lieutenant and the job of XO was usually assigned to a First Lieutenant. I had already been promoted due to having spent a full year with good recommendations as a Second Louie. In addition I had been an assistant S-4 Officer with the 82nd Airborne and had received high efficiency ratings for that job, so I was assigned that role in the Wolfhounds.

I was fucked and now it was clear. An initial refusal to go out to the field led to being sent to an Army lawyer, prior to being Court Martialed for refusing to obey a direct order and cowardice in the face of the enemy. "You'll do five years hard time in Leavenworth, Lieutenant Lumbert. And believe me it will start today," the draftee attorney said, despite my story of Diamond II being used as bait because we could not find the enemy...and being wounded by the beehive fleshettes...and that such a weapon was against the Geneva Convention...and anything else I could think up.

The next day I was scheduled to go out to a small Company-size Fire Base located near the HoBo Woods – well known to be a spooky, dangerous place. This ex-XO felt betrayed by the organization to which I had given my best efforts. Simple anger did not even approximate the feelings boiling inside me. Furious did not describe the depth of these feelings. What made matters worse was there was not even anyone to directly blame. The Artillery CO was not available, being in another Battalion entirely.

Major Stinson would shoot me for sure if I pursued that route. There was not even an admission of guilt, nor did anyone in command ever describe the incident as a mistake. I resigned myself to my fate. Shit.

Evidently this young man was a major rebellion looking for a cause and perhaps had been that way since childhood. From that day in late April 1969 when this disgruntled Lieutenant shipped out to the field to take charge of an Infantry Platoon in a war that already seemed an unwinnable mistake, I was a changed man. Distrustful of all authority, resentful towards all superiors, resistant to all pressure. And it is tough to succeed in the military or the civilian world with such an internal mindset. It is next to impossible to live happily with such ideas swimming around in one's head like ugly, warty, grouper fish befouling a pristine bay. I began a very destructive habit of self-blaming due to the obvious circumstances in which I found myself, and it would get a lot worse in the coming months. *I joined this fucked up organization to begin with...I volunteered to come back for a second tour like it meant no more than a toss of the dice...I deliberately stayed out at Diamond II when any fool could have predicted a major ground attack.* Yep, I was screwed, blued, and tattooed.

I got stoned one last time with Tom and Filbert. There was no intention of smoking weed when in command of an Infantry Platoon. Simply no way. "Hey, cheer up L T," friend Filbert said. "You'll be back in no time...soon as we get a shipment of newby Second Lieutenants." It was probably true but no matter what

Filbert said, the feelings of resentment and anger remained. Obviously the anger was unreasonable and was manageable. *I have to snap out of this shit and lead an Infantry Platoon like I was trained to do...like I expected and wanted to do when I arrived just a month ago.* And deep down inside somewhere there was still a scintilla of self-esteem and confidence. I could handle the job.

CHAPTER III.

The Platoon Leader

Summer of 1969

First Lieutenant Lumbert was definitely not a "happy camper" when he flew out in a Huey to take over the Third Platoon of Bravo Company, recently reduced in numbers as a result of the two Diamonds. He knew he was in for some hardships, to say the least, and his attitude had been substantially altered since the Army had virtually shot his face off with a Howitzer. The physical scars were minimal and ephemeral though when compared to his mental and emotional changes.

"OH, HELL NO!" I silently and automatically repeated my mantra of maniacal negativity when exiting the helicopter at a small Company-size perimeter near a dense forest. The Commander of Bravo Company was a lantern-jaw West Point Captain named Roger Dodgely, whom his new Platoon Leader immediately and irreverently connected with Dudley Do-Right of the Royal Mounties, a cartoon character. Dodgely even had the same throaty tension in his voice as his namesake on television. "Lieutenant Lumbert...welcome to Bravo Company. I understand you were a bit reluctant to come out to the field where we are fighting the real war," said the CO condescendingly. "I'm sure you will find I run a tight ship here, Lieutenant, and I sincerely hope you are ready to command men in combat."

"Captain, I have already commanded men in combat...where is my Platoon?"this ex-XO replied tersely, not about to take any shit off the guy, *West fucking Point or not*."

"You will command the third platoon...their sector of the perimeter is over there," said the career Army man, evidently well informed of my initial refusal to come out to the field.

I turned and walked in the direction indicated without another word to the prick and our relationship would rapidly deteriorate from this rocky beginning. The base was a scaled-down version of a Battalion Fire Base, with a mortar Platoon in the center instead of 105mm Howitzers. There was no berm line or concertina wire and only a few bunkers had been completed. The men were living in scooped-out fighting holes with poncho coverings for protection against the weather. The rainy season was just beginning. At night, two or three men would occupy each fighting hole, getting what sleep they could in the dirt or crouching ass deep in mud and water.

The Platoon Sergeant and Squad Leaders were somewhat subdued in their greetings, which was understandable since there had been recent heavy loses. The Platoon Sergeant was E5 Alton West, from Lubbock, Texas. He looked and spoke like a cowboy despite the helmet instead of traditional Stetson. West introduced himself and the Squad Leaders and welcomed his hew Platoon Leader. "Welcome to the third herd, sir...we're mighty glad to have you. Now we got twenty men again." An Infantry Platoon normally numbered almost forty men. Twenty was far short of the optimum number expected and only about half the troops in all the training exercises and schools I had attended back in the States. These men were a desultory lot, seemingly depressed, dejected, and disinterested in meeting me.

The stony faces surrounding me suggested that these men knew of my initial refusal to take on the role of Platoon Leader and they probably knew of my being wounded by the beehive fleshettes at Diamond II. Most of them and been at both Diamonds and had already seen two or three Lieutenants rotate through their job site.

"I wish I could say I was glad to be here, but we both know better," I responded honestly as I regarded the impassive faces around me. The men of this platoon probably had some of their own also wounded or killed by the beehive fleshettes at Diamond II, whether they knew it or not. I was certain I had been perforated by the darts only because the destruction of eight molars had slowed one of the projectiles enough for it to have stopped just beneath the skin. I might have been the third or even the fourth Lieutenant some of them had seen during their tour of duty.

Infantry Platoon Leader was one of the riskiest jobs in the war if a man performed his duties properly. The only positions considered more dangerous were door gunner on a Huey or Medivac pilot and crew.

That afternoon I called an informal meeting of my Squad Leaders and anyone in the Platoon was welcome to attend. Almost all the men sat in to acquaint themselves with their new Lieutenant. At one point, after discussing general tactics and experiences, I said, "I'll tell you what I learned from a very experienced Lieutenant with a Silver Star and two Purple Hearts (Manly). The most important element in our continued survival is avoidance of booby traps and one way to do that is to move slowly. Now I am open to suggestions from anyone because some of you have spent more time in the bush than I have. Anyone? Any suggestions or opinions?" No one appeared to agree or disagree. "My most important mission with you men is to send as many of you home with all your fingers and toes as possible," I stated with conviction. Still very little response.

"Roger that," came a halfhearted reply, and there was a murmur of agreement.

"When I was with the Rangers on my first tour we would sometimes spend a whole hour, moving in silent slow motion, just to set out one or two claymores and several trip flares." Nods of agreement went around the group as they listened to their new leader. It occurred to some of them that maybe this Lumbert would be a little better than most of the dipshits they had seen come and go. "And I'll tell you something else I have learned," I lowered my voice and spoke conspiratorially, "sometimes the mission sent down by the brass is uninformed bullshit. I intend to get myself and all of you home safe and sound, as much as possible." I probably stepped way over the line between the accomplishment of the mission and the welfare of the troops; but that was absolutely a truthful statement of my feelings at the time.

"All right!" came a more enthusiastic response from the men. "Hey, three-six, we're behind that idea all the way, sir," my RTO Pete said, using the ID I was to adopt as a radio call sign and a common nickname applied by my soldiers. Everyone seemed to loosen up a bit and I noticed respectful nods toward Pete McDonald, who would be the man closest to me both physically and personally. Pete was the oldest member of this group, at twenty-three, and seemed even older due to his calm demeanor and, as I would later realize, his deep understanding of our circumstances. He was from San Francisco and carried himself with dignity and intelligence. He seemed larger than his 5'6" physical self and he had a serene manner when looking out of his pale gray eyes. I was glad to have him close by from the start.

The code name "three-six" indicated the Platoon Leader of the Third Platoon, and "three-five" was the Platoon Sergeant. "Bravo-six" indicated the Company Commander of Bravo Company. Sgt. E5 West had divided the eighteen men of the platoon into only two squads due to the shortage of personnel. Names or ranks were never mentioned over the radio because the

VC could be listening on radios and had code books they had removed from dead US soldiers. Rank designations on uniforms were subtle black and dark green instead of bright yellow and many troops in Vietnam wore no patches at all on their uniforms because they would wear the same thing for weeks and weeks, then trash everything and get a new uniform from supply. Anyway, nobody was carrying needle and thread in the bush, so the whole system was ignored.

The American military troops were constantly facing enemy combatants who were more experienced than we were, and any additional disadvantage could tip the delicate scales in a life or death situation. We faced soldiers with years of combat experience in their own territory. They were there for the duration; we just wanted to live through a one year deployment. Any tactic American troops could employ to give them a slight advantage was firmly grasped and established, so a seemingly simple concept such as not having rank designations clearly visible was extremely important. Sometimes years and years of continuous combat experience was the main differentiation between the two sides in any confrontation, leaving American troops at a personal disadvantage in many aspects of the war in Vietnam. The helicopter was the principle advantage the US had in Vietnam; but helicopters and aircraft of every description were shot down by the hundreds by the Vietcong and the North Vietnamese Army.

Private First Class E3 Pete McDonald, my RTO, engaged in the very unusual activity of meditating twice every day regardless of the situation. He explained to his new Platoon Leader that he had met the Maharishi Mahesh Yogi in 1964, before he had been drafted, and had taken up the practice of Transcendental Meditation. Twice a day, for almost exactly twenty minutes, Pete would sit with his eyes closed, smiling slightly, and meditate. This was the only time in a 24 hour-a-day job when he would allow someone else to monitor his radio. "I'm going to meditate now, three six," he would say, as if it were as common as taking a shit, and he would pass the handset over. Then he would sit quietly, apparently oblivious to everything for exactly twenty minutes, then open his eyes and go about his business.

Pete's meditation practice was especially intriguing to me because I had studied Judo when I was seven to ten years old at the downtown YMCA in San Antonio. As a despised minority "gringo" I was beat up by two or three "Mexican" kids after school when we had first moved to central San Antonio from Mansfield, Ohio. When my younger brother started first grade and started having the same problem, the family had to move to the far northeast side of town where the minority "Anglos" could live in peace. I remember reading about Sir Edmund Hillary climbing Mount Everest in about 1954 when I was in the first grade. Seeing a photo of the Sherpa guide, Tsensing Norgay, calmly meditating before the final ascent, I had become teary-eyed for some reason I could not understand. When I looked at pictures of Tibet and Nepal in National Geographic in the fourth grade I had a longing to go there. I had entertained fantasies about Tibet and Japan when I was only ten years old. My judo instructor spoke about the importance of regular meditation. He had been with the Air Force during WWII and had been stationed in Japan after the war and had studied Judo and Ju Jitsu for several years with a Master in Kyoto.

During the first few days of watching Pete meditate I asked him again and again to tell me the secret – teach me to meditate. But Pete would smile and benignly say, "only the Maharishi can give you your mantra, three six," in a friendly and somewhat paternal manner. Pete had served under three previous Lieutenants during his eight months in Vietnam. He was the ideal RTO – calm, alert, and generally happy despite our predicament.

After two days of organization and improvement of our positions at the fire base, I had thoroughly acquainted myself with the men and discussed tactics with Sgt. West. I felt prepared to lead the men out the next day on what was actually my first sweep and clear operation. Our area of operation consisted of a dense forest, irrigated agricultural fields, and villages and trails – most of which was more or less accurately depicted on my topographic map. I felt confident in land navigation skills and knew, despite what I had told the men initially that my primary mission was to clearly and precisely know where we were to within 50 meters as we maneuvered through the varied terrain.

When creeping around the perimeter that night to ensure one man was awake at each position, it was impossible not to recall creeping around the bunker line at Diamond II and the mortar and ground attack that followed. I was <u>always</u> awake at

0300, having developed a sleep pattern that would continue long after my return to the civilian world. I did not sleep very deeply at any time and did not sleep for very long at a time each night, so it was easy to check on the men at night. On that night the men were alert as I whispered the pass word and held brief conversations with shadowy figures at every position on the perimeter. My hearing was so acute at night that I could hear an insect crawling over a nearby leaf in near total darkness.

The next day I led the Third Herd on a sweep and clear mission toward a hamlet about three clicks to the east, skirting the edge of the Ho Bo Woods. We were supposed to search the village then select a night ambush position somewhere near the fire base on our return in the afternoon. The men would clear the site of any possible booby-traps before coming back into the perimeter, then later that night, after full darkness, we would sneak back out to the ambush position and remain there all night.

About mid-morning my keen-eyed point man held up his fist then squatted down. The men all stopped and automatically set themselves to watch in every direction. I went forward to the head of the file and the point man indicated a thin wire tied to a bush and stretched across the trail at ankle level. "Booby-trap, sir," he stated the obvious as the demo man and Sergeant West came up. They quickly discovered a Chicom (Chinese Communist) hand grenade wired to a nearby bush, the pin barely held in place. The demolition man began preparing a small piece of C-4 explosive to place next to the grenade and blow it in place. Sgt. West dispersed the men while I called in the SITREP.

"Bravo six, this is three-six, over."

"Bravo six, go," came the reply from Capt. Dodgely.

"Three-six...have found booby-trap...fire in the hole in one zero, over," informing the Captain that the explosion he was about to hear in about ten minutes was no cause for alarm, just the safe removal of a booby-trap.

"Roger three six...Bravo six out."

We would never try to disarm a booby-trap of any kind, regardless of how simple and obvious the mechanism, because the VC were very ingenious in booby-trapping their booby-traps. The safest thing to do was to have one experienced man blow the whole thing in place without disturbing anything. Specialist 4th class Charles "digger" Yardley, my demo man would do the job. He walked around casually with about two or three pounds of C-4 on his person, and usually carried the blasting caps as well for the sake of convenience. He humped with enough explosives on him to blast himself and anyone else nearby into indistinguishable smithereens if he took a hit or tripped a surprise himself. Oddly enough though, there was no shortage of volunteers willing to take the job. It was very enjoyable to blow something up after days and days of inconsequential trudging through the jungle. A demo-man sometimes became the principle hand grenade hurler for some reason too, so there was that added prestige to the position. Some of the men would carry specialized grenades, like "willy peter" (white phosphorus) and would pass them over to the demo-man when asked. He was the official Destructo-Squad Leader, an important position in the Platoon.

I watched "digger" press a blasting cap into a small chunk of the malleable C-4 and carefully place it next to the grenade. He looked to his leader before lighting the fuse with a cigarette because we would have only about ten seconds to move back out of harm's way. It was extremely important that neither of us trip another surprise after he had lit the fuse on the first one. I was about to give the signal to light the fuse when...BOOM...a shock hit me from behind. Sergeant West was writhing on the ground and another man nearby was screaming and clutching his right arm that was spurting blood.

"AAAUUHHH, NO, no, no," West screamed as he looked in horror at what remained of his left foot, which was flopping spasmodically in an impossible manner, the toe of the boot knocking against the shinbone with a sickening "klock-klock." Portions of the calf muscle and the heel of the foot had been blasted away entirely. The other man had minor shrapnel wounds and would require a dust-off along with Sgt. West.

"Bravo Six, this is Three Six, over." I immediately called in as the medic attended to the wounded men.

"Bravo Six, go."

"Three Six. Need a dust-off...have two WIA, over," I ordered, trying to maintain a calm demeanor even though feeling revolted and angry and temporarily unsure of myself and the situation.

"Roger Three Six, On the way. Out." Dudley's voice was unemotional and uninvolved. The Captain would call Cu Chi on another radio and order an immediate Medivac helicopter. There was no reason to explain our position because we had only gone about one kilometer and the CO could tell where we were from the sound of the explosion.

The men were cautioned to move in slow motion as they set up briefly into a perimeter around the two casualties. Nobody triggered another dreaded surprise. I looked sadly at Sgt. West...as careful and alert as a soldier could be...a man I had come to respect and rely on in the previous two days; and I wondered if I was somehow at fault. The calm Texan had already taught me a lot with advice and the manner in which he conducted himself at all times. When noticing the concerned look on Pete's face, I asked him, "Goddamn, Pete...what the fuck?"

"Not your fault, sir. It happens," my sagacious RTO replied consolingly, intuitively sensing my frustration and tendency to take personal responsibility for every occurrence.

Within about thirty minutes a Medivac Huey came roaring in with a radio tuned to the Company frequency and correctly identified the yellow smoke grenade Digger had thrown out. Sergeant West, a fine man and a good soldier, gave us a brave thumbs-up as he was strapped to a litter and said, "move slow and stay low," as they slid him into the chopper. He was a hell of a man.

The inexpressible weight of responsibility dropped onto my shoulders like a soggy mildewed blanket as I looked at the eighteen men looking at me expectantly. Turning to the most experienced Squad Leader, I said, "Break for chow, Sergeant. Let's think things over," thus promoting the Specialist 4th Class to E5 Sergeant on the spot. Filbert would put the paperwork through.

Digger blew the first booby-trap in place, then everyone took a good long break and ate crummy C-rations. I met with the Squad Leaders and asked for input or advice. "I don't ever want to see anything like that happen again. Now, what can we do differently to avoid such a thing?"

"Move even slower, sir?"... "Stay off the trails entirely?"...were the uncertain replies.

It was impossible to never use the trails and footpaths. We wouldn't be able to make any progress fighting through the jungle in places. When we passed over cultivated fields and rice paddies, we had to either walk along the paths on the dikes, or slog through knee-deep water and mud while carrying at least forty pounds of gear. It was a tough call for an Infantry Lieutenant to make at times – how to move through the varied terrain in Vietnam.

"Well I'll tell you one thing. Today we are not going to reach our objective and I'll just take the heat from the CO," I decided. This was a complete reversal of the rationale an Infantry Officer should follow. Following any and all legal and rational orders to the letter without regard to the safety of the soldiers or yourself was the irrefutable dictate of the military. It would certainly not be the only time I would make the wrong choice in the coming months. Wrong according to the Army and wrong regarding my future in the Army. I understood that but chose the welfare of my men over the accomplishment of the mission at times...not always...but occasionally.

I embarked upon a course of action that would continue for the next three months as a line Platoon Leader. I would adhere to this plan regardless of the effect on my now forgotten possible career in the military. I began to realize I was not cut out for this shit and wondered about the entire concept of conquering and occupying this Country.

Halfway back to the perimeter, I signaled for a halt at the edge of a hedgerow of thick bushes that bordered some rice paddies. "What do you think, Sergeant?" I asked Buck Sergeant Thompson, my newly promoted, nineteen year-old Platoon Sergeant. "Looks good to me, Three Six," the man replied, referring to setting up the ambush there that night.

The men very cautiously examined the bushes for booby-traps until everyone was convinced it was clear, provided the VC did not plant some dreaded surprises after we left. There was seldom any degree of certainty in such matters. One had to expect the worst while hoping for the best. When we started back to the perimeter, I felt the sudden loss of my experienced Platoon Sergeant was a definite sign of severe difficulties headed my way. On that very first day of operations in the field the thought crossed my troubled mind of what a complete idiot I had been to volunteer to come back to Vietnam. Each time I caught myself immersed in such negativeness, I banished all self-blaming and resolved anew to stick to the present moment and live one day at a time, minute by minute – as if death was just seconds away. Much later in life I would discover that this was the mindset of Samurai warriors and was one of the most powerful forms of practicing continuous meditation while engaged in daily activities.

Captain Dodgely was not at all sympathetic to the tragedy of losing my most experienced man and focused instead on my failure to reach the assigned objective. "what do you mean you didn't get to the village, Lieutenant?"

"Well Captain, it took quite a while to clear those booby-traps..." I began lamely, thinking the man would understand my plight and not having devised or rehearsed a more plausible story.

"It takes five minutes to blow a booby-trap Lieutenant Lumbert and I didn't hear you find any more of them." The lantern-jaw twitched in irritation as the straight-laced West Pointer continued his reprimand. "That village is full of VC and we have been ordered to clear that village Lieutenant...you know what on order is Lieutenant?...it's what you carry out to the letter regardless of a couple of men tripping a booby-trap," the cold, remorseless – but correct – Captain concluded. He did not really know any of the men in his command nor did he want to. He was interested in the Army, his career track, and following orders without a thought of the consequences to the men. Dudley was simply a balls-to-the-wall lifer, I realized clearly as I listened to the practiced cadence of the berating.

"We'll head over tomorrow..." I began.

"Tomorrow your platoon will stand down. I'll have Lieutenant Kolo search the ville. Dismissed Lumbert," Dudley said with all the exasperation and irritation he could muster.

The man likes giving reprimands. I crossed the perimeter to my makeshift bunker/fighting hole, repeating my mantra automatically. "Oh HELL no!"

"The CO wasn't too happy, huh Three-Six?" Pete asked rhetorically when his Lieutenant stepped down into their fighting hole and sat heavily on his poncho liner.

"Fuck him. I got as much time to listen as he has to chew my ass," I replied casually. "What do we need to do to get ready for the ambush patrol, Pete?"

"Not much, sir...the men pretty much know what to do." And I knew they knew and was glad of it. I memorized my maps while eating some chow and planned the necessary steps to call in an artillery strike in various directions around the location if necessary.

Lieutenant Kolokai, from Molokai Hawaii, strolled up and introduced himself and we two Platoon Leaders discussed the general situation, berated Dudley, and became instant friends. "Dudley, huh Lumbert...that's a good one." The easy going, good-looking Hawaiian laughed. "I've had several run-ins with the man over the same type of thing. He's a real asshole, all right...looks like the cartoon character, too...ha ha. He's one cold mutha though, I'll tell you." Kolo quickly lent his support. "And hey, Lumbert, you did the right thing out there today. Losing a man like Sergeant West is tough on the men." A small Company enclosed within an isolated perimeter was much like a small town. Everybody knew what was happening to everyone else.

"Yeah, well what about me? This was my first day on the job, you know...running this type of operation. When I was with the Lurps we didn't traipse around in the jungle that much. We hid out and stayed put." I was still feeling confident enough...just a bit shaken by the rush of events in the past few days.

"You can handle the job. Hey, ain't nothing." Kolo assured me with a common grunt expression meaning it's no big deal...it's easy.

Early that evening I watched one of my machine gunners clean his M60 and the big muscular Black man glanced up from his meticulous labors, cracked a toothy grin, and said, "nuthin' to it, sir." We had to develop expressions like this to minimize the serious nature of the situation in which we found ourselves. The machine-gunner, PFC E3 Charles Edwards, was the acknowledged leader of the three other Black men in the Platoon and I had already appreciated the solidity in the big man. There was a lot more to him than just his physical size. Edwards was calm and steady, with a hearty sense of humor as well as a serious understanding of our combat milieu.

"You got that M60 looking fine, Edwards...you plan on using that thing tonight?"

"I hope not, sir...ever' damn time I do, some muthafucka start shootin' back."

"Yeah, and they always be aimin' right at you...Ed Man the head man." Pvt. Johnson quipped, one of the other Black soldiers sitting nearby cleaning his M16.

"Big as you is Eddie, I can't see how Chaley keep missin," Johnson added, chuckling in a deep throaty manner.

"I get a whole lot smaller when the shootin' start." Eddie smiled at the image of himself shrinking in size and sunk lower in his seated position.

They continued their friendly banter, trying to ease some of the tension of the day...of the past few weeks...of being in the 'Nam. They were trying not to think of losing their beloved Platoon Sergeant and all the experience and leadership he represented. They were trying not to mention or even think about that most disparaging, despicable, discouraging and disheartening of all the dangers they faced in Vietnam – Booby-traps. They were probably also wondering about the capabilities of their new Lieutenant, but were polite enough to not mention it.

It was times like this that the "Mad Minute" had been developed, when the men would burn ammo for a solid minute as a purge of their accumulated frustrations at not finding anyone to hold responsible...anyone to shoot in retaliation for what had happened to their friends. Big Eddie knew the men needed a Mad Minute, but he did not mention it to his new Lieutenant.

I stood there thinking, once again, of my almost complete ignorance of my situation. I did not really know what the fuck was going on or how I should act in this new role. I felt like a newby. The common sense explanation of what Eddie had said about the natural hesitancy anyone would have of breaking the stillness of the deep jungle night by popping an ambush and opening up with the enormous chattering of an M-60 machine gun just hit me like an awesome slap in the head. *Yep, you shoot at Charlie and you got yourself a firefight...the "muthafucka" right away starts shooting back.* The man made sense, Edwards did. I fell into the good-natured banter.

"Ed Man the head man. You sure carry a lot of ammo for a man who doesn't want to shoot."

"Yeah, well sir, once I do get started it's kinda hard to stop...huh-huh" The man once again stated a simple yet profound truth about American troops in general during that part of the war. We usually had plenty of ammo, and we also had plenty of frustrations, so nobody hesitated to expend some ammo at the least provocation and just hold that trigger down...just burn it up.

"'Course you don't notice the extra weight, huh...look at the legs on this man. Not to mention a bicep the size of a softball. How much you weigh Private Edwards?" I stayed with them in the conversation.

"I'm down to a trim two-twenty now, Three-Six...and six foot four, to answer your next question, L T."

"Well now you're way ahead of me...good man, Edwards," I said, honestly and deeply grateful to have such a man in my Platoon.

"Yessir," Eddie replied, flashing that big grin while still working diligently, carefully cleaning the bandoliers of ammunition link by link, round by round.

I solemnly reflected on my training and experience and asked the Squad Leaders about their standard operating procedures (SOP) to ensure we were all thinking along the same lines regarding the ambush. For example, I found out that even though it was close to the rainy season they did not use their waterproof ponchos while out on ambush because the wet shiny material could be seen too easily. They used only poncho liners, which were made of a camouflaged cotton/rayon blend that did not shine when wet. I listened carefully to the SOP regarding using a rear listening post, which I had been trained to do but which was not being done by that Platoon due to the shortage of men. Instead they tried to choose an ambush site that afforded some type of natural protection from the rear. That idea made sense and I certainly intended to go along with any such suggestions.

After full darkness had enveloped the jungle and just before the rising of the moon, which was two days past full, I led the Platoon out to the ambush site. They were not as quiet as Rangers, but they were good, I had to admit to myself as the eighteen men silently paced along with me under a starry sky. I found the spot without difficulty and we set ourselves for the night. I crept along the border of the hedgerow checking the placement of the machine guns and whispering words of encouragement to my men. Settling in beside Pete, the sounds of the night enveloped my awareness during the start of my first ambush patrol. Adjusting the greenish images in the starlight scope on a treeline the other side of some rice paddies, I breathed deeply to quell my nervousness, being the soldier who actually needed some encouragement that night.

About an hour later while looking through the starlight scope, ears attuned to the rumble of distant artillery, my attention was suddenly arrested by a very faint but distinctly identifiable sound -BOOMPH- a mortar round coming out of the tube. *Mortars? From that direction? Naw.* Then, KA-CRUNCH! There was no doubt. A mortar round exploded about 200 meters away, across the rice paddy. *Holy shit...we are in for it now!* There was a brief image of wide eyes and tight lips of the men in the flash of the explosion. KA-CRUNCH! Another round landed and every one of us jumped a foot off the ground even though lying flat prone. The second explosion was closer. I did not know what to do. Should we get up and run for the bunker line? *Fuck! There is no bunker line!* Embarrassed for having such a cowardly idea, I immediately got on the radio.

"Bravo Six, this is Three Six, over," I said much too loudly.

"Bravo Six, go," came the reply from Dudley's RTO.

"Three Six. I got mortar fire from about one click to the north, over."

"Roger Three Six...we heard it...I'm checking it out. Hold your position, over." came Dudley's voice, as if he knew what his Lieutenant had been briefly considering.

KA-CRUNCH! Another round landed in almost the same place as the second. There is a unique sound a mortar shell makes as it drops almost perpendicularly just before it explodes. It makes a "whirring" sound for a second before the impact as the shell drops at about 400mph. The crater from the explosion of one of the smaller rounds is about four feet in diameter, and shrapnel of various shapes and sizes will shred anyone standing within about fifteen or twenty feet. Through a strange dynamic in explosive projectiles however, there is a blank space in the killing zone of a mortar round. If a man was flat prone, hugging Mother Earth, he might escape unscratched from a round exploding only a few feet away. It is a mystery to anyone unfortunate enough to observe the confusion of battle...a mystery of life and death and of those who live through the deaths of others nearby. A riddle...it is a mystery of life and why some continue living and others do not.

Probably every one of us nineteen men damn near passed out from oxygen deprivation before we drew another deep breath, listening for that "whirring" sound we would hear an instant before the next explosion. But it did not come. I wracked my brain trying to decide on what we should do before the ground attack started. I could not think of anything, but lay there for an eternity in excruciating expectation. But we did not see or hear another thing for the rest of that long, long night.

After about an hour, taking a long deep breath, I whispered to Pete lying wide awake beside me, "what do you think, Pete?"

"Could have been RIFs Three Six," came the all-knowing unhesitating reply.

Random Interdictory Fire. I had not thought of that, only thinking that it must be the North Vietnamese Army preparing for another ground assault like at Diamond. It turned out Pete was correct, as usual. It was the "Arvins" - the South Vietnamese Army. Our allies had fired those mortar rounds. Third Platoon had just come in after dawn, a tired and bedraggled lot, to be sure.

"Arvins?!...there's no Arvin post shown on my map," I told Captain Dodgely a few minutes after we had entered the perimeter. The CO had explained the source of the mortars.

"They have just set up this past week and liaison hasn't been firmly established as yet." Dodgely lapsed into military jargon and was really pissed off over the event. The Captain was not tolerant of mistakes by anyone. He had probably been on the radio all night chewing ass to even get that much information. To me, it was just another dangerous insult in a growing list of offenses against me and my men. A growing list of offenses committed, not by the enemy, but by the US Army through carelessness, stupidity, and pure accident. I could not care less about the official explanation of the event and thoroughly resented every straw on that camel's back.

"So these Arvins don't even know where we're at...they're just popping out mortar rounds at random? Captain, that is a bunch of SHIT!" I exclaimed, even less tolerant of that particular mistake than the Captain ever could be.

"The situation will be straightened out to my satisfaction before I send any of you out on another ambush I can assure you, Lieutenant Lumbert."

"What a bunch of bullshit!" This disgruntled Lieutenant muttered, trudging back to my position, the mantra effortlessly revolving in a tormented mind like a tired rusty weathercock. The Platoon had the day off, and I sighed with relief, easing the body down to rest...more tired than I could ever remember. The first full day of leading men as a Platoon Leader had been worse than the bleakest expectations. Barely sleeping, and unable to just lie there after awakening, I began studying maps of the AO, then restlessly walked around the perimeter and looked at the men sleeping or quietly tending to their equipment. *I am personally responsible for what happens to every one of these men.* No course of instruction in Officers' Candidate School had been an adequate preparation for the tremendous responsibility of leading a Platoon in a combat zone. Perhaps the course had been designed with the presumption that a young Officer should not be overly concerned about the welfare of his men. But I <u>was</u> concerned.

Lt. Kolo and his Platoon came in from their sweep in the late afternoon. They had not found anything suspicious in the village I was to have reached the day before. They had found two more booby-traps just a short distance down the trail from where Sergeant West had been mutilated. They all walked back in with their limbs intact, having blown both devices safely in place. *Hooray for our side* I thought morosely, unable to accept the job of Infantry Lieutenant yet. There was a schism between the priorities of the mission and the welfare of the men and this dilemma was nowhere more apparent that at my personal level of command. I personally knew the men and actually led and participated in the missions.

In the early evening we two Lieutenants spent a long time talking and a very close bond began to form between us. It is safe to say that a conspiracy was launched before either of us knew it. We were not strongly committed to the "war effort", either of us; however we were both firmly committed to the welfare and health of the men in our command. This was immediately apparent in conversation as Kolo proudly enumerated the names of the men he had seen reach the natural end of their tour of duty under his command. "I've got twenty-two men now and to tell you the truth, I mean to send as many of them home as possible with all their fingers and toes." the dark Hawaiian eyes flashed with defiance as he added, "I don't care what happens between me and the Army anymore."

I had some level of appreciation for what this man might have gone through during six months on line. Having just barely survived my first 24 hour day on the job without making a major mistake gave me some idea of the reality of our situation. "That's almost exactly what I already told my men the other day...that my main mission was to send them home alive and well."

"You told them that?"

"Yeah."

"Did any of them say anything?"

"They said 'all right, roger that' in full unison like a boys' choir" I replied honestly.

"You gotta watch it! There're some gung-ho assholes out there like Dudley. I've had a couple of guys in my Platoon who just about accused me of malingering at times," Kolo advised seriously. "They think they're for Mom and cherry pie and all that shit."

"Apple pie," I corrected.

"We don't grow apples in Hawaii," Kolo countered.

"I can imagine what kind of cherries you grow, though."

"Hawaiian women are known throughout the world for their beauty and grace," Kolo said smoothly, his eyes taking on an entirely different gleam. The conversation lightened up a bit for a while.

During several days of relative inactivity, when the Captain was in Cu Chi attending tactical briefings, Lt. Kolo became the acting Company Commander in the field. We had just received a fresh shipment of ammo and nobody had fired a shot through their weapon in weeks, so it was the ideal time for a Mad Minute. I participated, jamming magazines through my M16 with the rest of the men and thoroughly enjoying it. It really did ease the tensions that had accumulated like bales of straw on the proverbial dromedary.

The two of us, as Platoon Leaders, made friendly wagers on how many rounds could be launched by our grenadiers fire with their M79's within a minute; how many magazines could be fed through an M16 on full auto in a timed minute; and whether one of our M60 machine-gunners could chop down a distant tree in one minute, firing from the standing position. Big Eddie won that bet, cutting down a good-sized tree about a hundred meters away...laughing like hell as he fired his favorite weapon from the hip, gangster style. He definitely burned the maximum 600 rounds in that minute, smiling and laughing all the while. We also had a contest over which grenadier could get the most rounds in the air before the first one hit. One of Kolo's men won that bet by launching four grenades incredibly quickly, snapping the breach open with a flick of the wrist, inserting another, and even placing all four rounds within a few meters of the target – a white tombstone about two hundred meters away. Maybe he awakened the anger of whatever ancestor lay buried there. We did not care. We were reckless boys playing with toys.

Being a natural left-hander, and having played center field in Little League baseball, I lofted the little grenades from an M79 like pegging a throw to home base. There was no need to use the sights. I fired accurately by just looking over the barrel and firing away. Rifles were best fired right-handed because of the direction of the shell ejection, so that is how I usually fired them. A pistol could be fired with either hand and it made no difference to me. I fired the M79 left-handed. The Demo men tried to cut down a tree using det cord, an explosive rope-like material used to tie several charges together. "Digger" cut down two trees causing them to fall in a perfect "X" just as he had predicted. Everybody was mighty impressed with that. The munitions suppliers, probably all friends and cronies of LBJ, would have been very appreciative of the practice of the Mad Minute. Maybe they had invented the idea.

Ever since that official 0300 creep around the bunker-line at Diamond II had been interrupted by the hellstorm of an estimated 200 mortar shells, I had not slept well. Within three weeks of being shot through the face by our own Howitzers, I experienced our allies The South Vietnamese Army shooting mortars almost right on top of my first ambush patrol. Nobody had ever admitted to any sort of mistake in either instance and in fact, many wheels were being greased to bring about a cover-up of the firing of beehive fleshettes at Diamond and attribute all the casualties to enemy fire. Anyone who said otherwise was scheduled for some type of dangerous assignment...like being assigned as a Platoon Leader when a man was already a First Lieutenant. The Army does have its off-the-books protocols for whistle-blowers.

This vigilant First Lieutenant began to like the night. There was a pleasant high that resulted from fatigue, tension, and long, long nights. I never smoked pot in the field, although I knew some of the men did and they knew I knew. That issue was yet another discrete conspiracy, launched like a ship that slipped its mooring lines due to natural tide action. Nobody was responsible. Things were just the way they were.

During several days of relative inactivity I held meetings with the Squad Leaders and also spoke individually to every man in the Platoon. It was important to find out more about each man. I asked them how long they had been out in the field, what they had done and seen, and whether they had any questions or problems I could help them with. Most of the men were somewhat subdued emotionally, some barely responding with more than one word answers to specific questions. There seemed to be no support for the "war effort" or any semblance of gung-ho attitude from any of the eighteen men in the Platoon. Several expressed regret at the manner of searching villages and destroying food supplies. Some felt bad about all the bombing which was irreparably damaging the agricultural landscape and natural habitats. Not a single man thought we were doing anything to help the people of South Vietnam. I became increasingly troubled over the whole affair.

I called Filbert on the radio when Dudley had flown into Cu Chi on a resupply chopper and asked him to take care of the promotion of Spec4 Thompson to E5 Buck Sergeant. My good friend Filbert said he would handle it, then he gave the Platoon a gift that was to spark hope and amusement in everyone of us. "I am looking for a good swimmer, over."

"Say again, over." I thought I could not have heard that correctly.

"I say again, a swimmer. I have a lifeguard job open, over." Now I was certain I was not hearing that right...*a lifeguard?* Filbert came back. "They have opened a swimming pool here. I can promote one of your men to lifeguard, over." He said it plainly and simply enough. Now I thought it was a joke...a late April Fools shenanigan.

"You gotta be shittin' me, over."

"This is no joke, Three Six...pick a man and send him in, over." Filbert made it as clear a directive as the Company clerk of Headquarters & Headquarters Company of a Battalion possibly could. I could not help noticing Pete, who was grinning hysterically and making gestures like praying and giving thanks, so I said, "Roger Filbert...pick a good swimmer and send him in. Uh, thank you. Out."

Suddenly all the tension of the past few weeks broke when I looked at the radiantly smiling face of my RTO and we both burst into raucous laughter. We quickly got silly on the laughter and were choking on tears and snot as several members of the Platoon walked up. We could not get two words out before collapsing again in hysteria, and were surrounded by the whole Platoon by the time we could clearly state the nature of the radio transmission. Pete noticed the way his Lieutenant was looking at him and said, "Not me Three Six. I'm not a real good swimmer...but I know who is."

"Who?"

"Maldonado there, he told me he almost joined the Navy Seals," Pete said out of a wildly grinning face.

"I ain't volunteering for nothing!" Private Maldonado said unequivocally.

"You'll volunteer for this job, Mike," Pete assured him, his face absolutely glowing.

"Are you a good swimmer, Private Maldonado?" I asked, feeling like Santa Claus.

"Yessir Three Six. What's this all about?"

"A lifeguard job in Cu Chi."

Minor pandemonium erupted and not another coherent word was heard for quite some time. Most of the men knew about the swimming pool the Engineers were constructing in their "spare time"; but I did not know a thing about it. *Maldonado looks kinda chubby, but boy can he jump!* I was totally and satisfyingly amused at having created this cacophonous release of tensions. The men pounded each other until they were sore. Maldonado cried like a baby. Pete forgot to meditate. That night I slept a little better.

PFC Mike Maldonado had been out in the bush for almost ten months, lugging extra machine gun ammo in addition to his standard issue weapon and personal gear, and sometimes serving as Squad Leader due to attrition. He had survived both Diamonds and dozens of minor firefights and encounters with booby traps. Now there he was, a filthy, fatigued, everyday grunt...going in to be a lifeguard the next day. I sat dumbfounded at the incongruity of it all...at the impossibly ironic events. I sat mystified.

As the weeks passed during that summer of 1969 – the busiest months of the war – I became more and more convinced of the futility, stupidity, and dishonesty of the "war effort." However, my Platoon seemed to be under a cloak of protection. We did not see anyone on our sweeps except the farmers and householders who were trying to live out their lives in the midst of the madness of war. We did not spring any ambushes and we did not get ambushed. Both the other two line Platoons had some kind of contact. Either a sniper fired at them or they detained a suspected Vietcong then shot him when he tried to escape, or they popped an ambush and killed some VC carrying supplies in the night, or something...something was happening all around us; but nothing happened to the Third Herd for weeks and weeks.

The men had become so accustomed to moving in slow motion that they even chewed each mouthful of tasteless food 32 times before swallowing. They turned their heads in slow motion during everyday conversations, just for practice...to keep the mind-set going. They were very good at waiting. When walking, they placed each foot down separately in a process seemingly unrelated to moving forward. For this reason, we found many booby traps and blew each one deliberately. Not another man was lost. We sometimes did not complete our scheduled trek through the woods and I took heavy recriminations from Captain Dodgely. Through no fault of mine and unbeknownst to me at the time, I was drawing unwarranted suspicions from my "superiors."

One day, as the Third Herd was moving along a treeline bordering some rice paddies, my flank man, Pvt. Willie Wilkerson, stopped and held up his fist. I watched as the man retreated carefully in his exact same steps, then slowly made his way over to the column. He was tight-lipped as he reported, "I found a bomb, three six...a fuckin' five-hunert-pound bomb." Then Willie's chest collapsed, like saying it took away all his breath.

"Are you sure?...is it rigged?" I asked, incredulous.

"Absolutely, sir. There's a frag wired to the nose...and a wire...goddamn that freaked me out, man." I conferred with

"Digger" and Sgt. Thompson as Wilkerson slumped nearby, sweating and shaking visibly.

"Jesus, what do you think, Digger?"

Digger was a country boy from Alabama, keen in the woods and alert in the hunt, actually very much in his element when compared to any city boy, regardless of training or experiences in Vietnam. There was no training to elicit the skills some of the men already possessed on entering the military. They were good hunters, aware of the flow of nature around them. I was interested in Digger's notions about things anytime.

"Shee-it, you ever see the crater one a' them things makes? If you drove a jeep down in it, you'd never get out. Shee-it. We gotta clear way the hell back out a' here, L T!"

Digger was reliable and likable and carried his own load of mayhem – three pounds of C-4, ten blasting caps, about six feet of fuse...not to mention two fragmentation grenades, two smoke grenades, and a loaded flare gun. "If I knew for sure we could get away, I could light a five minute fuse on that sucker, Three Six, I got enough fuse here...but." He left the rest of the sentence hanging because we both knew what the "but" was. Another booby-trap.

"Sarn't Thompson, move the men back about 200 meters the way we came and set up a tight perimeter. No extra movement." I had an idea about blowing up the bomb and, despite the danger, I really wanted to have a look at it. Digger removed all his explosives and gear then led the way, stepping exactly where Wilkerson had stepped and moving in ultra-slow motion. I followed, trusting in the sharp eyes and steadiness of my demo man.

And there it was – slightly dented and with the nose crumpled a bit. It looked like a malignant, finned, five-foot long aluminum beer keg, with an American fragmentation grenade wired beneath the nose. A thin wire was holding the handle down, attached to another wire that was stretched between two bushes. Any movement of any branches in the area could slip that wire off the handle and the whole thing would blow.

Digger had only a single word to express not only astonishment at the mere presence of the bomb and the delicate trip mechanism, but the fact that the two of us had walked right up to it. "Sheee-yut," drawing the word out even longer than usual. I did not say anything. I could not summon an appropriate word. Digger had expressed my response. We both turned and painstakingly stepped our way back to the trail, neither of us able to speak until we had reached the rest of the Platoon. Digger described the bomb to the rest of the guys as I called in the SITREP.

"Bravo Six, this is Three Six, over."

"Bravo Six, over," came the response from Dudley's RTO. I knew the CO was nearby listening. Captain Dodgely was an assiduous worker and keeping track of his Platoons was one of his principle jobs.

"This is Three Six. I got a booby-trapped five hundred pound bomb here...request a Huey come out and hit it with a rocket or something, over." It was a purely ridiculous request and Pete chuckled along with scattered "guffaws" from the men nearby.

Dudley came right on the horn. "This is Bravo Six, follow normal procedure, over."

"This ain't no normal booby-trap...I cannot approach, over." Profane oaths against the Captain and all his ancestors were muttered aloud by someone in the group.

"This is Bravo Six," like identifying himself again would make his bullshit more palatable, "what's the problem, Three Six? Blow it in place. Out." *The problem is your pigheaded stupidity you son of a bitch.* I would not give in. The thought never crossed my mind now in my daily bouts with my Commanding Officer. I was used to going head-to-head with the asshole West Pointer by then. I even enjoyed it.

"Ah, this is Three Six, will stand by for the inbound and mark with smoke, over." Then I gave an approximate location based on checkpoints. As usual, we had not gone far. As usual, I audaciously ordered up support from all possible sources and was happy to wait for it until it arrived. It was actually not a bad plan. Dudley had to relent and call for a chopper with rocket pods. Much to his amazement, chagrin and vexation, the chopper liaison Officer loved the idea and said he wished he could fly the mission himself. The incident certainly did not endear this "demanding bastard lieutenant" to my Commanding Officer, that's for sure.

"The goddamn Captain just doesn't understand that discovering booby-traps <u>before</u> we trip them is one of our primary objectives," I grumbled to Pete, my captive audience.

"You got that right, sir." Pete readily agreed.

The men settled down to wait. Some of them ate while they waited, others smoked, others just sat and waited, absorbed in their thoughts as they automatically watched the jungle directly in front of them – their sector. Waiting meant not moving and not moving meant not tripping a booby-trap and waiting was an integral and substantial part of every man's time in the Army. They all damn sure knew how to wait. It was a lot easier to wait with the knowledge that their rascal Lieutenant was conscientiously and audaciously looking out for their best interests. They could wait comfortably, happily, with Three-Six up at bat for them.

From about 200 meters away, hitting the bomb with a grenade from an M79 would have been an easy shot; but there was too much foliage in the way. Nevertheless, I took a few shots with one of my grenadiers, just to keep the eye, just to get the feel of the weapon a bit. The rounds were designed to arm themselves in flight no less than 15 meters in front of the barrel, so in theory we were not in any danger as we popped the monkey-fist sized grenades up through the canopy of assorted trees. Just monkeying around while we waited.

About an hour later, Dudley called. "Three-Six this is Bravo-Six, over."

"This is Three-Six," Pete answered, glancing at his smugly smiling Lieutenant.

"Bravo-Six. You got an inbound ETA in one zero. Go to your channel, over." The Captain's voice was clipped as short as a first military haircut, as if calling in a helicopter had cost him some money directly out of his paycheck. I took the handset, confirmed our location based on checkpoints, then Pete switched to "your" channel, a prearranged alternate frequency. Digger and Sgt. Thompson moved up about halfway to the bomb and popped a smoke grenade when the Huey began a high circle overhead.

"Three Six, Three Six...this is lazy buzzard, over," came a relaxed, modulated voice. We could say just about anything because these frequencies were set up through an underground network of disgruntled RTO's that crossed service lines and protocols as easily as our transmissions crossed forests and rivers.

I gave Digger a hand signal then answered, "This is Three Six...identify smoke, over." We watched expectantly as a cloud of purple smoke expanded and rose in the still air.

The pilot or perhaps the co-pilot/sharpshooter reported, "Uh-heult...identify Goofy Grape, over," he said in the cartoon character's voice, obviously not too distressed to be flying that day. They were cool, they were high, they were pilots.

"Grape is affirmative. Your target is about a hundred meters west of smoke. You know what it is?"

"We know, Three-Six...I see you and confirm the target...duck your heads, boys."

Nobody ducked down very much. We all wanted to watch. The Huey came in smoothly from the south and fired a rocket...and missed, blasting some bushes near the bomb. We all exhaled. The Huey circled then came in again, smooth and steady...and the copilot fired another rocket on target. KA-BOOM! A thrilling thump passed through our bodies as we watched whole trees topple, clods of dirt and roots thrown high in the air to filter back down through the canopy. One man tried to get a photo of the destruction caused by the detonation of 500lbs. of TNT High Explosive in a forest; but the percussion of the thump caused him to jerk too much. "Considerable havoc" could be a possible description of the scene we observed as the Platoon advanced past the crater.

And sure enough, we found several smaller, regular everyday booby-traps a little farther down the trail. If Digger had lit a fuse on that bomb and we had tried to hustle on down the trail, chances ore one of us would have tripped another surprise while the fuse was burning on the first one. Not a cool scenario and one that Digger and I had already discussed. Several of the men personally thanked me for using such good judgment and standing up to Dudley's "by-the-book" directive. I had the distinct impression I had saved some life and limb that day.

The Captain would be pissed that we had not made our objective, once again; but I now had a firmly established personal SOP for handling an ass-chewing. I simply waited. When Dudley was finished, I went about my business. My business was keeping myself and the men directly under my command "alive and kicking"...period. An ass-chewing by a mere Captain meant nothing, absolutely nothing, more than the time spent waiting. And I felt the same way about waiting as my men felt. It was just a time you had to accept in the Military.

Captain Dodgely and I were not in the same Army. The difference of one gradation of rank in the Infantry could be a quantum leap in one's everyday reality there in Vietnam in the summer of 1969. The Captain had a bunker, complete with steel-planked roof and sandbag walls. He even had a damn cot to sleep on, probably a regular pillow for his weary head, too. A Lieutenant Platoon Leader endured the same circumstances as his men. In this case, not enough sandbags to build bunkers, no concertina wire perimeter in which to set trip flares and claymores, and no real way to defend against the weather while nervously expecting to defend against an invisible, insidious enemy capable of untold ways to kill and maim.

I did not rejoice in the wondrous technology of America on that memorable night when, in the summer of 1969, someone hit a golf ball on the moon. I was squatting in my scooped out fighting hole in a drizzling rain, my profane mantra the most optimistic of my mental ruminations. My mind was swirling, my vigilance whirling...out into the jungle night...long into the night. I sat vigilant long into the night. I cursed that hero on the moon.

The question: "Where were you when they walked on the moon?" would remain a signpost for me later in life, indicating a vast chasm of disconnection between most of my age group and myself. Some went to college during the late 1960's, some went to Vietnam. For combat veterans this disconnection was all the more evident and clearly revealed to friends and family alike.

A few days later the Platoon was clearing an ambush site in the afternoon, when I was stunned into temporarily believing in God, or at least Guardian Angels. I had become complacent, even clumsy, after several weeks of humping without incident. Walking carefully, looking down directly at every step, I was about to step on a brownish patch of grass...when "whoosh"...something seemed to pass by and slightly upset my balance. I stepped down just beside the brownish patch of grass. While wondering about that inexplicable "push" the realization hit me as to why I had reacted, on whatever level, to what my eye was seeing. A brown patch of grass?...in the midst of a lush tropical jungle during the rainy season when plants are running riot with growth? I signaled for a halt.

Digger came right over, seeing the incongruous patch of ground as he approached. A careful examination revealed, beneath a half-inch of soil, a claymore detonator. A line of slightly disturbed grass led to a natural berm line about eight feet away. Digger immediately pointed to the mine, set into the berm and plastered over with mud. That claymore mine would have cut me in half if I had stepped on that detonator.

A rush of heat hit my face and my knees trembled at the thought of the consequences of a momentary lapse in vigilance. I had failed to see what my eyes were looking at. I resolved to learn a stern lesson in just one instantaneously imagined photograph of myself torn apart, scattered pieces of body parts strewn in twitching heaps. I graduated from a very dangerous school in one split second.

The image of bloody possibilities floated in my mind as I watched Digger prepare to dispose of the booby-trapped Claymore mine. There seemed to have been some sort of "push" or rush of energy that had kept me from making a terrible mistake. However, it was easy to dismiss any possible explanation of otherworldly influence and explain the enigma as some sort of deep reflex or autonomic survival response. The notion of ethereal forces, or God and Angels, did not make rational sense from my perspective, engaged as I was in a futile, unconscionable war. An ephemeral belief in Guardian Angels was less substantial than a child's belief in the Tooth Fairy.

This disillusioned Lieutenant found it impossible to believe in a God or any forces of righteousness that could be watching over such a bloody pointless war and allow it to continue. A God I could believe in would not have to rescue some temporarily blind, careless Lieutenant from blowing himself up during a misplaced endeavor such as the one in which we were involved every day...*every day and every fucking night.* I sat considering contradictory belief systems as Digger safely blew the Claymore in place.

There was plenty of time to consider the matter all that night lying awake at the ambush site. I deliberately set up by the berm, right where we had blown the Claymore, in order to think things over as I glanced from tine to time at the gaping hole left by the explosion of the booby-trap. Nighttime awareness was as natural as night vision...automatic. A nap in the afternoon was usually the only time I relaxed into anything resembling normal sleep.

At about 0200 on that dark and moonless night I detected noise and movement somewhere directly in front of our position. Before I could even focus my starlight scope, Edwards opened up with his M60 and held the trigger down. Instantaneously the air was filled with deafening small arms fire as the whole Platoon started jamming magazines through their M16's, everybody on full automatic as if they had all been wide awake and waiting. I could see muzzle flashes about fifty meters out, indicating that the suspected VC were probably behind a dike. I immediately decided to call in some Artillery, in keeping with my personal SOP of demanding all the support available at every opportunity and then just observing and waiting. It was still not a bad plan.

"Bravo Six, this is Three Six, over." Since we were only about 600 meters from the perimeter, Dudley could already hear the shooting.

"Bravo Six, go."

"Fire mission. I got Charlie pinned down a hundred meters south of my position, over."

"Roger Three Six. Wait for one, over." Dudley replied immediately. He would order a single round first for adjustment of fire. I knew it also meant to wait for one minute, because that's about all the time it would take. The CO insisted on perfect planning and coordination, one of his better character traits on the job, and had already connected with the nearby Artillery units in preparation for just such a possibility. He prided himself on the rapid response he could initiate...how soon he could bring in some Howitzer shells. It was a personality trait I appreciated. Within one minute Dudley came back, "On the way Three Six. Adjust fire, over."

A single round came whooshing in from the rear and crunched about 300 meters out, probably behind Charlie's position. I made a correction and ordered "fire for effect." In about another minute, six rounds would come sailing in, hopefully just a little bit closer. Having your Artillery directly to your rear and firing over your head was a bad situation, but I could not pick and choose which unit would respond to the call. I fervently hoped those gunners were alert and precise in their adjustments. One slight turn of a crank would be the proper shift, but a twitch more would bring the bombardment down right on top of us.

A rocket-propelled grenade exploded nearby and one of my men began screaming for the Medic. Then there was a pause in the shooting. Shirt buttons were pressed into the dirt and everybody "got smaller" as Edwards had so aptly expressed it, waiting for the Artillery. A sound like the rushing of a freight train was heard briefly overhead then we were bounced off the ground by multiple explosions right on target, about 100 meters directly in front of us.

There was a moment of stillness as profound as the incredible noise an instant before and I was focusing the starlight scope when … "pow-crack," the VC fired another round from an AK and the whole Platoon up again. I yelled to the Squad Leaders to slow it down and save some ammo then called for another salvo, same target. Big Eddie managed to get his thick finger off his trigger momentarily as we all wormed our way down into the dirt once again. At a time like this, a man just about wanted to rip those shirt buttons off in order to gain another eighth-inch of "smallness." The six 400mph freight cars whooshed overhead again and exploded right in front of us, maybe even closer. Screaming hot shards of metal filled the air and I ordered, "end fire mission," confident that the CO would relay the message.

We waited. I tried to discern something definite through the starlight scope but there was still too much smoke. We waited some more. In that silence of waiting after the noise and incredible tension of calling in Artillery so close to your position...in the silence when every eardrum was still vibrating, every retina still frenetically flashing signals...we listened for one more shot. It was a listening with a hope of hearing nothing. When that listening noticed the normal jungle sounds begin their buzz and chirp and hum, a man wanted to jump for joy at not hearing another shot. Something inside really wanted to jump and yell; but there could be no jumping...no yelling. When the silence continued and the jungle resumed its normal full-scale nocturnal cacophony, a man could just about shit for joy as his rectum finally dropped back down into its normal configuration.

I crawled over and found the Medic reassuring Pvt. Wilson, one of my Black soldiers, who had sustained a minor wound from the shrapnel of the RPG round. Wilson was smiling grimly, maybe going back to the world with all his fingers and toes – just a manly scar. At gray dawn I ordered one squad out to check for bodies while the rest of us waited tensely. Cpl. Grant, an experienced man almost to the end of his tour, led five men out, quickly signaled "all clear," and the Platoon advanced to view the result of the engagement. It was on our way back to the perimeter anyway.

I exhorted the men not to move any of the bodies or collect any souvenirs. A single survivor might have booby-trapped his dead buddies somehow. The smell of those charred, bloody, shitty sacks of rags was indescribably atrocious and I could not help remembering my glimpse of all the bodies around Diamond II when I was dusted off. A man wanted to gag, cough, blow snot, anything to remove every molecule of that stinky, death-saturated air from his body...from his being. Later in life some of us would attempt to remove such memories with drugs, alcohol, and risky behavior; but all forms of self-medication would prove to be ineffective.

Despite a strong internal revulsion, I kept my outward composure as we approximated the number of former human beings that had once been constructed out of the strewn body parts we found. It was hard to tell exactly because everything was shredded, even the weapons. We found one AK47 almost intact, but that was about it as far as recovering anything definitely identifiable. There were probably three or four bodies to report.

I saw everything in shades of gray that early dawn. Gray lifeless sacks of rags; gray unidentifiable body pieces flung about in the dirt of the craters; gray, smoky soil and plants. Everything was gray, silent, and lifeless,. I felt fractured emotionally, being so glad to still be amongst the living and at the same time feeling so sad about removing so much color from the world. So much life was just...gone. *Where does the color go? What is life anyway, and who am I to remove it?*

I called for a Medivac even though the wounded man was ambulatory and I continued to witness the morbid, grotesque scene as we waited for a Huey. Thankfully only one man had been wounded, apparently not very seriously. I could not stop looking at a headless torso and for some reason kept trying to discern if the man had some type of rank or insignia on his clothing. It was not that it mattered to me either personally or militarily. I just wondered what that man had been like when he still had all his color and all his pieces were still attached. Another memory for later viewing.

When we returned to the perimeter I reported in to Captain Dodgely to turn in the body count statistics and I intended to thank my CO for his prompt and expert actions during the night. I was stopped with cold sarcasm.

"Well Lumbert, finally set an ambush in the right place, huh?"

"What's that supposed to mean, Captain?"

"Only that in almost two months on line, that's your first contact to speak of," the CO said condescendingly.

I did not know what to say. The comment was so completely unexpected.

"I suspect you and Kolo of avoiding contact with the enemy, Lumbert, and if I can pin it on you, believe me, I will."

"I don't know what the hell you're talking about, Captain." Other than a few casual conversations, I had not spoken to Lieutenant Kolo in several days. We each had a full time job running missions and ambushes day and night, after all. "Are you saying I'm afraid…?"

"I'm saying you have less body count than any Platoon in the Battalion, Lieutenant…"

"I also have less causalities."

"This war will not be won by molly-coddling the men – no war is. You don't reach your objectives half the time. This is your first successful ambush out of how many, fifteen or twenty?...just what the hell do you think you're pulling, young man...you think you're fooling me?"

"Fooling you? This is bullshit, Captain."

"You got a bad attitude, Lumbert. You think you've had a hard time of it so far? HA! I'll show you what a hard time is, Lieutenant. Your Platoon will stand down today, then tonight you and Kolo will be going out on an ambush patrol to a site I will select. Report back to me this afternoon...dismissed."

The last part of the conversation was held at sufficient volume that the members of the Platoon heard every word. I went to my personal position to repeat my mantra and try to get some sleep or at least rest for a while. I dozed off with the pleasant, comforting awareness of Pete sitting nearby meditating on his mantra, whatever the hell <u>it</u> was. I awoke four hours later feeling tired, the mantra turning itself on again inside my head as I ate some crummy rations and drank weak instant coffee. *The HELL with this bunch of goddamn shit.*

Lieutenant Kolo came over to discuss the upcoming ambush patrol. "He's trying to get me wiped out, Three-Six, I know he is." he said without prelude.

"Come on man, whatever you might think of the prick, he is on our side."

"He's after me. I know he is," Kolo continued, still not bothering to name names.

"Why would he be after you? What's he think you've done?"

"Not being at my ambush sites."

I paused to consider the times we had not set up exactly where we were supposed to due to heavy rain or a bad feeling about a place after getting out there. I had made slight shifts at times, always aware that we could not stray very far from the plan because we could get blasted by RIF's or walk by another ambush patrol. "Are you at your ambush sites?...I mean generally?"

"Well, Lumbert...I trust you." Kolo lowered his voice. "Me and my men have had enough."

"Yeah, well I've had enough too...what can anyone do about it?"

"Do you think your men want to get into a firefight?"

"Hell no. I can't think of a single one of them that does," was my no-bullshit reply.

"I think the last newby I got in is an agent or an informer or something."

"And you think this guy snitched you out?"

"I don't know...I just don't know anymore," Kolo said, looking at me imploringly.

The man has been out in the bush too long. Lieutenant Kolo had been defying the odds for a long time. Months ago he had crossed a statistical line and had started becoming a longer and longer long shot of a bet as to whether he would finish the race – survive his tour. And he knew it.

"Hey Pete...come over for a minute, will you? Kolo, I trust this man with my life every day and every night. He's been an RTO for longer than you've been a Platoon Leader. Talk to him, okay?"

My sagacious RTO walked over, already aware of the conversation, as usual. "Sirs," he said, in mock formality, issuing a salute, which nobody did in the field. "What do you think, Pete?" I asked my standard question, not bothering to elaborate. I never had to explain anything to the astute meditator; but I had to ask Pete for his opinion, otherwise the considerate man would say nothing, just watch and learn.

"Nobody wants to get shot at, Three-Six." He stated an obvious fact in a manner that allowed a lot of room for interpretation.

"Yeah, but we're in a fuckin' war here," I stated another obvious fact.

"My war now is with Dudley and all the lifers he represents. They're trying to wipe me out. I know they are." Kolo finally expressed his true mental state...his suspicions...his anger.

"Jeez, we got a fuckin' problem here," I said, realizing the extent of Kolo's admission. I was dealing with a fellow junior Officer in near total revolt...damn near mutinous.

"I don't have a fuckin' problem except Dudley, the gung-ho mother-fucker," the Hawaiian said, uncharacteristically profane.

"All right. But what do we do about it?...Pete?"

"Well Three-Six, if Charlie is walking right up on us like last night, we have to open up on him...but."

"But otherwise?" I asked, knowing the answer.

Kolo elaborated, "we're not winning this war, Lumbert, don't you see that? There's more VC than ever. We're going to spring an ambush on the lead element of a whole division of NVA. They come by my position, me and my men might let it slide. We are done getting shot up in this <u>fucking</u> war!"

"Jesus Kolo, you're startin' to cuss like me." I wondered how much of the current stress and tension was due to the simple fact that Second Platoon had not made any contact lately, but Kolo had lost two men to booby-traps. We were all frustrated and depressed, the troops and their junior Officers. Maybe even Dudley was depressed.

"Fuck this shit!" Lieutenant Kolo said under his breath, with the same inflection as I occasionally used. Pete looked back and forth at the two concerned young Officers – his "leaders"- with compassion and understanding.

"Where do you think he'll send us tonight," I asked openly.

Jeffrey Lumbert

"To the fuckin' river," Pete immediately responded, <u>very</u> uncharacteristically.

"Oh Jesus." Kolo put his face in his hands and heaved a huge sigh.

The three of us sat for a long time, saying nothing, each man absorbed in his own thoughts. Finally, I looked expectantly at my wise RTO and Pete said, "let it slide, Three-Six." And an unspoken conspiracy was born out of disillusion, fatigue, and simple observable facts that we three soldiers knew to be true even though the "Brass" would not get the message until years later. Our war was futile, the way it was being conducted. The troops could see that at the time – at least some of us could. Some of us were seeing the true forest while hiding behind a single tree. Later, most historians would agree that some of us everyday soldiers were correct. The Vietnam war <u>was</u> unwinnable the way it was being fought. In 1975, when our government finally gave up, we survivors knew that every man lost in the effort had been lost for nothing; and some of us knew it at the time...while we were there in Vietnam. We definitely had a very serious, what the Army would call, Morale Problem, that's for sure.

Morale problem or not, I knew we had to coordinate the two Platoons so I opened my map and pressed ahead with the issues at hand as if the matter were settled; but had an uneasy feeling it was a can of worms, just opened. We decided that Kolo would set up by an obvious bend in the river and I would

168

set Third Platoon at the edge of what looked like cultivated fields about 200 meters downstream. It was going to be tough because we had not scouted the exact sites. It was absolutely crazy to go out there in the dark without having first cleared the area of booby-traps the same afternoon, as per unit SOP. We had both been past the river on daily sweeps, but neither of us had investigated the exact sites we were planning to occupy that night. It was nuts. I had the foresight to also plan alternate sites and devise a system of breaking squelch on the radio at precise hours to indicate whether we were at our primary or alternate positions.

After receiving the expected orders from the Captain, Pete being correct again as usual, I faced another morale problem. I had called for a general Platoon meeting to honestly explain the dilemma, if possible, between the Captain's orders and my own plans and priorities for the night. "All right, tonight we're going to set up by the river, about one klick..."

"Aw HELL no!" One voice came through the chorus of groans. "NOT ME...ain't goin' to no muthafuckin' river," Pvt. Jones said, one of only two Black men besides the Big Head Man Eddie.

"Jones, let me finish," I began.

"You finish if you want to...I'm finish now!" Jones said, folding his arms defiantly over his chest.

"Hold on Jones. You remember what I said that very first day?...about my main mission being to get our asses out of here in one piece?" I tried to continue.

"Well my main mission be not gettin' no more leeches on my ass. I AIN'T GOING!"

"Jones just listen a second..."

"Naw you listen muthaf..."

"You don't talk to this man like that," Edwards broke in, grabbing Jones by the shirt and jerking him around.

"Hey..HEY...everyone chill out for a second," I said, aware of a possible full-scale mutiny at hand and noticing quite a few of the men showing signs of being on Jones' side. "Now listen up goddammit!" I lowered my voice to a conspiratorial tone. "Now listen up. The Captain told me to take a patrol to the river...but he didn't say how close to the river we have to set up." Undisguised murmurs of "fuck what he wants" went around the group. "The Captain wants his body count...the Captain wants us poppin' ambushes...but Edwards here taught me something on my first day on the job, and now I know he was absolutely correct." I paused now that I had their attention. "Ever' damn time I shoot at someone, the muthafucka starts shooting back...right Ed Man?"

"HA-ha...a plain fack sir." Eddie replied with a straight face and a level gaze, not smiling at all and maintaining a calm brow and relaxed posture.

"Well boys, if we play it cool and stick together, I got a plan to get us all back in the morning, believe me." I said as convincingly as I could without giving details.

"Yeah, we all come back wit' leeches on our ass. I am not goin', Three Six." The man Jones did not back down an inch once he had his mind made up. Another obvious "fack."

"Well Jones, if you don't come with us, I'll have to report it to the Captain officially."

"Fine wit' me. Send me to LBJ (Long Binh Jail). I got lots of home boys there already."

"Suit yourself, Jones," I finally replied. *He just cast his dice again.*

Late that evening in full darkness I led my small group of men – not a Platoon by any standards – out to find an exact spot on the ground that we had never scouted during the day and set up an ambush position in a place we had not cleared of booby-traps. It was just plain crazy. After about two hours of painstaking movement with frequent stops while I dropped to the ground in order to discern vague shapes and silhouettes of memorized tree lines against the starry horizon or looked through the starlight scope at the distorted images, the Platoon finally started sloshing through ankle-deep marshy water somewhere near the river.

Pausing to consider our rotten predicament, I absentmindedly scratched a slight itching sensation on my calf. Under my pant let was a hard, squiggly, slimy leech, crawling up my leg. "Fucking leech," I muttered, snatching the disgusting thing off even though we had been told to burn them off with a cigarette or something. There were no cigarettes on ambush patrol. Suddenly there were more of them on my pants and even in my waistband. I quietly freaked out. Everyone was cursing and gasping as we pulled leeches off our bodies. "Pull back a hundred meters," I whispered. There was no hesitation from the men.

The Platoon retraced our steps and I set them up Ranger-style at the corner of two berm lines where it was fairly dry and there was good cover and concealment. Lieutenant Kolo and his men were supposedly about 200 meters to the north; but I had no idea of their exact whereabouts. It was an extremely dangerous situation, caused by Captain Dodgely for no military reason. The two Platoons could shoot at one another if we moved around any more and I could only hope Kolo was thinking the same thing as Pete and I monitored the radio, waiting for a coded clicking from Kolo's handset. Finally Kolo coded that he was also at his alternate site. Now we both could only hope that our land navigation skills in near total darkness were accurate and we were really where we thought we were.

"What a fucked up mess, Pete."

"Truer words were never spoken, Three-Six."

Sometime during that very long, very fucked up night, we heard a single distant explosion back in the direction of the fire base – our perimeter. *No point in speculating.* As I lay awake all night long my heart hardened against Captain Dodgely, the US Army, and anyone involved in the "war effort." *The gung-ho lifers are killing us hope some hero fragged Dudley.* I realized Kolo was probably correct in his assertion that Dudley was trying to wipe him out because here we were in a dangerous mess for no other reason than what Dudley had explicitly told me the day before: to show Kolo and me a "hard time." The very idea that the Captain had deliberately ordered us out on this ambush due to personal spite, or whatever nonmilitary reason, just chapped my ass...*that son of a bitch.* The conviction arose that the US Army was every bit as dangerous to us as the NVA or VC. These bleak realizations were not mere paranoia on my part, as would be revealed later when I saw what the CO had in mind for Lt. Kolo.

I lay awake that whole night, as usual, angrily recounting the insults and injuries committed by the Army against its own troops, which mental machinations took at least an hour's time. Then I started counting the acts of stupidity, which took damn near the rest of the night. Then I started into the ironies, some of which were not caused by the Army other than by the simple fact of being there. And finally I meditated on my mantra - "oh HELL no" – for a while. Thus my disgusted mind occupied itself while sitting on that ambush site, listening and peering, feeling the jungle around me...awake...wide awake all night long during a very long, very fucked up night.

The repeated experience of sitting in a remote jungle, fully armed and with malice in the heart, waiting for...anything...and the excitement and shear adrenaline rush involved, would forever set these men apart from their social peers – the ones who spent the Summer of Love in high school or college. There would never be a day nor a night when these combat veterans would not be survivors of ambush patrols, just as there would never be a time in the parallel lives of their peers when they would not be college graduates. Never the twain would meet.

Next morning I led my two squad "Platoon" back to the perimeter, as promised, with no casualties. I had done my job and felt justifiably proud to have made the decisions I had. When we were about half way back, we saw a Medivac chopper descend into the area of the fire base. *Someone got hit last night hope Dudley took a rocket up the ass.* The men were cautious as we slowly made our way back to the fire base. Reaching the perimeter as the chopper rose and turned in the direction of Cu Chi, I reported in to Captain Dodgely. I felt uneasy for some reason.

"You fucked up, Lumbert...you and Kolo both." It was somewhat surprising to hear the Captain use profanity. "Your man Jones was killed by a rocket last night...what the hell was he doing here?"

"He refused to go out Captain. I was going to report it to you this morning." *Goddamnit a good man died...was willing to go to jail and ruin his future all because of you lifers, DAMN YOU.*

"Well this morning is too late for Private Jones, Lieutenant. Now, you mind telling me exactly where you were last night?...how you could have missed a sampan full of arms and equipment that came down the river last night?"

"We didn't see a thing all night," I stated honestly. *You ignorant dog. You couldn't walk a mile in Jones' shoes you asshole.*

"Because you were not at your ambush site by the river," Dodgely said, pointing an accusatory forefinger at my chest.

"Bullshit Captain. We were there, by the river, and we did not see a thing all night." Not an entirely accurate description; but close enough for navigating in pitch darkness. We were there by the river, close enough to have seen anything happening...for about half a minute...then we had pulled back, pulled leeches, and hurled silent curses. Our position was only about a hundred meters from the river and we could have heard any traffic during the quiet night. *You rotten bastard. You won't survive now that I know my life means nothing to you, you rule-book asshole. I've been thrown out of several schools and clubs already for kicking the good boys' butt. I'll frag your ass myownself, save one of my men the trouble.* Despite my rather horrendous internal dialogue, I kept a straight face and stuck to my story. Looking the Captain directly in the eye at the end of a ten minute interrogation, I showed appropriate anger and indignation. I was insulted to be accused of such a thing.

"I'll be dealing with Kolo when he comes in then I'll get to you later, Lumbert. Dismissed." The captain concluded the interrogation, unable to penetrate my story because he was basing his accusations on presumptions and suppositions. And he knew it.

I fumed my way back to my position, cursing Dudley and all his ancestors... again. There was never a time when I had intentionally malingered to avoid contact with the enemy. The Third Herd had simply not seen the enemy in a few weeks. And furthermore, many of my men would be flat out hunting someone to shoot if they were having a bad day and someone was always having a bad day. The only thing "wrong" I had been doing was moving slowly in a heavily booby-trapped area in and around a very dangerous VC infested forest – the HoBo woods.

I watched disconsolately as Kolo and his men dragged their asses back to base about mid morning, looking depressed, exhausted, and barely able to place one foot down in front of the other. My heart went out to the ragged, filthy men of the Second Platoon, particularly my fellow Officer, whose head hung so low he could not wear his helmet...he carried it. *Kolo my friend, now I know you were right. They're trying to wipe me out too...and whatthefuck are we doing here and whothefuck put Dudley in charge and where is Major Stinson when I need someone to shoot...you bunch of rotten bastards sitting at a desk listening to me on the radio as we lose chunks of our bodies then demanding we move faster you goddamn rotten sonsabitches.*

My ranting, rampaging mantra was becoming more complex, able to show disgust and anger towards larger and deeper aspects of people and institutions. Such a mindset would become a major impediment to later integration into the society that had stayed home while each lonely man went to war and was changed forever. And Society – the civilians who had stayed home – might wonder what had brought about such an angry, negative disposition; but none could understand what it felt like to be in a wet scooped-out fighting hole looking up at the moon when a hero was up there playing super putt-putt golf. Lacking first hand experience, and being continually misled by the mainstream press, American society had no way of knowing what had gone wrong with these men – these Vietnam Veterans.

We had engaged in a seemingly righteous effort; but realized it was all for naught. This realization was especially apparent to me during that Summer of 1969. My country was losing the war and I definitely knew it. It was all for nothing.

And a deep protest arose within me against the war, against the Army, and against all institutions and authority figures. A network emerged in Vietnam as a calculated anti-war effort, composed of men who had simply had enough. Enough of the danger and killing, enough of seeing American lives wasted, and enough of the Army and all career men engaged in the war while sitting at a desk. Supply personnel, radio and communications operators, and disgusted, rebellious men of all ranks and job descriptions began to question their role in the War...began to question the very idea of war.

Supply and transport personnel surreptitiously packed and shipped souvenirs, weapons and military equipment, and of course, dope of all descriptions, to a soldier's home address without a search by customs. Opportunities for making money were difficult to resist when morale was low and a man's time in-country was drawing to a close. With an average age of only nineteen - compared with twenty-six in WWII - soldiers in Vietnam were more prone to the excesses of youth and grew up in a time when rebellion against authority was common in their age group. It was The Sixties for those in uniform as well as for those in high school or college.

Pete and I looked helplessly at each other, exchanging chagrin, embarrassment, anger, and "D" all of the above, as Dudley briefly interrogated Lieutenant Kolo. Then an unscheduled Huey came flying in and Captain Dodgely and Lieutenant Kolo boarded and departed in the direction of Cu Chi Base Camp. The Captain's RTO came walking over to speak to Pete and when he caught me looking said awkwardly, "Uh, the cap'n says you're in charge, Three-six." *Yeah, well if I'm in charge I'm calling off the whole damn war.* I knew I was the ranking Officer in the field and just nodded at the information. Then I heard yet another ironic story as Dudley's RTO told Pete everything he knew about what was going on.

Jones and another man were killed while smoking reefer on the perimeter. They were shredded by a 122mm rocket that burst in a tree directly in front of them. Both were killed instantly and it was hard to get what was left of one of them into a body bag. More memorable mental photos that would last a lifetime were formed on that particular morning.

Some memories would stay in a mental box, neatly compartmentalized, as the Psychologists would say; but some images would not always stay in the box. They would leap into an unsuspecting mind like a leopard in the night, slicing and rending conscious connections to time and place. Internal questions will arise having nothing to do with a situation. Questions such as: Why did I survive when my buddy did not? Why not another guy we all thought was an asshole?

Unanswerable questions and involuntarily memorized photographs of exploded friends could never be buried or forgotten for long. There were many visual, auditory, and olfactory cues one would encounter later in life. A walk in the woods ten years after the war might awaken an unnecessary alertness for booby-traps. The slightest noise or movement at night brings instant full consciousness with combat readiness. Police or EMT helicopters elicit memories of chopper rides in the 'Nam with the connected emotions and adrenaline responses. The "bang" and "pop" from firecrackers and the smell of ignited gunpowder will call forth similar sensations created during life or death circumstances.

Pete's cohort told him, with me obviously eavesdropping, that the Captain had taken Kolo in to face charges and we would not be seeing the overwrought Lieutenant from Hawaii coming back out to the field. Knowing a little about the Army's Uniform Code of Military Justice, I sadly reflected on the fate of my friend, who like every man facing a Court Martial, would be assumed guilty or someone would be in deep shit for wasting the Court's time. It irked me no end that the Army had waited until Kolo had been out in the field for over nine months – much longer than the statistical law of averages of the life span of Infantry Lieutenants – then they had shafted him. Oh, and I had no doubt that Kolo was deeply shafted...he was fucked.

Naturally, I gave a good deal of thought to what the CO had said regarding my own actions, but was not really worried because I knew nothing I had done was remotely punishable. Maybe Dudley was guessing that I was "up to something" because we had not made contact with the enemy for a long time. The Third Platoon had been extremely lucky, that's all. I constantly expected something to happen, but nothing did happen except the tension incurred through maintaining such an expectation day after day. What could I say to charges of malingering? We simply had not seen anybody except peasant farmers and villagers. Nobody shot at us, except the one time a few nights back when we had popped the ambush. The main danger we had to deal with on a daily basis, other than booby-traps, was heat exhaustion. Third Platoon was leading a charmed life that nobody wanted to explicitly mention due to fears of bringing up some bad shit.

Being the ranking Officer in the field – in fact the only Officer at that Company-sized perimeter – I was technically the Acting Company Commandeer that day as the three Platoons rested, cleaned weapons, and talked quietly in small groups. This discouraged Lieutenant could not initiate or sustain a conversation with anyone all day, not even Pete.

That afternoon, Dudley came back out with three newbies, one for each Platoon. The CO called for a meeting of all the Platoon Sergeants, thus eliminating me from the meeting. He was showing me a complete lack of respect and ignoring the normal chain of command by doing so. Later I listened as Sergeant Thompson informed Pete and me what had been said at the meeting. It seemed the upper echelon of command had reached the conclusion that troop morale was very low and all sorts of allegations were flying about that some men, including Officers, were shirking their duties and conniving to avoid the enemy. The Navy had intercepted a shipment of arms down river and the Captain had surmised that Charlie must have come by the ambush sites during the night. The fact that neither Kolo nor I had popped our ambushes just proved, in Dudley's manically military mind, that we were not at our ambush sites. It was an empty speculation on his part however, because there were many tributaries the VC could have used to get down the river and it was possible they could have shown up downstream without having passed our ambush positions.

Lieutenant Kolo was facing serious charges and I had to wonder if he had been correct in his suspicions of there being an informer in his Platoon. Naturally the next thought to come into my mind was whether my new replacement was an informer or investigator of some sort. Nothing more could be ascertained regarding my friend Kolo though, and the events of the next day eclipsed any concern I might have had for him or my actions as Three Six that Summer of 1969.

Sergeant Thompson assigned and oriented the new man while Pete waited restlessly for an opportune moment to interrupt his Lieutenant's dour reflections with a little more good news from our pal Filbert. "Hey L T, look what Filbert sent us," he said, displaying a brand new PRC-25 radio and a strictly classified book of codes and frequencies, forbidden to mere Lieutenants in the field.

I perked up a bit. "Great. Now I can call in my own artillery and cobras."

"Right, and I can eavesdrop on the Captain and the Colonel on the Battalion net and find out what they're up to," Pete realized immediately. Filbert was taking care of us – a good friend hinting that we should stay informed and giving us the means to do so. "You've got a right to have two radios anyway, Three Six, being acting CO now and then," my faithful, perspicacious RTO informed me cheerfully.

"Well let's be careful about having any more antennas visible, okay?"

"Roger that," Pete agreed as he began fiddling with the new radio like a kid with a new toy.

Captain Dodgely finally summoned me to the Command Post early that evening to meet one of the replacements – a recently commissioned Second Lieutenant named Rasko. I murmured some sort of welcome while surveying the plainly scared newcomer. *You have no idea what you have gotten yourself into, you dumb fuck.* "Lieutenant Rasko will be commanding the Second Platoon and I will take charge of First Platoon temporarily for a very important mission beginning tomorrow." The asshole paused for effect then continued, "we are to begin clearing the HoBo Woods," he declared proudly, seemingly thrilled to draw such a dangerous near impossible mission. I felt somewhat gratified that Dudley was finally going out on a mission though, and looked forward to finding out if he would hold up to it. *You'll never last out there...your rule book don't mean shit in the bush.*

The plan called for Dudley to lead First and Second Platoons on a loop through the woods, which one or another of the three Platoons had been skirting with minor contact for over a week. The Captain had no real knowledge of the area. He had been monitoring the radio and coordinating with support units, as was his proper job. Third Platoon would set up a blocking position and ambush the VC as Dudley's "forces" flushed them out. Charlie would be caught in a pincer tactic and be mowed down from both directions. I relayed the patently absurd plan to my Platoon Sergeant and Squad Leaders.

"Fuckin' ridiculous, Three Six," Thompson said immediately. "The man thinks he's fighting World War Two."

"Yeah, like everything's going to work according to diagram three, page ninety-four of some college textbook," I replied with a smirk of disgust.

"He'll probably get lost in there. It's awfully hard to navigate in those woods," Pete commented, once again cutting right to the truth of the matter.

"All right. For the sake of the poor souls he'll be leading, we gotta be ready for anything tomorrow. Pete, I want you to memorize the codes and frequencies for the Battalion, the Artillery, the Cobras, the Navy jets..."

"The Marines, sir?"

"The fucking Marines...everyone! If we get in some shit in there, I want to be ready to call down the whole world on that place." I had a hard knot in my stomach that did not occur very often and expected big trouble. Something just did not seem right about the sudden idea to try to clear the HoBo Woods with a single Company. The place had been a guerrilla stronghold twenty years before when the Vietnamese were kicking Frenchy's butt out of Southeast Asia.

"Yessir, Three-Six," Pete said, a light of pride and affection gleaming from his eyes. He could not take the code book out on a sweep, so he would have to memorize a considerable amount of information then leave the code book hidden deep in his personal effects at the fire base.

That evening the men of the Third Herd, by now confident in the good judgment and maybe the personal luck of their Lieutenant, quietly prepared themselves. There was no groaning, no quibbling. They removed every round from every magazine, carefully cleaned each bullet, and then reloaded it. They loaded all the grenades, ammo, and articles of war they could possibly carry into rucksacks and web-belts and checked each other out. They knew what they might be confronting the next day. Serious-faced, yet still joking and poking, they stayed busy late into the evening. I watched these men with pride that evening, consciously imprinting the memories of one proud moment in an otherwise detestable situation. I had a definite premonition that I would never again be a part of a better group of men.

In the gray dawn the Captain led his two "forces" - totaling about forty men - out of the perimeter while Third Platoon waited for portions of Charlie company and the 4.2 inch Mortar Platoon to arrive in Hueys and occupy the fire base. About mid-morning, after the support personnel had arrived, the Third Herd moved out to our planned blocking position just inside the Woods. The men slowly cleared the site of possible booby-traps and set themselves in an excellent ambush site as Pete and I listened to the Captain on the Battalion frequency reporting every move and decision like he was making a minute to minute life or death combat decision. Pete commented that it sounded like they were up to something. *Dudley probably hasn't qualified for a CIB (Combat Infantryman's Badge) yet, the officious bastard.* And sure enough, a few days later when the fiasco was over, Filbert informed me that both the Captain and the Colonel had more than one scheme cooking on that day. They also had more than one misconception regarding the conduct of combat operations.

About noon Dudley's Platoons were ambushed with heavy small arms fire from well fortified and camouflaged bunkers. From the sound of the firefight I estimated they were about one click (a thousand meters) from our position in a thick portion of the forest. Suddenly the shooting escalated and within minutes the Captain was reporting that the newby Lieutenant was shot dead and there were numerous others dead and wounded. From the frantic urgency in his voice as he ordered an Artillery strike, it was obvious to me that the Captain was not where he thought he was. The Artillery came in way off target. Then Dudley tried to order a Medivac chopper when it was clear they could not fly into that thick forest, especially in the midst of a raging battle. Finally the CO called for help.

"Three-Six, this is Bravo Six, over," he came in over the Company frequency, not knowing I had been listening to all his transmissions on the Battalion net.

"Three-Six, go."

"Bravo-Six. Where are you, over?"

"Three-Six, in the planned position, over." *You fuckin'
idiot!* The sound of the shooting was muffled by the forest, but I
could tell the Captain was not where he thought he was or he
would never have called in an Artillery strike where he had. He
was lost, ambushed, and pinned down by steady effective fire.
He was in a very serious situation but he was too proud and too
ignorant of his reality to admit it. He truly had no idea what he
had gotten himself into.

"This is Bravo-Six...I want you to reinforce my right
flank...get your ass over here, over."

"This is Three-Six...*asshole*...I can adjust your
Artillery...where are you, over."

"Bravo-Six...by an unused road, looking east across a
clearing. Charlie is dug in about one hundred meters from me...to
the east. Over."

Studying the map for a moment and judging by the sound
of the firefight, I could pinpoint Dudley's probable position by a
trail indicated on the map. I had the advantage of knowing
exactly where we were because we had not traveled very far and
the area was familiar after a week of sweeps nearby. Calling in
an Artillery was problematic because the triple canopy was so
high and thick that the shells might burst up in the trees and if
Charlie is in well-fortified bunkers such a barrage would have
little or no effect.

"Three-Six, this is Bravo Six...did you get my last? Over."

"Roger Bravo Six...I have your position...do you want artillery? Over." That pissed off Dudley royally. A goddamn Lieutenant was going to call in artillery for him.

"I can adjust fire!" came the egotistical reply. "Three-Six, I order you to move up on my right flank. Out!"

"How can he adjust fire when he doesn't know where the hell he's at?" I asked Pete.

"We better try to help out, Three-Six," came the reply from my conscientious RTO.

I passed the word to "saddle up" then called the artillery frequency and gave them Dudley's exact position. I called the Cobra team and requested air support because it might take them a while to arrive on the scene, but once they did they could be much more accurate with rocket and cannon fire than the artillery could from 2-3 miles away. Third Herd humped steadily in the midday heat for an hour then positioned ourselves behind a slight berm line next to an unused, overgrown road. The firefight was steady and I could see the Captain's radio antennas about 100 meters off on my left. It appeared the NVA were dug in securely in well fortified bunkers about 80-100 meters across an open field and they were still pouring small arms fire and rocket-propelled grenades on Dudley's two Platoons. The Captain had the men firing in coordinated bursts, putting out as much fire as possible at a sustained rate, just like he had been trained to do; but their fire had little effect against the sturdy bunkers. The

NVA were not slowing their fire, which meant they probably had plenty of ammo already stored and ready at hand.

This was not good. I ordered the men to take their time and aim for the muzzle flashes and puffs of smoke in the bushes across the clearing. First and Second Platoons were pinned down and still taking casualties. This was bad. Very bad. And it would get a whole lot worse if we could not get out of here and had to spend the night at a known position in the Hobo Woods. A whole lot worse.

Pete was monitoring the radios and informed me that the Colonel was on his way out from Cu Chi and he had just told Dudley he had requested the Navy come out and drop napalm. Phantom F-4 Navy jets would be on the scene sometime during the afternoon. That meant soon, hopefully. *Shrewd move, Colonel, but what the hell are you coming out here for?* A cynical thought occurred about whether the Colonel needed a Combat Infantryman Badge in his resume, since he had missed plenty of other opportunities to come out to the field and find out first hand what his men were involved in while he sat in his air-conditioned office in the Base Camp. I was jerked out of my negative speculations by the Captain screaming at me on the radio.

"Three-Six, this is Bravo Six, over."

"Three-Six, over."

"Bravo Six. Move forward and attack the enemy's flank. Do it! Over."

There was a moment of stunned silence as I, along with all the men nearby who had heard that order, stared at Captain Dodgely in disbelief. *Are you completely fuckin' crazy?* The man must have felt it even from 100 meters away...a dozen hard faces glaring at him...some of them thinking about firing the next burst in his direction by mistake.

"This is Three-Six...ah...I got good fire on him from here, over."

"Bravo Six...I say again...move your men around and attack the enemy's flank. Out!"

I looked at the men who were looking at me, shaking their heads in disbelief and not thinking for one instant I would order them to do anything so suicidally stupid. And many of them did not even know the napalm was on the way and would probably settle this day of mistakes and arrogance. My Platoon would be cut down before they took ten steps beyond the berm we were crouched behind. Charlie was already sending quite a few rounds in our direction, no doubt in response to that damn Ed Man rattling off rounds at them with his favorite machine gun. I could not think of a response to the Captain's clear, direct order.

There was no way I was going to lead my men on a charge across a clearing towards those bunkers. If we moved around to the right and approached the "enemy's flank" that way, we would be in the wrong place if the F-4's came in with napalm. The enemy might not have a "flank" in the military sense...might just be more and more bunkers filled with NVA regulars. The jets could not remain on station very long. You had to identify your location, direct their fire, and then get your ass down. *Jesus, what a mess.*

Pete was positioning himself and the radios in such a way as to keep the antennas flat and I was looking right at him thinking how lucky I was to have such a radioman and what the hell was I going to do about Dudley's order. Suddenly Pete was thrown backwards, flat onto his back with his arms and legs splayed, a look of stark disbelief on his face. I did not know what had happened. I could not see that Pete was hit. I was shocked when the medic ripped open Pete's shirt and revealed a neat black hole right in the middle of the sternum. My Medic glanced at me as he eased Pete onto his side, then gasped in surprise and growled in anger when he uncovered the fist-sized bloody exit wound. Probably an AK round...straight through the chest.

Right before our eyes, Pete lost color and changed from pink to gray to lifeless without a word. I entered a dream world – an altered state of consciousness – and was looking down at myself sitting there in shocked disbelief. Voices I did not recognize were speaking in unintelligible basso-profundo syllables and I had the strong sensation I could hold Pete in this world if I could just concentrate hard enough. I returned to the present reality with Dudley screaming at me on the radio and reached over to turn the damn thing off.

The whole Platoon was completely still, staring in grief. Then someone screamed and held his trigger down and everybody followed suit. I did not consciously recognize what I was doing as I jammed one magazine after the other through my M-16, firing on full automatic. Sergeant Thompson brought me back to awareness shouting in my ear and jerking on my arm. "Hey Three-Six! Slow down...get down sir!"

"Yeah. Okay Sarn't," I replied as I awoke to the present and everything resumed its normal dimensions and speed. From a level of deep calmness, I remembered firing five magazines, aiming the whole time and holding a tight shot group, seeing the bullets impact over the barrel...laying heavy lead into the base of a clump of bushes where there had been a muzzle flash an instant before.

"Get down, Three-Six...stay low sir," Sgt. Thompson said, definitely keeping his cool in a chaotic situation. He pointed down the berm line and here came Dudley scrambling along with both his RTO's in tow.

"Take these radios over to the right there, Thompson, this is going to be trouble," I directed, ducking down. I had not realized I was standing up while firing.

"Yessir, I'll have a man take over as RTO...stay down, L T, be cool sir...we're backing you up one hundred percent," the good Sergeant said, moving down the berm line as bullets popped and zinged overhead.

Captain Dodgely came low-crawling up, red-faced, grimy, and screaming. "Did you get my order Lieutenant? I told you"...POW...he was thrown over backward by a shot through the neck that blasted away the whole back of his skull. He died without a twitch.

"Oh yeah? You told me what?...YOU STUPID FUCK!...HUH?" I insanely got in Dudley's instantly dead face and shouted obscenities at him nose to nose. I was completely lost in my tirade until I heard, out of a remote corner of the mind, Edward's big deep voice, laughing and chuckling in his normal relaxed way.

"HAAA_HA HA. That's telling the muthafucka Lieutenant...HAA Ha, huh-huh. Shit."

I once again had the sensation of waking up to the present reality and, odd as it might seem to remember it, collapsed in hysterical laughter. I crawled over and punched Ed Man in the shoulder and the big man hugged me to his chest like a huge mommy for a second, then said, "It's all right, L T. We gonna make it." And I believed him and I felt fine.

"Well shit, Sarn't T. What do you think?

"I think Charlie's dug in and ain't going nowhere..."

"Let's barbecue the sons-a-bitches in place, right?"

"Sounds like a plan to me sir. I just heard the Colonel try to tell Dudley the Phantoms are on the way."

"All right!...stay down...napalm on the way."

A Cobra gunship arrived on the scene and I directed his fire on Charlie's positions. Within minutes, two Phantom F-4's roared overhead getting their bearings from the actions of the Cobra. They made a wide banking turn and the Cobra drew back as the Phantoms came screaming in and dropped several canisters into the treeline...BOOMWHOOSH. The whole section of the woods erupted like a huge over-primed barbecue pit and the wall of flame singed eyelashes all the way across the clearing.

We cheered. We laughed. And we cursed Charlie for killing Pete, a man loved and respected by all. Everyone was quiet as the immense inferno burned itself out in the moist tropical jungle. I gathered statistics then reported to the Colonel that I, Three-Six, had assumed command of Bravo Company. Sergeant Thompson sent a squad to the rear to set up an observation post and locate a possible landing space for a Medivac. The Colonel would call for choppers based on my report of dead and wounded. We had four dead, three seriously wounded, and five with minor injuries during the three hours of fighting. Among the dead were two of the three Officers present, a fact that was both painful and frightening to me. *Each event...a toss of the dice?...*

I was startled from a reverie by the Colonel on the radio unnecessarily ordering me to move across the clearing and conduct body count, which my good Platoon Sergeant was already coordinating. Two squads moved out while the rest of the Company held in place, ready in case any enemy had somehow escaped being roasted. The entire hedgerow and nearby trees were a charred smoky rubble. I waited with my men, automatically poised and trigger-ready for another shot. I really wanted to burn up the rest of the ammo I had been hauling around for weeks. I only had three magazines left and I was not done killing for Pete.

The Colonel unexpectedly had his chopper land right in the middle of the clearing and got out with two other Officers. *What the hell?* The three of them joined the men of Bravo Company and approached the treeline unprepared for combat...not even holding weapons. *He wants to see the results of "his" operation.* Suddenly a small, filthy, barely recognizable humanoid creature emerged smoking from the ground and held up its hands, croaking "Chew hoi" - I surrender.

The little figure looked at the approaching group of Officers, now only about fifty feet away, and his eyes widened in recognition. In an instant, the scorched little soldier picked up an AK-47 at his feet and fired a burst into the three Officers. The Battalion Commander, a Division Major, and a liaison Captain were all shot within a fraction of a second. A hundred rounds from a dozen weapons instantly pulverized the charred little soldier; but he had the last laugh...he had personally shot some enemy Officers.

Stunned into mere observation after witnessing the final expenditure of ammunition, I gratefully just watched as Sgt. Thompson took charge of the Platoon. Two Medivac choppers landed in the clearing to evacuate the dead and wounded from the initial firefight, then another came in to pick up the Colonel and the two combat-ignorant Officers, all of whom were shot due to stupidity, pride, and dishonesty. They were on the scene to make a claim for a CIB, which would enhance their advancement in the military. They were Infantry Officers looking for their first enemy engagement so they could be "awarded" the Combat Infantryman Badge. They engaged one enemy, one time...and all got shot. Congratulations.

After the Colonel had been evacuated, I became the Acting-Battalion Commander-in-the-Field. I was too tired to feel any pride or sense of accomplishment as we dragged our sorry asses back to the familiar perimeter. I was not even glad to have survived. Two men had been shot dead right beside me, one of whom I loved, the other I despised. I had seen an ill-planned operation get worse as the day went from poor planning to chaos to ... NOTHING. Nothing was gained. Charlie still owned the Hobo Woods and would still be there six years later when this latest group of foreign invaders finally gives up and allows this country to settle its own civil war.

The next few days passed in a fog of depression and self-blaming. The Battalion was pulled into Cu Chi Base Camp for a major restructuring while replacements were shipped in. I coasted, avoiding contact with almost everyone except Filbert, who supplied me with superb reefers to be smoked out on the bunker line which was largely deserted during the day. I had a lot to think over.

For no reason I could think of, I was transferred to Headquarters&Headquarters Company of the 25th Infantry

Division. If I had still been considering a career in the Army, this assignment could definitely lead to recognition and advancement. I smoked weed and for the first time really malingered and avoided contact not only with the enemy, but most certainly with other Officers.

When considering the Summer of 1969, my time as an Infantry Platoon Leader, I felt even more frustrated at my performance as Three-Six than I was after the brief one-month tour with the Rangers. Every aspect of my time as Three-Six was overshadowed by that last day in the field...by the death of Pete. Every time memories of that day occurred, an entire series would unroll like a connected film: Sergeant West's face as he stared at the way what was left of his foot flopped impossibly against his shinbone...the smell and even the taste of the exploded bodies after we had popped the ambush...the inert face of Captain Dodgely, looking like he was about to continue in his reprimand even though the whole back of his skull had been blown off...and the look of incredulity on Pete's face as his color faded.

Somehow I forgot about sending Maldonado in to become a lifeguard; and I lost my perspective on how many men still had their limbs attached due to my continual exhortations to move slowly; and all the pride I had at being commissioned a Second Lieutenant at age nineteen was forgotten. I could not remember what it felt like to graduate from Airborne Training; and had no clearly recalled memories of the awe and respect fostered by the Rangers I had supposedly been in charge of. There was no pride at having volunteered for this shit. No pride at all. As the parade of horrendous photos floated past my inner eye, I simply felt the senseless shame of it all.

The fact that I was still suspected of malingering to avoid the enemy served to deepen my overall sense of failure as a Platoon Leader. Dudley's numerous, demeaning reprimands still echoed in my head. *Fuck him...he's dead.* Whatever meager respect I had for authority figures or the Army in general...or Generals in general...dropped to zero.

At the young age of twenty-one and a few months, somewhere deep inside, I knew I had already experienced the most powerful and memorable days of my life. True or not, it was a mindset liable to lead to the development of an anti-social, risk-taking attitude later in life.

CHAPTER IV

The Renegade Lieutenant
October 1969

In piecing together the possible reasons behind my transfer to Headquarters&Headquarters Company of the 25th Infantry Division, I became increasingly disgusted with the Army. Filbert learned of the Colonel's plans and he informed me that if the Colonel and Dudley had not both been shot that day in the HoBo woods, I would have been facing an investigation and possible Court Martial, just like Lt. Kolo. Based on Captain Dodgely's speculations, the Colonel had assigned guilt by association and assumed that both Kolo and I had been shirking our duties. Since my Platoon had made very little contact in a few weeks, I was suspected of avoidance and malingering. My refusal of a direct order in a combat situation, however unsound the order, would have been the final nail in my coffin. And Captain Dodgely certainly knew it at the time. He was setting me up for a fall by issuing such a ridiculous and futile order. I really blew up at the assertion that I had been avoiding contact with the enemy.

"What a bunch of shit! We were careful and lucky, that's all, Filbert. Other than one time about a week ago when Dudley sent us out into a leech-infested swamp we hadn't even scouted, I was always at my ambush sites," I stated emphatically. The combat truth of the matter was that nobody could stray too far from their planned position. And no matter how reluctant my men might seem before a mission, I knew they would be alert and ready to pour out the lead and they would follow all but the most suicidal of orders. There were men in my Platoon who did not even need an order to sacrifice themselves without a thought of personal safety – just do whatever the situation demanded. I considered some of my men to be definitely heroic, in an every day unassuming manner. If I had ever seen anyone walk by one of the ambush sites, I would have been the first to open up on them as a matter of survival and I was certain every one of my men would have done the same thing.

"I can understand why there is low troop morale though, I tell you. I had about as much chance of being killed by so-called friendly fire as I did from the VC, you know?...and then I got someone like Dudley giving me stupid orders all the time...fuckin' stupid orders!...like did I tell you about the time he wanted me to blow up a 500lb. bomb by lighting a regular fuse on it?...what a complete idiot." I was able to unload on my understanding friend Filbert, who had been there long enough to know the score. He handed over a nice fat reefer rolled with real Zig-Zag papers that he had received from one of his college chums. What a guy.

We were at our usual evening smoking area by a bunker beside the Supply shed. About a dozen Black guys were down inside the bunker listening to Motown music and getting really stoned, having more or less commandeered the premises on a regular basis. They did not tolerate very many "white boys" hanging around – just Filbert, Tom, and now a rebel Lieutenant. I was still playing the role of a misplaced person for a week or so before reporting in to Division. I no longer had any duties with the Wolfhounds, so I just drifted. I felt I had earned a break.

Distinct polarities among the US troops became apparent during my first week back at the Base Camp – even more pronounced than just a few months before. The Black guys definitely hung together, probably due to peer pressure and sociability, not true racial animosity. The White Southern-type "good ole boys" formed a distinct group and were generally beer-drinkers and hell-raisers apt to cut loose with rebel yells whenever the mood struck them. The "Radicals" were often well-educated, usually draftees, and habitually stoned on pot. These "Radicals" were engaged in many surreptitious forms of protest and resistance to the war and against authorities in general and many of them chose to go to jail for their beliefs, just like Private Jones had been ready to do – before he was shredded by a rocket.

The fourth distinct group formed only a small percentage of the overall combat troop population in the rear areas and an even smaller percentage of the men in the field. These were the "Lifers"- the career Army men. There were practically no lifers out in the field personally conducting combat operations. There were very few Platoon Sergeants with ten or fifteen years experience leading men in combat as there had been in other wars. By the Year of the War 1969, most of the E5 and E6 Sergeants in the field had received their rank by attending rapid-advancement schools in the US similar to Officer Candidate School, whereby I had been commissioned a Second Lieutenant after only six months of indoctrination.

The career Army men who were not out in the jungles during that war were sitting behind desks in air-conditioned offices making speculations and allegations and wondering why the troop morale was so low. They concluded the cause must be rampant drug use and the fact that American youth were just going soft. They were certainly correct in some ways and these generalities were shown to be true through informers and investigators which were infiltrated into the groups of men the Lifers were not personally leading. They prosecuted and incarcerated men instead of leading them through example. They prosecuted young men for drug use then they went to the NCO clubs and drank themselves into a state of near unconsciousness each night. They never did, and still don't, consider daily alcohol inebriation to be a form of drug addiction.

The men in the rear areas I characterized as Radicals – the pot smokers – were a relaxed bunch of guys who seldom found any cause for personal animosities. Generally, whatever tensions might build up were short-lived. Nothing another joint wouldn't help. The Blacks certainly had their reasons for being pissed off at the White authorities who had sent an unbalanced percentage of them to the War. The beer-drinking Good Ole Boys would fight at the drop of a helmet but were usually more interested in having a good time. Almost everybody had seen the effects of bullets and grenades first hand, so whenever a serious disagreement arose, there was intervention and calming words from friends on both sides and it usually did not take long before everyone remembered to look after his own survival and allow others to do the same.

The blatant reality of the message "live and let live" could never be more apparent than when everybody had weapons and grenades close at hand, and almost everyone had already survived brushes with death, and most of those present already felt like a killer. When two men disagreed and were standing there ready to kill each other...then they let the moment pass...they truly and literally understood the meaning of the saying. They understood on a deep visceral level that they still lived and they had allowed someone else to continue to live. The ugly realization of having been ready to kill another American over some comment, or a ten dollar bet in poker game, or some perceived insult, might generate yet another grim memory for a

19 or 20 year-old to add to his war experiences...another dent in self-esteem...another possible pit of depression gaping before him when he returned from the War.

There were many subtle warps in morals and odd behaviors that these incomprehensible men would carry back to their families and their society. There were many unstated, unrecognized differences that would forever separate these veterans from their peer group. Some veterans would never sleep through the night for the rest of their lives. Some would isolate themselves, internally by showing a numbness of feeling, and externally by retreating into the woods and wilderness areas to just be alone. Speaking for myself, when I returned from Vietnam, I felt in some ways invincible and completely unafraid of risky behavior and I certainly did not sleep well. Mute depression could instantly turn into angry tirades and violence against any animate and inanimate objects immediately at hand. At times, isolation could be a good thing.

The real social and psychological statistics the Vietnam Veterans would compile when they returned to society would eventually become a cause for concern among Psychiatrists and Psychologists but that concern and the help engendered would come much too late for many. A large percentage of the combat veterans would be in jail within one year of returning from Vietnam. Many years later when some of us finally applied for compensation for PTSD, we were denied a disability rating by the VA Psychiatrists, who ascribed our emotional problems to having been in jail or prison. We were in jail and/or prison BECAUSE we were affected by PTSD and some of us undoubtedly had suffered Traumatic Brain Injury (not definitely diagnosed before widespread MRI and other imaging techniques).

I finally reported in to HQ&Admin. Co. of the 25th Infantry Division and met my immediate supervisor – a tight-assed, screaming little prick of a Major: Thomas Walner. He treated me with contempt from the start because he had read the reports of the unfounded allegations against me that had been sent up through channels. The Major informed me, "you will be the bunker line control Officer of the eastern half of Cu Chi Base Camp responsible for taking a detail out to repair the wire and make general improvements to the bunkers. And you will also function as Officer-of-the-Guard at night, ensuring the manning of the perimeter each night. Any questions Lieutenant?"

He assigned his new whipping-dog to a virtually 24 hour/day job just so he could have ample opportunity to prosecute any failure to perform all the assigned duties. "That's fine with me Major, thank you," I replied to the overwhelming job description, making no attempt to hide more that a trace of sarcasm in my voice. I watched in amusement as red patches of irritation spread across the Major's pale, freckled face and ears, and decided I liked my Major with come color in his cheeks. Walner was a fair-skinned redhead with blond eyelashes, features I had for some reason disliked all my life. I winked and grinned at the Major's "hooch-girl" Lan as I left the office. She had entered with a pair of freshly-shined jungle boots for the Major to change into just in case he got his boots dirty during his strenuous day around the office.

"Oh HELL no!" My sincere and automatic mantra cruised through my mind like a huge, dilapidated 1948 Hudson Hornet in an exclusive modern subdivision as I supervised a group of men out on the bunker line the next day. They were all misfits like me, doing shitty Base Camp work because they were in transit, or were awaiting judicial proceedings of some sort. The job required them to go out into the concertina wires beyond the perimeter and reset trip flares that Charlie would often steal or set off from a distance at night just to harass the Americans. Nearly every day the bunker line detail would find a Claymore anti-personnel mine turned around backwards or even booby-trapped. There was also the ever present danger of snipers, even in broad daylight right beside a major base camp like Cu Chi. It was about as bad a job as any base camp commando could possibly have.

My current driver was a wise-cracking Black guy, Private E1 (busted) Russel Tolbert, who was trying to figure out his new Lieutenant as we sat in the cab of a deuce-and-a-half watching the three man detail load scrap metal from a demolished bunker into the back of the truck. Tolbert remarked, "you know, L T, sometimes I don't know whether I fucked up or got lucky with this here job...know what I'm saying, sir?"

"Ah yes, my good man, a curious conundrum I must say. So I figure we might as well get fucked up while we ponder the predicament," I replied in the voice of W.C. Fields, having already figured out the man Tolbert. I produced a Havatampa Jewel joint Filbert had packed the night before with powerful Thai weed, lit it up. It was becoming an amusing ritual – the first surprise joint with my drivers.

Tolbert cracked up. "Haa...ha,...yeah, my brothers over to the Wolfhounds was saying as how you been smoking reefer over there, Lieutenant Lumbert. Goddamn, I ain't had no Officer-in-Charge like you before, that's a fack." Tolbert took enormous hits off the cigar-joint and glanced again at his at his new CO, totally amused. "We the fuck-ups they couldn't catch at anything serious, you know. I think I heard mention of the word "incorrigible" in my case, L T, how 'bout yourself?"

"Well, with me I guess I repeated my mantra too often...OH HELL NO!...something like that," I answered between hits of the Havatampa. "You see, I developed sort of a bad attitude after they shot my face off with a fuckin' 105 Howitzer at Diamond two."

"Understand sir...understand how that might change a man's mind just a bit."

"Fuckin' right it changed my mind. And I'll tell you Tolbert, at this point, I'm not sure I was ever Officer material to begin with. Now I truly don't give a shit, man," I replied honestly, taking yet another hit even though my ears were already buzzing. The truck was not even half full of trash, but being the lackadaisical Lieutenant I had become, I decided to head on out to the dump, taking as much time as possible to do very little work, as was my personal SOP. I directed Tolbert to head out the gate to the dump, which was located outside the perimeter.

As Tolbert eased the big truck through the village beyond the gate, I looked with compassion at the squalor and dire straits the people endured. I also could not help wondering about all the inherent possibilities, knowing what I now knew from accompanying Mac to Saigon. The dump was run by a private enterprise and manned by Korean civilians who in turn were supervised by American Military Police patrolling in a jeep with an M-60 mounted in the rear. The Korean guard glanced in the back of the truck then directed us to the scrap metal pile. I automatically scanned the nearby treeline for any signs of the enemy and studied the Base Camp from that perspective.

Thinking about what it would take to crawl through the concertina, avoiding trip wires, soundlessly rearranging delicate traps and mines in near total darkness, I decided some of these people have a hell of a set of balls, for sure. And these were not trained North Vietnamese Regular Army soldiers. The local populace, untrained, would sneak around in the dark and mess with the minds of the invaders – the Americans. And they were very, very good at it.

My mind drifted with a speculation on what it might have been like for one of the NVA soldiers who attacked Diamond that night in April. I wondered if they had any individual men who refused to go out on a mission, like Private Jones had, and whether the men who attacked us had any idea how many of them would surely die that night. A Lieutenant in that Army would probably shoot a discipline problem on the spot, I imagined; and they damn sure did not have guys going off to jail where they received three-hots-and-a-cot...see the "home boys".

After leaving the dump we fired up the joint again and as we passed through the village the boom-boom girls and hustlers waved and called out to us. "Hey GI...numba one boom-boom today. Umercan numba one!" Tolbert looked at his new boss and wiggled his eyebrows then flicked the Havatampa like Groucho Marx flicked his cigar and said, "What's the secret woid, L T?"

"Yeah, well, as long as one man stays in the back of the truck, I don't care if the others jump out and buy a coke or something...what the hell...we got plenty of time." Tolbert parked in a side "street" next to a jeep. It seemed safe enough, with American troops strolling the dirty lanes buying trinkets and black market items, or drinking cokes and beer while eating some unidentifiable forbidden roadside food from the numerous stalls and vendors. Two of the men went off with some girls and came back about twelve minutes later walking in that relaxed way guys do after getting a load off. *Oh well, boys will be boys...everybody's got to make a living, even in a war.*

After seeing numerous mistakes made by the Army, I could not be a stern disciplinarian on minor matters. The military was committing a major blunder every day of the week and I was certain that lies and cover-ups were as commonplace as bad coffee at mess halls. These men had about the worst jobs in the Base Camp except for burning shit, which was done be old papasans. Of course, besides their occasional trips to the dump and working out in the wire every day, the men could go to the PX and they had movies, the steam bath, and many other luxuries that some men in the field would just about give their left nut for. The word was out that I was a pot smoker anyway so the men figured they might get away with some minor indiscretions as well.

I could relate to any of the polarized groups, but the only group that felt comfortable was the draftee pot smokers. The Blacks accepted me to some extent, and I could understand the White Southern Good-ole-Boys; but I did not get along with most Lifers. I was an openly disgruntled renegade who expressed contempt towards other Officers and anyone I thought was using the war to advance their careers. The mannerisms of Captain Dodgely often came to mind as I reflected on the fate of other "Gung-Ho" Officers like him.

There were substantive rumors of certain brainless – or heartless – Officers who were "fragged" by their own men during incoming mortar or rocket attacks. Although I had taken little notice at the time, I did recall several of my men taking casual pot shots at the Colonel's helicopter when it was circling high overhead and we were shooting it out with NVA Regulars in the HoBo woods. Whenever a memory of that day occurred, by whatever circuitous route the mind took to start that memory bank...whenever I thought of Pete being killed in that pointless attempt to "clear those woods"...I would burn with rage. I could bite through nails when I thought of that day. Then I could sink into a mire of depression and self-blaming thinking about those months as an XO and a Platoon Leader. *I'm a complete idiot...I volunteered for this shit...hope Dudley is burning in hell the goddamnsonofabitch.*

Tolbert was intelligent and fairly well-read and we engaged in philosophical discussions on a wide variety of subjects. I gained a better understanding of some of the reasons for the instinctive and general revolt of the Black Man in Vietnam. "There's way too many Brothers over here, L T...something like twenty percent of the troops fighting the White Man's war. And for what, huh?" My driver felt free to express his own tirade, not expecting any answers from me, just venting.

"Hey, I understand what you mean, Tolbert. I can't see any sense to any of us being over here. And I never thought of it before, but there do seem to be lots of Black guys over here, more than I was used to seeing. Growing up in San Antonio, the Mexicans were the majority and I was a minority. The city of San Antonio was very segregated as far as what side of town you lived in and what school you went to. I don't remember a single

Black person in my whole high school, man. Plus, I grew up half-Jewish and I always felt like I didn't belong anywhere."

"Half-Jewish? What does that mean, Lieutenant Lumbert? Uh, pass that Havatampa, please."

The two of us were having our customary late afternoon smoke after dropping off the detail men who had been assigned to bunker line punishment that day. We were parked out on the far east perimeter of the Base Camp, an isolated area until I posted the guards later that evening. We were sitting in the deuce-and-a-half listening to Jimi Hendrix, a shared passion, on a small cassette player as we looked out across "no-mans' land" - our work area – towards the dump about a mile away.

"Well it means my Mother was Jewish but not seriously involved in the religion and my Father was raised Methodist or something, but converted to marry my Mother just before he went away to World War Two. I never heard him talk about religion though, except to tell me I could make up my mind later in life. He died about a year ago." I had become confident in the understanding and open-mindedness of my driver.

"So what did you do on Christmas and stuff..." Tolbert honestly inquired.

"Didn't celebrate Christmas and I always felt left out at that time of year. We had another celebration about the same time of year – Hanukkah."

"Didn't celebrate Christmas? Oh yeah, the Jewish people didn't think Jesus was the Savior, right?"

"Oh, a lot of them did at the time...and others later. They were the first Christians...the followers of Jesus. But the Jewish leaders didn't like him because he was upsetting their whole apple-cart. And you know Tolbert, it was fine upstanding Christians who enslaved your people and pointed out a passage in their Holy Bible to back up what they were doing. I doubt you'll find any Jewish slave owners, man, we got heavy teachings about when we were slaves in ancient Egypt. You know, Moses and that whole story. In fact some of the Old Testament is about the Jews wandering around suffering persecution...when they weren't kicking butt, that is."

"Understand there, L T...and what was he the savior of anyway?...he didn't save his own self...he didn't save the Jews from a lot more suffering...and when you look at what the modern so called Christians are doing...shit...makes me wonder about everything, you know?"

And so the conversations would go, ranging from politics and religion, to Black Power, to grousing with the hooch girls who came in to clean the barracks and living quarters. Young men thrown together in stressful circumstances and subjected to demands and decisions regarding life and limb, alternating between extremes in a time of possible deadly daily consequences. Even for Base Camp "commandos" like ourselves, there was really no time day or night when we could rest assured of our safety.

Well-known hooch girls were suddenly found to possess booby-trap materials. The old respected papasan barber at the PX was caught at the gate smuggling out two hand grenades. Rumors abounded concerning ambushing of convoys, poisoning of cokes, and hiding razor blades in the vaginas of boom-boom girls. I thought that one was probably untrue. The US troops in Cu Chi Base Camp lived each night wondering when to expect the next ass-clenching, breathless moments of hearing mortar rounds "KA-Crunching" around inside the perimeter like King Kong on a drunk. Ten thousand soldiers would be lying in their bunks trying to decide whether to run for a bunker or not during a rocket or mortar attack at night. Ten thousand personnel whose job description placed them "back" from the fighting – in the rear areas. Every American realized that the enemy was close, very close, at all times.

During one period, for instance, I kept strict records of the incoming rounds at night. For four nights in a row, at 0200, three mortar rounds would drop into Cu Chi. Then for two nights nothing happened. Then a new cycle started with a single rocket fired in at about 0600, usually in the direction of the airfield. The Vietcong would intimidate every American, regardless of rank, job, or ideology, and damn near every American Soldier had no real way to directly retaliate. There were no "safe rear areas" in Vietnam in 1969.

The enemy was invisible because the enemy was ubiquitous. The "Asian" in these Asian Peoples resisted this latest invasion by foreigners. Every South Vietnamese person, whether they were receiving help from the Americans, or threats and violence from the North Vietnamese, resented the presence of the Americans. And how could they not? The malleable masses might eventually enfold this meager invasion as easily as the mighty Yangtze river inundated vast fertile plains in China. For in true numbers, even at the height of US troop commitment, we were a mere half-million among tens and tens of millions. Within all of Southeast Asia, an individual American was outnumbered at least a thousand to one everywhere he looked. There was no way to not feel humbled and somewhat unnerved by this fact, depending on one's experiences. It made for some jumpy responses at times from just about everyone.

This overwhelming sense of inferiority in numbers probably had something to do with the amount of piracy, larceny, smuggling, and black marketeering that occurred when anyone knew they could get away with it.

"Hey there, L T...just the possible Officer-in-Charge I was looking for...heh-he," big Sergeant Mac said, strolling up as I was dismissing the morning detail men. Mac took a deep breath and rubbed both hands down the sides of his twelve-pack belly then leered at me conspiratorially and continued, "come on over to my office Lieutenant. I got a proposition for ya."

I hopped in the jeep without a question, always ready to hear whatever the sneaky supply Sergeant might have on his mind. We drove over to the Wolfhounds' area and after entering the bliss of the air-conditioned back office I asked Mac, "what's up Sarn't Mac? Another tradin' and requisitioning run?"

"Something like that sir, thought you might like to go along...make a little spending money too, you know?" Mac said, laying bait like a Cajun fisherman.

I was intrigued of course. "Well I have a reason to maybe justify a trip down to Saigon for a project I got going on over at Division. I was going to come over and talk to you today as a matter of fact. What's on your devious mind Sarge?"

Subtleties were never Mac's strong point so he came right out with it. "Remember those Ration Cards, sir? There's still a stack of 'em in the safe at Alpha Company...uh, you still remember the combination to that safe?"

"It was just a few weeks ago, Sarge. Fortunately my good man, I have an excellent memory for numerical sequences." I slipped as easily into larceny as I could my W.C. Fields imitation. "You reckon you could scrounge up some enamel door and trim paint for me in some nice colors? I'll tell Major Tantrum that's the reason I have to go to Long Binh or Saigon." Sometimes it did not take long for a plan to come together.

"Oh yeah, I got paint right here in Cu Chi I can lay my hands on...no problem."

"Something besides olive drab or gray, please."

"Nice pastels, lieutenant really...oil-based enamel from the Navy, sir. Sign this here gate pass as, uh, Alpha Company XO...and off we go...heh-heh."

This larcenous Lieutenant quickly coordinated with Filbert, who relieved the Alpha Company Clerk for noon chow then he let me into the Company Commander's office. This ex-XO made short work of opening the safe. "Holy shit, Lieutenant Lumbert! Look at that payroll." Filbert shuffled through several stacks of cash – Military Payment Certificate, or MPC – not US greenbacks.

"No way Filbert. I'm only taking a little of what I know won't be missed," I wisely decided, and slipped a hefty stack of Ration Cards from a large bundle. Seconds later, blithely out the door, I headed over to the Motor Pool where Sgt. Mac was loading up the ¾ ton pickup.

Mac grinned expectantly. "How'd we do, L T?"

"Pretty good sarge," I said, pulling out a stack about an inch and a half thick and slapping it down on the hood of the truck like a deck of playing cards.

"Hooboy. Way to go Lieutenant! Them's worth about twenty bucks each, depending on how we unload em'...hee-he. Reckon we can get a decent room for the night, sir?"

"I feel certain we will find suitable accommodations my good man, drive on Sergeant."

All it took was a call to the Company Clerk at HQ&Admin. to curtly inform him that I had to go to Long Binh to requisition some paint and should be back before dark. As we were checking out at the gate I remarked, "Gee Sarge, I should feel bad about missing some sort of meeting this afternoon over at Admin, but somehow I just don't give a shit anymore...know what I mean?"

"A meeting with that flaming prick, Major Walner?"

"Major Tantrum I call him now. Yeah a meeting about beautifying the Base Camp for some type of inspection coming up...big brass and politicians or something...shee-it. All I really need to do is finish painting the new BOQ and he's got nothing to bitch to me about."

"Well Three-Six, it seems to me that Major Tantrum is going to be on your ass either way. Shit. And you know what my main mission is today? To trade for some regular PRC-10 radios that my men need in the field and I can't get through regular channels. How you like that shit, huh? Is that any way to run a fuckin' war, lieutenant, huh, is it?...shit."

"I tell you sarge, sometimes I feel so damn mad I just want to rip things up. I pity the fool who gives me any problems. I'll punch his lights out."

"Yeah well, whew...you got good reason to be pissed off there, Lieutenant Lumbert. And by the way, if you don't mind me mentioning it, you look about as bad off as you were the first time I told you, 'hey, you look like you need to get laid, sir'...remember that?"

I grinned. "Do I remember?...shee-it. We going to redistribute some flack jackets this trip sarge?"

"Yessir. I tell ya', I don't know how the country could run without me. I even re-upped for another year because so many guys owe me favors I can't afford to go home, hee-he." Such was the manner in which the Supply field operated.

"We going to requisition anything interesting?"

"Oh, no more of that for a while, sir, the CID (Criminal Investigation Division) is coming down with some big-time investigations and shit. We just redistribute the items we already got, lieutenant."

"I see. Then we re-itemize the redistributed items and everybody's happy. Is that how it works, Mac?"

"It's how the Armed Forces has always operated in a war zone, is about how I see it, lieutenant."

"I reckon so, sarge. Any chance we might see your buddy the Sergeant-Major-in-Charge of all the booze in the country?"

"One of the first stops, L T. I'll get us set up right, leave it to me." And I knew he would, so I rested comfortably during the fifty or so miles to the outskirts of the conglomeration of Long Binh, Tan San Nhut, and Saigon. Mac pulled in at the familiar warehouse to unload the numerous flak jackets that the men refused to accept and carry in the field. After a brief conversation with the same E9 Sergeant Major, Mac went inside the building with the man who controlled all the alcoholic beverages in the country, and naturally returned with drinks for everyone.

"One of these two bottles of Jack Daniel's finest is a gift for the bartender at the Hilton, sir, then you see what kind of service we get tonight. This other one here is for you, Lieutenant."

"And that bottle of Gilbey's Gin?"

"For the girls, you know...hee hee." The crafty Supply had all the bases covered, as usual.

"Hey thanks a lot, sarge. You really know how to take care of your troops."

"I do my best, L T. My very best."

Negotiating the streets of Saigon, this introspective Lieutenant reflected on my first trip to this confusing, clamorous city, a mere six months before. My eyes had certainly been opened to the sorrows of war which were all too evident in the Vietnamese people, both in the countryside and in the city. Pangs of pure undiluted grief assaulted me as I viewed the hopeless cripples, the heart-rending amputees, the ragged filthy children, and the tired prostitutes lining the sidewalks. I looked more attentively into the alleys and side lanes at the poverty, the filth, and the misery written on the faces of the people. Many of the Vietnamese smiled readily enough; but the mere change in the shape of a mouth could not disguise the grief and pain etched deeply into the lines of a face...a face too old for its years yet too proud to give up entirely...a face reconciled to mere survival and mute acceptance of hardship. I had to turn away from Mac to hide the heaving in my chest and the mist washing my eyes. *How do they do it? How do they face each day like this?*

Mac parked the truck in the usual guarded enclosure near the center of Saigon and we walked the several blocks to the Hilton. The same worn-out, skinny "cyclo" drivers were perched atop their bicycles, towing their rickety contraptions, wearing the same toothless grins and little else. The same nattily dressed black-marketeer cab drivers suggested the same shady possibilities as the last time I was there with Mac; but now I saw deeply into the tawdry realities and dire straits of these people. A clear glimpse into the utter desolation that lay behind the scene was unavoidable, given my experiences. It was like a peek backstage at a gaudy sideshow in a grimy, run-down traveling carnival. I felt the disillusionment a boy of ten might experience when he excitedly peeks into the clowns' dressing room at the circus and finds depression, depravity, and decay. *Are we causing this suffering or are we here to alleviate it?* It was impossible to reconcile or understand the human suffering and fracturing of a society which I was witnessing.

I watched disinterestedly as Mac sold the ration cards to a group of cabbies for about $800 and was noncommittal when Mac handed me half the money. I felt apathetic and was not having as much fun in this scam as expected. There was no humor to be found that day. There was no longer any imagining of myself as Milo Minderbinder (from Catch 22), masterfully scamming and scrounging for the troops. There was really nothing I wanted with the money we had apparently just accumulated. There was nothing I could get for "my men" because I did not have any men in my command. I had no command except leading a varied group of misfits in a shitty, dangerous, and thankless job. *The hell with this shit and shoot the donkey Jesus rode to town on, and the hell with all the lifers and politicians who put me here goddamnit!* The mantra had complexified itself in a stressed and twisted mind and I still did not sleep well.

Mac did manage to lighten my mood a bit with a guided tour of the main Post Exchange though, where I bought a possibly ersatz Rolex Oyster Pearl wristwatch for under $400. *What the hell...it was free money.* Sergeant Mac picked up two expensive cameras, two Seiko watches, two deluxe binoculars, etc...and after assuring that a certain known accomplice was on checkout duty, quietly said, "see that blond-haired PFC in the far checkout lane, L T?...he'll take two cards for an extra ten bucks...watch this." Mac bought two of every item that each card limited to just one.

A nod of recognition passed between Mac and the cashier as Mac gave him two ration cards with a folded ten-spot between them. Without a blink or a pause, the clerk rang two of each item, palmed the ten, and punched the cards together in the appropriate blank, all nice and legal. Mac had sent home a dozen high-quality Pentax and Minolta cameras, expensive wristwatches, and stereos in this manner.

"You ought to make you an investment, L T...for the future. You can double your money on this stuff easy."

"Yeah, I might give that some thought Mac, thanks." Somehow scamming a camera or wristwatch did not seem like a good way to spend my last few months in country. Not that I could formulate a better or more coherent plan.

We proceeded to the Saigon Hilton, which had been a rendezvous for plotting and scheming among politicians, journalists, entrepreneurs, and generals from at least eight different nations during it's forty-some years of operation. Sometimes listed as a Four-Star International Hotel, now it was simply stately, just plain and functional. It was still there and it was still the Hilton of Saigon.

The top floor bar and ballroom was a huge cavern enclosing an assortment of oddly-lit dance floors, deep enclosed booths, and arrangements of small round tables and chairs. There were still occasional floor shows on a stage at one end; but the era of the big bands of the Forties and Fifties had passed and the general ambiance now was of elegant dining, serious drinking, and discrete high-class hustling. At one end of a forty-foot mahogany bar served by several multi-lingual Malaysians there was a group of professional journalists and photographers seriously drinking and engaged in animated discussions. Along the back wall and other dimly lit areas there were friendly Asian women entertaining GI's for the evening...dancing, drinking, laughing, eating, and all evidently having a good time. Immediately on entering, one encountered the Bar & Grill inhabited by senior NCO's, where the career Sergeants, most of them veterans of the war in Korea, could congregate to discuss the daily life of the military and the conduct of that particular war.

These career military men were hard-pressed to provide quality leadership to the everyday men under their command due to the aforementioned regulation of a one-year tour of duty for most of the troops actually engaged in the war. If a recruit survived his apprenticeship and worked for a few months gaining experience in his job – whatever job that might be – then he would cross the halfway point in his tour and would begin to think of himself as a short-timer. He might think, "hey, I've done my part, now I'm too short for this shit detail...let the newby do it." Therefore, regarding any type of mission or work schedule, the least experienced men were often the ones performing the hardest yet most important tasks. This held true for machine-gunners and second Lieutenants in the field, and corporal/clerks in the Base Camps who were reporting statistics through channels and coordinating press releases. Most of the men in Vietnam were just there for their tour – not for the duration of the war – so the cohesive force of career NCO's was very important; but also hard to implement.

Sergeant Mac greeted several acquaintances as we entered the Bar & Grill and took a table in the restaurant area. The NCO enclave was created as much by architecture and furniture arrangement as by the tough-looking Sergeant-at-Arms who stood lurking and drinking and surveying the scene from the entrance. The old veterans glanced at this young Lieutenant tolerantly, the way an uncle might greet a young nephew at his first adult poker game at uncle's house. I was accepted because Mac was well known and was greeted loudly by the head bartender as he accepted Mac's gift with grace and facile charm. "Ah yes, Jack Daniel's...thank you Sergeant Mac...good afternoon Lieutenant." He greeted us in flawless English while grinning his broad Malaysian smile then turned and said something in Vietnamese to a passing cocktail waitress before barking some orders in a Chinese dialect to a young boy clearing tables. Drinks, appetizers, soup, and wine arrived within minutes and everything was choice...nicely done. Everyone was happy, even this formerly morose Lieutenant.

After food and drinks, I realized how depressed I had been earlier on the sidewalk and turned my full attention to enjoying the rare evening in the big city. "Hey sarge, check out this Rolex...says it's waterproof down to 32 atmospheres of pressure. You know how deep that is?. About a thousand feet, that's what...think about that."

"Definitely top-o-the-line there, L T. You deserve the best, sir. I've seen lots of lieutenants come and go and I'll tell you the truth, Three-Six...Lieutenant Lumbert...you've done a fine job since the day you got here. I don't care what anyone says...I know you."

"I'll drink to that sarge, thanks. I did my best, that's about all I can say," I said, my mind wandering into memories of being "Three-Six", the Infantry Platoon Leader. The memories automatically became pictures – clear photographic images in my mind: Dudley shot through the neck right in front of my eyes; Pete fading away and feeling that I was somewhere in that "away" and thinking I could hold on to him and keep him in this world; various shocks and explosive concussions; being lifted in the air by the blast at Diamond; convulsing on the ground and willing myself to take a breath...the hole in Pete's chest...the small black hole in Pete's chest.

"I'll tell you the truth Mac, half the time I didn't know what the hell to do. I mean, pullin' ambushes and shit, going out on search-and-destroy sweeps. I had some just plain good luck at times, that's about all I know for sure."

"Aw, you'll do all right. You always have," the good Sergeant assured me as he finished off an excellent lobster tail. We dined and we drank in a fine hotel while other men were facing the terrors of the night out in the jungle...waiting and wakeful. Sleeping like nervous cats. Pensive, touchy, and listening...always quietly listening. Others had the good fortune to sleep in barracks where they dozed in the exhausted consciousness of chronic anxiety, ready to haul ass down into the nearest bunker when the mortar shells start sailing in or a rocket roars by.

Sergeant Mac conversed with several other NCO's who dropped by the table and I laughed like hell at times listening to the bullshit and knowing most of it was true. I felt myself swept up in the magnetic and expansive nature of the good-natured wheeler-dealer. A feeling of peace and mental clarity descended on me that night, sitting there with plenty of money in a city of all possibilities and sharing the stories with these seasoned soldiers. I decided all lifers were not so bad after all.

These men seemed capable of conducting a war; but they were not in charge of many aspects of the war in Vietnam. They knew their jobs and they knew themselves, being mature men in their thirties and forties; and they were upset over many of the tactics and decisions under which they had to operate there in Vietnam. The morale problem affected seasoned soldiers as well as draftees.

Problem with me right now is I have no job...or my job has gone to shit, zilch. OIC of fuckups, Chief Slack and his slackers...fuck it. I've snuck out in the night with malice in my heart and come back terrified of what I didn't see. I've seen the dead and the living dead, and those who were cheatin' death and knew it...and men who simply did not care. Me, I'm any of the above. Shit.

"Hey lieutenant, cheer up. Here come the girls," Mac said as four beautiful young women slid smoothly into the booth, two on each side. They began to introduce themselves with smiles and silken brows, their delicate limbs and childlike size disguising what I knew was a tough, realistic survivor on the inside. I had a pleasant recollection of feeling MaryKay Brunsell's breasts in the eighth grade behind the scenery during drama class – my first fondling of that amazing forbidden flesh, a young breast.

I did not feel like acting out a pretense of love though, or even affection, with these women; although part of me had definitely raised its swollen head to scope out the possibilities. It just seemed, on thinking about it, demeaning for both people involved. I felt stifled and oppressed in facing the inevitable unemotional coupling that was the whole reason the women had come over to the table to begin with. I excused myself and headed down to the far end of the ballroom toward the rest rooms. Passing the journalists, who were still seriously drinking and gesticulating, I noticed one of them peering closely at my face and insignias. When I came out of the can the guy said, "Excuse me lieutenant, got a minute?"

"I got almost four months of minutes."

A short, intense, hawk-eyed man gestured to a chair amid a group of what I could see were photographers, there being stacks of photos arranged on the table, neighboring chairs, and in folders in their laps.

"Jake Bellcross," the guy said as he gave a nervous, wiry grip. "Combat photographer. We're all photographers here. Not to start up any war stories or bullshit lieutenant, but you look familiar, did I take your picture somewhere?"

"I don't think I have ever seen any of you guys in my neck of the woods, gentlemen, not when I was a Platoon Leader. Don't recall seeing any official photographers where I've been."

"And where have you been, lieutenant Lumbert, if I might ask?" Jake pressed ahead, automatically gathering information in a journalistic manner.

"Right now I am the official bunker line control Officer of half of Cu Chi Base Camp. Before that I was with the Wolfhounds, the Second of the Twenty-Seventh."

"Yeah, the Wolfhounds, hey...HEY...look at this! Here you are, lieutenant. Jeez, no wonder I thought you looked familiar. I took this friggin' shot here," Jake said excitedly as he smacked the cover of the September 1969 Stars and Stripes magazine. And there I was in the background, with Dudley's huge jaw line taking up half the foreground, in a photo that must have been taken on the one and only riverboat ride I had been on. I could not remember a photographer being there. There was only a sketchy memory of a one-hour uneventful trip down a muddy, stinky stream that was barely wide enough for the boat to pass in places. Once I thought about it though, I remembered the event as an ass-clenching, ambush-expectant, momentary novelty during weeks of inconsequential drudgery. Weeks punctuated by the occasional horrendously gory minutes after a booby-trap was tripped...minutes that were stretched into hours of internal imagery...seconds that were extended into lifetimes of stark anatomically explicit, horrific photographic memories...memories etched by shock into a psyche numbed by weeks and months of low-level terror and chronic fatigue...a body too tired to rest and a mind too exhausted to dream...a mind that forgot nothing commanding a man who forgot minding...and memories unwinding in a mind unbending brought indelible photographs from somewhere inside, suddenly into the light.

I involuntarily tallied up the twisted, mangled limbs I had seen as I gazed at some of the photos on the table. Each incident flashed through my mind like pages in a photo album turned by the wind: the foot of the dead Ranger flopping with the banking of the chopper; Sergeant West's foot knocking impossibly against his shinbone; the nameless young corporal convulsing limply after being hit by the beehives; the look of incredulity on Pete's face; myself being flipped through the air. And the photos turned faster, showing all the charred, grotesque bodies at Diamond when I was dusted off in the Medivac. I saw the bodies and the pieces of bodies my men sorted out after Edwards had popped the ambush, then I fixated on the appearance of the small black hole in the center of Pete's sternum – right through the chest. It was just a small hole...so very small.

"Hey! I said, what happened that time after I took this shot here?" Jake said loudly, repeating himself to break into my reverie.

"Not much. Just days and days of humping the jungle and nights and nights of listening." I replied to the question even though unable to shake off the images still flashing like neon signs in my mind. Pointing to the cover of the magazine, I said, "this west point captain here in the foreground, with the jawline, he got shot through the neck about two weeks later in the Hobo

Woods while ordering me and my men to do something totally stupid."

"How long were you out in the field, lieutenant?"

"Hey, it's not how long...it's the FUCKING QUALITY of the experience that counts, ha-ha." Initially taking a light tone and unsure how much to divulge to these guys, I wanted to respond in some way to the question while the photos were flashing in my head, but found it difficult to engage my brain to my vocal chords. I was swirling internally in a flood of visual memories while trying to focus on appearing to have a normal conversation. *Am I too drunk or something? The fuck is this guy saying?* Jake was saying something I could not quite understand, then before I could collect myself I began to rant about Dudley...then about Pete's death...then about the beehives being fired at Diamond II when we were being overrun...and by the time I could catch up to myself I was smacking the table with the palm of my hand hard enough to be scattering glasses, booze, and photos everywhere while shouting my litany of futilities...my tirade of fiascoes.

Suddenly I looked down at myself staring at the shocked journalists who were looking up at my now blank face, and said, "And THAT, gentlemen, has been the **fucking quality** of my experiences so far in Vietnam." Jake and the other photographers said not another word as I turned and walked back across the ballroom toward the NCO lounge. My heart was pounding in my temples and my eyes were dazzled by the lighting and I kept hearing distant artillery echoing in my ears. *Does Saigon take a lot of mortars and rockets?*

I might have appeared normal on entering the restaurant though, where I found Mac joking with an old First Sergeant and stroking the silky forearm of a smiling, pudgy woman smuggling up beside him, as expected. My buddy Sergeant Mac smiled and pushed a key across the table as I slid into the booth and said, "Your room's all taken care of there, L T. Have a drink with me and top here and maybe a woman will come by, hee-he." He was in fine form, with a wallet full of cash and a nice giggly pillow for the night.

Naturally, just as Mac predicted, my double Jack-on-the-rocks had no sooner arrived, when two gorgeous copper-skinned young women walked right up to the table and introduced themselves. More of Mac's meddling no doubt. Taking care of his troops, even Lieutenants. The wise Sergeant grinned as he watched his favorite Lieutenant get petted and fawned over by the two women, the pair pretending to compete for my attention the way not-quite-innocent adolescents might, instead of experienced ladies of the evening. Oh, and they were experienced all right. This young man found myself lost in the delightful clutches of "Mai", the more petite of the sloe-eyed beauties.

After venting some of my frustrations verbally with Jake I definitely felt more relaxed, so the natural energies of a young healthy male in close proximity to a perfumed, smiling woman took over and I realized how horny I was. The deeper more meaningful aspects of love might come later back in the World; but right then I simply wanted to get into bed with this cute, willing woman. That fact was abundantly clear from the regular spasmodic expansions occurring in my left pant leg.

I bullshitted with Mac and the Top Sergeant long enough to not seem too eager, then excused myself and my "lady" and floated off to my room. A room...my own private room. A bed...a huge, soft, clean bed. *How wondrous and fine!* A shower...hot endless streams of water. Soap...cleanliness. Even these simple pleasures were magnified into ecstatic novelties after a few months in the field, or even in a Base Camp. It was unbelievable how good it felt to stretch out on a big bed, naked and clean.

The sensations of coupling with a beautiful woman were such as only a horny, healthy, twenty-one year-old man could derive. Feeling somehow energized after a frenzied hour of sex, I showered again, dismissed the girl with my appreciation, both monetary and verbal, and then headed back to the top floor to see if those journalists were still at it. I felt the need for some intelligent conversation and intellectual understanding and wanted to find out what those guys knew about the war in other parts of the country.

Jake, the combat photographer, grinned and waved me over when I got close enough to recognize. He was completely sloshed. "Hey lieutenant! Hey...check your weapon at the door ya' goddamn hothead." He turned and slurred to his associates, "this man has seen some shit, believe me...don't piss him off, okay." Jake gestured drunkenly to a chair and indicated the row of bottles on the table. "Have a drink lieutenant and tell us something else about the war," he said, apparently unconcerned at seeing me get more than a little out of hand earlier.

"The war is a lie," I said, taking a swig directly from one of the bottles of scotch since all the glasses visible had been used. "There is no war I can find that everybody agrees on." I took another drink and stared sullenly at the group. "The war is a lie," I repeated.

One of them took the bait, said argumentatively, "if there is no war, what're all these photos of huh, a fuckin' wedding? We have been out in the bush, Lumbert. I've been under fire. I have watched body counts."

"Oh I believe you've been in the field. I said there is no war that I can find. I said the war is a fucking lie because there's not a single, defined, attainable goal or objective that everyone agrees will make a difference. Does it make a difference in any way that one day my men killed ten Vietcong and we only lost one man on our side? When there are thousands of them...millions of Asians. And every one of them is here for the duration and none of them is going to change centuries of tradition and suddenly do things the way we say they should. They <u>all</u> resent us on a purely racial basis. We are a foreign race coming into their country messing with their lives and destroying their countryside. You think old mamasan out in a village cares one way or the other? Shit. Half of them think we're the French coming back to work the rubber plantations."

One thing about journalists: they were good listeners. They heard and considered what this erratic, opinionated hothead was saying. They were all somewhat older than I; but they showed respect for my point of view since I had been out there in the jungle, slogging through the muck, sitting at ambush sites all night, fighting the war whenever I could. They knew what I had been through. They understood more than any civilian a returning veteran would encounter, ever in his life. Most of these men were against the "war effort" and had seen enough Americans lost in what they agreed was an unwinnable mistake. Even those who could not state exactly why they were against the war philosophically had seen enough dead bodies by the end of 1969 to want to call the whole thing off and go home. They stayed because it was their job to stay and they believed in doing their job. They wrote the stories and they snapped the photos and they, the journalists and photographers, knew that the war was not being reported to the American public in an honest manner. And they already knew of numerous instances of body count statistics being manipulated along the way up the chain of command, even before any type of official press secretary got hold of them. The war was not a lie – it was not <u>one</u> lie. It was a thousand lies...a hundred thousand. And they all knew it at the time.

Taking full advantage of the chance at meaningful dialogue with these men, who were also veterans of war, I found out how the war was doing elsewhere. The war elsewhere was a lie. The killing was definitely real; but the "war effort" was a lie. It was an understanding that gave little comfort. It was a confirmation of the applicability of my mantra. I drank and conversed long into the night with the witty, intelligent and realistic photographer, Jake, and awoke the next day feeling disgusted. *Oh HELL no,* I thought as I dressed and went out to find Mac and some coffee, not necessarily in that order.

I found both at the NCO lounge, now serving breakfast. Nodding at the crusty First Sergeant lurking and slurping coffee at the entrance, I mutely pointed to big Sergeant Mac as a way of communicating that I know somebody – I'm okay.

"Morning L T," Mac said with characteristic cheerfulness. "You look kind of run over, sir, that little girl give you a pretty strenuous night, or what?"

"No, I tipped her in great appreciation for a full hour of bliss then went and drank with the journalists all night. Shit, Sarge, those are some fuckin' A serious drinkers," I responded quietly, trying not to spark up a glittering headache behind my eyes.

"Well, what did you find out you didn't already know, anything much?" Mac asked with insight.

"I found out I'm not the only one who thinks the war is fucked up. Lots of lies and lots of flies and not a goddamn thing I can see that we're doing right – that's doing any good," I said, groaning with delight at the first sip of strong black coffee just placed in front of me. Probably another influence left over from the French, I thought, and thanked my French ancestors for any part they might have had in bringing the simple, civilized joy of morning coffee – strong, black, and scalding hot – to Southeast Asia.

"That's how I came to the decision a long time ago to scam a little on the side if I could, you know, L T. It's a natural part of trying to supply my men with what they need and everything is so screwed up anyway...morale way down, troops committing mutiny or worse...shit. I don't know what has become of the Army I knew, lieutenant, I really don't," Mac lamented, showing his disgust in a way I had not seen before. Mac was from the "old" Army and the days of post-WWII morale, and he felt a personal sense of loss at seeing his troops and his country engaged in a confused, misdirected effort at bringing peace and democracy to an area already torn by decades of strife and political instability. Just like this young Lieutenant, the career track of my experienced friend was being drastically altered by his tours in Vietnam.

"On a positive note, I did manage to arrange to trade for some radios the men need," Mac commented, shrugging and shaking his head. He had done all he could for his troops despite suffering his own disillusionment and depression. I admired him greatly. The men he cared for like family constituted an entire

Battalion – about 400 troops. He felt personally responsible for providing every piece of clothing, equipment, and armaments to his men. What a guy.

The friendship between two larcenous co-conspirators deepened as we commiserated on the miserable, inescapable inconsistencies of the war, and neither of us could come up with a consoling or mitigating factor. It was difficult to face the drive back up the highway to Cu Chi Base Camp. About the only thing that tipped the scales in favor of leaving was the pure and simple fact neither of us was really interested in what Saigon had to offer: the drinking and whoring and the sprinkling of past excellence in the Cholon district and the formerly fine hotels. It all smacked too acridly of the taste of smoke. The people were desperate for a good time, knowing they live on the fringe of war, or on the brink of returning to the war, or glad to be almost out of the fucking war. Saigon was not a pleasing place to visit, nor would anyone want to live there, given a choice. It was a chaotic and desperate city.

After we had eaten a choice breakfast, Sergeant Mac surveyed the tired, morning-after scene unfolding at a depressingly familiar cadence in the NCO enclave, and as he gazed off to the northwest towards Cu Chi, said, "I'm thinking about my nice quiet, sandbagged, air conditioned back office, L T. What do you say?"

"Sounds real good to me, Mac, let's hit the highway."

We joined a convoy out of Long Binh and spent the time on the road as tourists, unconcerned about someone else's war that might be going on somewhere else. It was an attitude of survivors. It was an attitude contributing to remaining sane in an insane environment. I decided: *hey, I'm a fuckin' tourist. What do I care about someone else's war.*

It is doubtful this new mantra would endear me any more intimately with Major Tantrum or the Army, though, as was demonstrated to me immediately upon my arrival at my room in the new Bachelor Officers' Quarters. The HQ Company clerk came trotting up as Mac pulled away in the truck and said, "the major wants to see you A S A P lieutenant Lumbert. He sure is pissed, sir."

Walking resignedly over to the office, I reflected on all the times I had been sent to the principal's office for discipline problems in school. There had been dozens of instances, perhaps a hundred in twelve years of school culminating with being expelled from high school six days before graduation for knocking a guy out in a parking lot scuffle. Even back then, in school, I had been aware of the metaphor of the last straw on the camel's back. *So this might be like shoving that straw up the camel's ass, I guess.* I was all too well acquainted with the role of being the bad boy going to the office to hear of my offenses.

Upon entering the office, I beheld a frowning, purple-tinged Major, nervously shaking a sheaf of papers above his desk like he was winnowing out weevils. "Lieutenant Lumbert, you have been ABSENT WITHOUT LEAVE...A W O L! I have a whole stack of complaints about your bunker line detail and...and...I've gotten a report of your failure to attend a meeting on the beautification of the rear area...."

"Major, I have just been on a requisition run down to Long Binh for some paint....."

"STOP INTERRUPTING ME GODDAMNIT LIEUTENANT! AND...and," the Major paused, gasping and grasping at the paperwork. "And...lieutenant Lumbert, I have a report here from a Division liaison officer, a Captain Davenort, who was present at the firefight in the HoBo woods. It refers to the fact that Captain Dodgely and Lieutenant Colonel Branson both had intentions of pursuing an investigation of dereliction of duty on your part and of refusing a direct order in a combat situation. I'm beginning to think you're not Officer material at all, Lieutenant Lumbert, but I'm going to give you one more chance to straighten out. Orders are being cut for you to go to a Fire Support Base near Tay Ninh and run road security with the Recon Platoon...should be right up your alley, right Ranger Lumbert? In the meantime, you will continue to be responsible for the bunker line detail; but I have a responsible NCO who will run the guard detail at night. Dismissed, Lumbert."

Goddamnit it...Tay Ninh...Rocket City...they're trying to wipe me out just like Kolo. The city of Tay Ninh and the associated Base Camp were close to the Cambodian border, west of Saigon, directly in the southern path of the Ho Chi Minh trail.

It was a very active infiltration route for soldiers and equipment and, being very close to Cambodia, the enemy did not have to carry mortars and rockets very far to unload them on US troops.

I was trying to think of a way to get back at Major Walner in my remaining few days at Cu Chi when Tolbert pulled up in a jeep with his little cassette player blasting "Paint It Black" by the Rolling Stones. This disgruntled Lieutenant realized I was not quite done requisitioning paint. Tolbert and I cruised several supply sheds before we found the color I was looking for: flat black. Dull, flat, primer black was exactly the artistic medium necessary for a "fuck you" finish to my decoration of the new BOQ.

I had personally supervised the professional level of paint job on the four rooms of the newly constructed Officers' Quarters and had been quite pleased with the work. Had been pleased that is, until I received word of my transfer. I had even gone to extra lengths to find some nice pastels for the doors and trim; but now that idea was out the window along with all care and concern. I had the best intentions of finishing up colorfully; but now I thought, *FUCK 'EM.* Tolbert and I repainted my room flat black...everything – the walls, the ceiling, and even the floor. We repeatedly played the tape of what was now my favorite song during the job.

Private Tolbert was completely cracking up when we were done, peering into the room at dusk. "That's for sure the blackest mu'fucka I ever did see...huh huh...you in some deep shit now, L

T. Goddamn, sir, I ain't never had no officer in charge like you before, Lieutenant Lumbert."

"Fuck 'em. What are they going to do? Send me to rocket city?"

We smoked another reefer while pondering the impenetrable gloom of the room. Even with the overhead light on (a standard military 60W bulb) it was so dark that you lost depth perception and could not distinguish where the walls and the ceiling met. The floor looked like a dark abyss through which you would drop into the bowels of the earth if you stepped onto it. It suited my mood exactly and I was extremely pleased with the work. It was the interior design corollary to the angry Infantryman's expression "kill 'em all and let god sort it out."

The next day was more of the usual bunker line shit detail. Tolbert and I smoked a bowl over at the motor pool before going over to Admin Company to pick up the fuck-ups who would be the crew for the day. We diddled and dawdled the morning away clearing some debris from a bunker that had taken a direct hit from a 122mm rocket a few days previous, then after a leisurely noon chow break we headed out the main gate to the dump.

At the entrance to the dump, the Korean civilian in charge told us cheerfully that we would have to go clear around to the other side of the dump because the scrap metal pile had been moved. Going clear around the dump meant driving on dirt trails that had not been cleared of mines, not to mention passing close to a thick treeline where snipers had been known to hide. *Where does he think they set up the mortar tubes and rockets at night?* I said, "hey, we dumped here a few days ago and we'll dump here today. You gotta be a fuckin' idiot to think..."

The Korean leaped up on the driver's side running board in an instant rage and said, "You no curse me! You go other side. You no curse me!"

I replied calmly, "I said we are dumping here. Now get off the fucking truck so we can back in."

The guard, a stocky man in his mid-thirties about 5' 10" and 180 pounds, was outraged that this young officer was uttering what he considered to be curses and showing such disrespect to him. It was not done in his culture – uttering such words – unless very dire circumstances were at hand. He hated these arrogant, foul-mouthed Americans, and he hated this skinny-looking young Lieutenant even more so. He was not about to cut any slack for a man who used such deplorable language to someone whom he should respect, if not because he was just doing his job, then certainly because he was older. He would not get off the truck until this man apologized and they would not put trash where it did not belong.

I told Tolbert to back the truck up to the edge of the pit where we had dumped the other day; but the Korean started grabbing the wheel and screaming at us, leaning through the window. Tolbert looked at me, unsure what to do. I said, "sit back a little more man, I'm going to pop this fucker in the mouth."

My driver's eyes widened a bit and a stiff grin spread across his face as he leaned back in the seat. I laid my left arm on the back of the seat and slid across the cab, then threw a sharp right jab and hit the guy right in the mouth. I could hear teeth chip as the man's head snapped back, but the sturdy Korean did not fall off the truck as expected. He ran his tongue along his bloodied lips, spit out some teeth fragments and said, in a fuming rage, "you come here. I KILL YOU!"

Without a word or a pause, I leaped out of the truck and ran around the front of the vehicle. The Korean had backed away and had dropped into some type of karate stance; but I did not pause to square off. I ran right up and threw a right front snap-kick to the area of the groin that was instinctively blocked. The kick was not a committed move, however, it was an opening for what was coming next. Being skilled in balance from years of Judo training early in my youth, as my right foot came down, I launched a straight left from the shoulder with all my weight behind it, twisting smoothly at the waist. I hit the Korean flush on the jaw, knocking him immediately senseless. I momentarily marveled at seeing the man's eyes flip up, only the whites showing, as his head shot backward and his body followed. He flew halfway down the slope before he hit the ground then slid like a sack of potatoes to the bottom. *Goddamn it. Killed the gook sonofabitch,* I initially thought, categorizing the poor guy in a thoughtless irrational manner. Maybe I hit him so hard because he was Asian and I had not had sufficient chance to retaliate for all the harm I had seen done to me and my men the past summer.

For whatever reason, I put all my pent-up aggression towards all the enemy soldiers I had seldom ever even seen and had never been able to personally strike back at. I put a lot behind that punch and I had been trained to punch. Being a natural left-hander, I had completely surprised the man. Maintaining proper bone alignment, it did not even hurt my hand. Almost immediately, a jeep came roaring up with two American MP's in it and one of them, obviously a New Yorker from his accent, began exclaiming, "what a shot! Jesus Christmas, what a fucking shot!" I liked the guy right away. He noticed I was an Officer, so on the next repetition, added, "what a shot, sir! Jesus Christmas what a fuckin' shot," and started slapping his forehead in awe for added emphasis.

Meanwhile the Korean, a Mr. Pak I would later be told, was unsteadily regaining his feet. He could not make it back up the slope without the help of a couple of other civilian employees. They glanced nervously at this dangerous Lieutenant and were none too comfortable that the three American soldiers in the back of the truck had all locked and loaded their M16's and one of them was fiddling with the pin on a hand grenade. Mr. Pak kept looking in wonderment at my hands and sizing me up as if to ask how this skinny foreign devil had so quickly overwhelmed all his years of training in his national martial art, Tae Kwon Do. He had never been knocked out completely by anyone, not in his childhood fights nor even in some serious sparring matches during his military years as a younger man.

I stood six feet tall and weighed about 175 pounds at that time. I was naturally fast and had been trained to be ambidextrous, though left-handed. A narrow face and high hairline marked me as an intellectual in the mind of some, and any type of clothing hid a slim, but very well developed musculature. Anyone who knew what to look for could have seen the bulging veins in the forearms and at the elbow, and the well-defined insertion of the biceps that came from years of steady exercise; but few people knew how to judge these attributes. I was a left-handed riddle and a surprise to many bullies throughout my life. Often underestimated from the start, before an opponent could revise their opinion of me, they found themselves on their ass, wondering what had hit them. That is just how I naturally operated when faced with a fight.

The Military Police apologetically explained that there would have to be a report filed and everyone would have to come down to the station and make official statements. Tolbert and the men in the work crew all lied and exaggerated the story so it seemed that the Korea had really been the aggressor and had forced the situation by cursing the Lieutenant and threatening to kill him. Lieutenant Lumbert had justifiably smacked the guy after fending off several punches by the Korean. This pugilistic Lieutenant and his incorrigible driver laughed like hell later as Tolbert recounted what he had put in his statement. He told me for the umpteenth time, "Goddam, sir, I ain't <u>never</u> had no Officer-in-Charge like you before, Lieutenant Lumbert...haahaa...you somethin' you are."

"Yeah, I'm some kind of trouble all right." We shared another bowl late that afternoon out by the bunker line. I had to face Major Tantrum the next day, then appear before the Division Commander, a two-star General, to explain why I had almost caused an international incident between two friendly nations. It appeared to me everyone was overreacting to a simple smack in the jaw. *Jesus, it's not like I got him down and pounded on him...he threatened to kill me. I didn't kill him for god's sake, I just hit him once, big deal...big fuckin' deal."*

But it was a big deal because it was, once again, the single straw that fucked up the camel caravan. The familiar factors of being the bad boy going to the Principal's office naturally came to mind as I considered meeting an even more important authority figure – a US Army General. I had cruised through Major Tantrum's tight-lipped, purple remonstrations with aplomb, but was not looking forward to meeting the General under such circumstances.

It turned out the General was not a bad guy though, and I told my slightly altered version of the story animatedly, as if talking to someone in a barroom. I was stoned. For some reason, we both wound up chuckling at my description of the MP and the way he was still repeating that exact phrase down at the station half an hour later. The General laughed out loud at my perfect imitation of the guy's Brooklyn accent. For no apparent reason, the General asked, "what is your family background, Lumbert? You got some Irish blood or something?"

"Actually, General, I do. My father was half Irish and half French." I lied, having no definite idea of my paternal ancestry.

"Did you ever hear of the Koreans being referred to as the Irish of the Orient because of their temper and their constant fighting?"

"Nossir, I never did." I almost used the formal "Sir" appropriately for the first time since being shot through the face, thinking it might be a good time to forego the total rejection of the term.

"Well it seems to me that if you would apologize to Mr. Pak for your foul language and pay his dental bill, I don't see any reason why the whole incident can't be chalked up as a disagreement between two Irishmen."

And that was the conclusion of the incident. I paid almost $200 in dental bills – an exorbitant amount in a country where a simple filling might cost five dollars – and wrote the man a formal apology. Major Tantrum lived up to his nickname when he found out I had gotten off so lightly after committing such a serious violation of the decorum expected of an Officer in the US Army. And he still did not know what "color" I had painted my room in the brand new BOQ.

I found out later, after my transfer, that a Black Lieutenant had rotated in from the field to take over my job and my quarters.

I could only imagine the Black Lieutenant and the Purple Major cursing this renegade Lieutenant from afar.

They probably missed the general and totally blank rebellion expressed by painting it all black, like in the song. The Black Lieutenant was a completely innocent apparent victim due to circumstances, and could not understand how someone could do anything so blatantly racist. The Major undoubtedly figured out some way of reporting the horrifying nature of the offense. He probably added quite a few pages to my records...all negative.

I was gradually enhancing a dubious capability of provoking others into a rage, deliberate or not. I was a loose cannon for sure. I did not give a shit and some people still did, is about what the problem was, stated in the vernacular of the times.

That evening, this disillusioned Lieutenant, now known as a left-handed knock-out artist, went over to the Wolfhounds' area to get high with Filbert one last time...again. Filbert was celebrating being short – only one more day and a wakeup. He was so short he could "look a grasshopper in the eye." I was completely slaphappy at seeing another face there I did not expect...a man too short to mention it even though he stood six-foot four. Big Edwards, my machine gunner, as steady and reliable a soldier as I had ever known, erupted into a grin and a hearty welcome, lifting me off the ground in a bear hug that about broke some ribs. He warmly took both my hands in his huge paws and said tearfully, "I'm going home tomorrow, three-six." We laughed against each other's shoulders and pounded backs affectionately like brothers.

"Hey! Listen up." The Head Man did not have to raise his voice to stop everything, he just stood up straight and took a deep breath and people took notice. "I just want to say clearly and for a absolute fack, that this here is one lieutenant who's okay with me. Lieutenant Lumbert, when the chips was down, I felt like you were lookin' out for me...for all of us...and you kep' your head up too and never even got us lost. I was glad to a'been with you sir, I really mean that."

"Edwards, I was mighty glad and relieved to know you were nearby with your thousand rounds of ammo at the ready and your big finger on the trigger, let me tell you for sure. And you spoke simple truth to me, man, and I learned from you when I definitely needed some advice." It was easy to return the admiration honestly because The Head Man was a hell of a man and an easy guy to admire and respect. We all loved big Eddie, and he had served a whole year out in the field without suffering the slightest scratch. God must have loved Edwards a lot too.

That evening I was able to be "just pals" with several men I knew and liked. We were all too short to notice. I was off to Rocket City and unknown new experiences. Filbert and Eddie about to go home – back to The World...and unknowable new experiences. We had a raucous time recounting making Maldonado a lifeguard, and Edwards laughed wholeheartedly – whole bodily – at hearing about the ration card escapade. He looked once again in amused respect at his former leader. Nobody mentioned Pete's death. Then Tolbert showed up and told everyone how the rambunctious Lieutenant had cold-cocked a Korean karate expert at the dump the day before, exchanging conspiratorial looks at me as he lied about it a bit. We all laughed until we could not stand up and we smoked reefer until we had belly aches.

I somehow managed to stay out of trouble for the next few days, waiting to ship out to Tay Ninh. Dropping in on good ole' Sergeant Mac, we had the usual sort of conversation soldiers are accustomed to - "good luck...see you when I see you." Mac had a contact in the Supply field in Tay Ninh of course, and made me promise to contact him and use Mac as a reference if I needed anything whatsoever. *It always pays to get along with your Supply Sergeant.* The good Sergeant also issued me some "tiger" fatigues, normally given only to Rangers and Snipers, the jungle camouflage design just becoming available to regular Infantry units. And he just happened to have a brand new pair of deluxe binoculars that were not listed on inventories, so he offered them to me as a straight gift. Mac expressed appropriate concern over my assignment as Recon Platoon Leader and gave what advice he could, not being an Infantryman. He gave advice the way an uncle might to a wayward nephew about to hitchhike across the country for the first time and I accepted his words with appreciation. We had the type of relationship seldom found in civilian life, and this was probably true for most soldiers, especially in a war zone.

"Rocket City" was an appropriate name for the Base Camp near the ancient city of Tay Ninh. Rawlins Forward Fire Support Base Camp had the known record for consecutive nights of rocket attacks and often as many as a dozen 122mm – the big ones – would roar in every night. Charlie did not have to hump them in very far from Cambodia, and was probably glad to get them off this hands, or shoulders, as soon as possible. Fortunately they were notoriously inaccurate. Situated out on a dusty plain about three miles from the city of Tay Ninh, the Army had constructed a major Forward Fire Support Base. The North Vietnamese could bring in rockets and mortar rounds from Cambodia in about three hours in total darkness, and evidently enjoyed the work. The local population was largely anti-American by that time and was not happy at seeing the war shift more heavily into their Province.

By that time, I could slip through introductions, job descriptions, and SITREPS with relaxed dexterity and immediately assumed command of the Recon Platoon. I settled a few personal effects into a cubbyhole sleeping hooch attached to the Battalion Radio Shack, since I was now assigned at the Battalion level of command. The Communications area was thoroughly dug in and sandbagged since it also served as the Command Post in times of activity – like every night. I was now a member of the First Battalion of the 27th Infantry Regiment, still a Wolfhound.

I immediately recognized the pot smokers among the RTO's in the Commo bunker, and had generally found them to be the brightest of the draftee enlisted ranks. We conversed while listening to the ragged conversations on the radios, and I fell asleep with the familiar hum and clicks and indistinct chatter. I slept well nestled deeply into our man-made cave in Mother Earth.

The next day I met with my Platoon Sergeant, E5 Ron Davis, and the group of men who would be under my command. I introduced myself in my normal manner, saying that I knew they were already doing the job before I got there so I was not going to change anything, just observe. It usually made for a good impression, something I was seldom able to do later in civilian life. As I broke the 100 days' mark in my personal countdown to freedom, the realization occurred that I might never again have a similar level of excitement and responsibility. There is no job in the civilian world comparable to being an Infantry Platoon Leader in a combat zone. Nor would I be likely to develop a similar level of friendship as I had there in Vietnam. At the tender age of twenty-one, I felt I had already been a part of the most rewarding, dirtiest, most gruesome, and most awe-inspiring experiences a man could have. These premonitions occurred to me at the time and inspired a measure of enthusiasm toward my new assignment. Something new and different. Definitely once-in-a-lifetime.

The day began with this recently reassigned discipline problem "leading" the recon Platoon out of the Base Camp to clear the road of mines and booby traps so the resupply convoy could safely proceed to the Base. The men of the Platoon walked, with two men handling mine sweepers out in front and about 25 men strung out behind. Sgt. Davis, the Platoon Sergeant, indicated to the Squad Leaders where to post men along the way, making alterations in the positions every day. Two or three soldiers were set up every quarter mile or so, depending on visibility. The men of this Platoon were very serious and obviously knew their job, so I concentrated on studying the map and memorizing artillery fields of fire as we rode slowly along in a jeep with a .50 caliber machine gun mounted in the rear.

"Don't see many of these old fifty calibers over here, Sarge, usually M60's nowadays," I commented, about half way into the three-miles of road clearing.

"Yessir...well, the M60 is a fine weapon, but you see these sturdy stucco houses we're passing, L T?... a fifty-caliber will chew right through them walls, but an M60 just won't cut it, sir," Davis replied, casting a wicked grin in my direction.

The ancient city of Tay Ninh and the surrounding hamlets clustered along the roadway were examples of some of the finest architecture I had seen so far in Vietnam. The houses were somewhat pockmarked and there was evidence of an explosion of some sort here and there, but the structures were of stucco and masonry designs and seemed to be very well put together. There were tiled courtyards, porticoes, fountains, and picturesque red-tiled roofs with ornate details.

The Buddhist compound within the city was a splendid sight. Not a single mark, nor scar, nor bomb crater marred the elegant grounds and beautiful buildings. I marveled at the saffron-clad monks as they calmly and happily walked to the marketplace from their enclosure. They had a serenity I found magnetic...entrancing. I saw a level of consciousness and wisdom sometimes demonstrated by Pete – only more so...a thousand times magnified. The idea that I could learn to meditate when I got back to the world bloomed like a bud of hope in my mind. If these monks could be so happy and unconcerned here in the middle of this war, then surely I would be able to cope with my memories when I returned from the war. The certainty of a method of regaining sanity gave ease to a mind caught up in uncertainties. A knot of tension suddenly loosened in the twisted coils of a traumatized brain.

After posting two or three men every quarter mile or so, Sgt. Davis parked the jeep beside the road in some shade by a small river. The scene before me was awe-inspiring: carefully tended, centuries-old, terraced agriculture, layered in graceful curves up the slope from the river. The people worked diligently and nature was flourishing under their care. It was amazing to see the continuance of the orderly life of a farmer in this part of the country. The people of Tay Ninh province had been innocently involved in one war or another for over two decades.

My Platoon Sergeant was a short-timer and openly expressed his desire to get his ass home in one piece, without any scars or aftereffects. He had only thirty-five and a wake-up and he readily agreed with me regarding the general philosophy of moving slow and staying low. He had already adopted his own version of the same idea. We agreed on having no idea what the war was all about, and we definitely agreed that the only thing that made sense at our level of command was to look after the welfare of the men directly under our immediate supervision. What else could we do? With these tactical and philosophical introductions out of the way, we cruised slowly back along the several miles of dusty road, nodding or talking briefly with each group of men.

About noon, the resupply convoy from Cu Chi and Long Binh came roaring by, some of the drivers and security guards exchanging banal comments with the men of the Recon Platoon as they passed. Part of the convoy route was the same road that had been used to supply Diamond II, which had been situated about five miles to the north during its brief intense existence. The main highway, if it could be called a highway, ran parallel to a river, with Cambodia just on the other side. There were numerous possibilities for ambushes, and there were hundreds, if not thousands, of North Vietnamese Regulars in Cambodia with more arriving every day and every night.

The mission of the Recon Platoon was to maintain the road against incursion by the enemy each day, after clearing any possible mines that might have been placed the previous night. It was a serious business and I observed an alert and serious group of soldiers meticulously going about their daily job. After the convoy sped by on its return trip the men would hike back into the Fire Base, then they would do the same thing the next day. After walking five or six miles with full combat gear, the men would take shifts guarding the perimeter at night, getting what sleep or naps could be found in between the incoming rockets, our own mortars firing an occasional flare, or our own distant artillery thumping and rumbling in the distance.

"And that's all there is to it, sir," Sergeant Davis remarked casually as we chugged along with the Platoon back inside the relative security of the Fire Support Base late that afternoon. Brick-red dust as fine as flour sifted and fluffed with each step the men took and they were covered by the end of the day, looking like they had been partially dipped in dye, with the deeper tints dripping down toward their sweaty, dirt-caked boots. "We haven't heard from Charlie during the day in quite a while now, lieutenant, but stay close to a bunker tonight, sir," he advised sincerely in parting as we dismissed the men for showers and chow, and "retired to quarters."

"I'll be closer than close sarge, thanks. I'm going to stay in a bunker...I'm going to live in a bunker and be glad of it," I replied, heading for the Commo bunker/radio room. But it was

257

hot and stuffy and noisy that evening down in the bunker, so this restless Lieutenant wandered around the perimeter, naturally sniffing my way to the pot smokers. A couple of men from Recon were hanging out nearby but I was way past making the automatic and authoritarian distinctions between officer and enlisted ranks that the Army insisted were necessary for the maintenance of discipline. How could I, being a discipline problem myself, not only in the Army, but throughout my life? The rationalization of the supposed contradiction between doing a good job during the day, then getting stoned at night, was easy to make, and it was going on all around me anyway. Another definite reason for grounds for dismissal as an Officer for conduct "unbecoming." I was becoming less and less fit for command in the eyes of the Army. Probably I had not been "officer material" to begin with. Sweeping roads during the day and smoking a little weed at night made about as much sense as anything else I could see going on around me as 1969 drew to a close.

In an occasional dark moment, 1969 seemed like the worst year of my life. A year later, back in The World, I faced even darker depths of depression when there was nothing really important happening...nothing even remotely similar to supervising a road clearing operation or checking the bunker line at night. A vague presentiment of this shift in reality led me to relish each day and every night in my position as Recon Platoon Leader. This would probably be my last job in a combat assignment. I made a conscious decision to remain constantly conscious. I began to take note of details in my surroundings and commit certain scenes to memory...the good scenes...the good men.

There would never be another environment that could approach the mystical beauty of that tropical setting – so different from anything I had known. So dangerously real and close. Living among a people whose daily realities could only be glimpsed at times and whose political beliefs could not be imagined. And there I stood, smoking and joking and getting stoned with a group of men, all barely acquainted yet congregated and fortified into a brotherhood of foreign invaders in a land totally unlike our own. What happened to these men that made them so different upon their return? Vietnam happened to them. We were there, simply enough. Even those who escaped wounds and injuries, who never caught malaria or were poisoned by weed killer, even those who never saw a friend shot dead right in front of them nor counted up dead enemies like so many bundles of mutilated meat...everyone who was there was changed into someone different. And how could it be any other way?

I felt tired, pissed off, and depressed much of the time; but so was almost everybody else, so it was not a state of mind to be changed or understood. It did not seem odd to be angry most of the time. One was just another tired, angry face in a crowd of similar faces, so it seemed to be the normal daily experience. It was not odd to be emotionally numbed by what some of us had been through. Psychic shock and subsequent social numbing will occur to any individual under extreme or prolonged stress. We had no idea we might be developing personality traits that would not serve us well back in the civilian world, not to mention becoming experts at jobs that had no place nor use in our society. Many of us would forever remain far removed from our peer groups who had lived out happy, hippy, collegiate experiences during that Year of the War in Vietnam, 1969.

A shocking percentage of these young combat veterans would die a traumatic death back in "the World" within a few years of returning home. We would not assimilate well, some of us. Our reality included the possibility of crashing a motorcycle at high speed; overturning a car during a police chase; or dying in a shoot out with friends and neighbors or the police. Vietnam veterans, especially combat survivors, would check out from drug overdose, alcohol toxicity, being run over while passed out on train tracks, or "D" all of the above. Years too late for most of us, psychologists and social scientists would start to wonder what was happening to all these young men – these "crazy" 'Nam vets.

Actual statistics were not gathered until the 1980 census, when Vietnam Veterans' Counseling Centers would open up across the country. But concern for the well-being and readjustment of the Vietnam veterans would occur too late for many. The most seriously affected could not seek help even when it finally became available. Many could not manage to turn the complicated wheels of the VA system because doing so required some semblance of hope and trust in authority figures, and we had none. Once one lost the hope of ever feeling better, <u>and</u> felt betrayed and lied to by the government, it became impossible to apply to that same government for help. We coped on our own, most of us, who survived the initial phase of readmission into an America much different than we remembered.

Every veteran could have benefited from counseling and deprogramming before being released from the Military, especially combat survivors. We had been taught to camp out in the jungle; build bunkers; fire machine-guns; and count up dead bodies when we were eighteen...nineteen years old; and had been programmed and indoctrinated to be emotionally unaffected. But no conscious human being could be unaffected by what some of us had witnessed and participated in, either willingly or as a matter of life or death choices. Many would try to fit in and some of us would die trying...back in the World. Many of us could not find the World we had left – it did not exist. Thousands would not even be listed in the accumulating statistics because there was no category for "missing-in-action" back in the civilian world. The 1980 census would not find untold numbers of returned Vietnam veterans.

There was no quantifying the loss. There was no way to replace what we were missing as we slipped off into the woods and remote areas and disappeared in our own country. Some of us disappeared deep down inside ourselves while trying to appear normal; but that disguise would not hold up for long. Psychologists would consider the "compartmentalization" of our experiences to be a state of "denial" and thought we needed to just talk things over and all would be well. We were lost and isolated and had no maps or guideposts. Our military compass did not work back in the old neighborhood. We easily went astray. Many saw the inside of a jail cell within one year of returning.

"I know what I'm going to do when I get back to the World," I said to an RTO from Pennsylvania, nicknamed "Strings." I am going to get my pilot's licenses all the way up to instructor rating. I've been flying small airplanes since I was a kid." Strings had just finished telling a story about an uncle who was a crop duster and longtime pilot from WWII.

"That's about what I plan to do, L T, settle in with my uncle's business...maybe seriously study electronics and open a little repair shop or something when I'm not flying," Strings mused as he handed over an ornate water pipe stuffed with Thailand's finest weed. My new smoking buddy was possibly named for his string-bean physique; but more likely for the strings he could pull to acquire any type of dope or off-the-record equipment anyone could ask for. I was unsure which was the case and was not concerned with such labels. Strings had a secret messenger service set up within the convoy system; a couple of friends with ties to the Black Market; and both American and

Vietnamese underground transport and information channels he could access. Of course, he knew Sergeant Mac in Cu Chi and we shared stories about that particular participant in unregulated and unseen enterprises.

I had naturally gravitated toward a wheeler-dealer individual like Sgt. Mac; but Strings was a daily pot smoker so he operated even further underground that Mac. We two immediately trusted each other, and this misfit Lieutenant was automatically accepted into the private bunker parties among the troops as I accompanied Strings and one or another of the RTO's in their stoned peregrinations around the Base Camp in the evenings. Strings took orders and handed out little packets of "medicine" along the way. *Oh well, somebody has to do it.*

Almost any stimulus, if repeated often with no effect, will become less of a stress factor. I found myself becoming irrationally accustomed to the rocket attacks after a week or so. Every night, and sometimes several times a night, one or more rockets would come roaring and spewing flames and sparks out of the treeline and thunderously crash somewhere in or around the perimeter. A guy got to where he would keep looking for an extra second before ducking into a bunker or trench though; because a rocket was an awesomely beautiful sight to a stoned eye...once you got over the initial wince and could halt the automatic flight of the body long enough that the eye might linger and capture some fantastic images.

Being in a bunker was no assurance of survival anyway. A direct hit by one of the larger rockets would devastate the average bunker, leaving the occupants dead or screaming in shock in a crunching flash. I knew that the more directly towards you a rocket comes, the less of it you will see, so I reached the point of just lingering outside, watching the rocket's red roar. To explain an apparent act of extreme bravado or brazen stupidity such as standing in the open watching a rocket attack, some would quote the well-known saying, "hey, you never see the one that gets you," meaning you night as well watch when you could. Nuts. I would never forget the first time I had seen a few men just squatting by a bunker grooving on the light show like it was the Fourth of July back in the States.

It wasn't that anyone would deliberately expose himself to a rocket attack; but if you were with several buddies, for instance, roaming the Base Camp when a rocket screamed in and exploded just up the road, crusty experienced men would just keep walking, chuckling at the newbies who were dashing about, bashing their heads on a bunker doorway, or falling and breaking an ankle while fleeing underground. We would continue walking nonchalantly, glancing at how much our companions were flinching and laughing at the scared newcomers. *SHHHWOOOSH...* **_KA-CRUNCH._** *Cool man, you see that one?* Craziness did not seem so crazy after a while.

I began getting stoned every evening so I did not notice nor give a shit where the rockets came from or where they landed. I strolled the Fire Base with total impunity, dropping into a bunker occasionally just to see who was there; but inwardly simply relying of my presumed luck. Nuts. I often thought about that single toss of five dice back in Oakland and began to seriously and numerically count down my days left in-country. Fifty-two and a wake-up the first time I computed the exact figure. Significant.

I bought a pack of playing cards at the PX and began turning the cards over one by one each day and slipping each sequenced card face up on the bottom of the deck, the Ace of Spades being the card I would turn over on my last day in Vietnam. There were rumors of men leaving the Ace of Spades on dead VC as a way of identifying their unit, and there had always been a special significance attached to that card in some card games. I wound up carrying that particular card with me for many years though, as a memento of not finishing my full tour. Instead, I embarked on a continuous series of half-finished stories and relinquished plans...of unplanned results and drastic steps along uncertain pathways to make up for having failed to reach each previous goal.

As it was, Tay Ninh and Rawlins Base Camp being what they were, and having experienced what I had, I came to resent new beginnings as much as surprise endings. I stayed stoned and let the war run itself...an unconnected tourist.

One day about a month after assuming command of the Recon Platoon, the convoy had already passed and the men were lounging by the roadside waiting to walk back in, when a jeep pulled up and a severe-looking Captain asked, "are you in charge of these men Lieutenant?"

This discourteous Lieutenant strolled over casually, not saluting or showing any sign of deference either in posture or tone, and replied, "this is my Platoon, Captain." I stood there arrogantly looking at what I considered to be a lifer and a "base camp commando"- a by-the-book asshole- and just stared at him as if to ask, "what about it dickhead?"

"Lieutenant, I have just observed one of your men drinking a beer back there by those hooches," and he began to indicate somewhere back down the road but he stopped and flushed in anger when Sgt. Davis snickered and I sarcastically replied, "drinking a beer Captain?...one of my men..." shaking my head and puffing out an exclamation between pursed lips in apparent displeasure and consternation.

"I'll sure look into that Captain." Something about the manner in which I could say the word "captain" now made it seem rude and offensive. Possibly the mantra was automatically chugging through my mind like a deuce-and-a-half truck...unmistakable and capturing attention even when not directly monitored. It so happened that this was the very Division Liaison Officer who had landed with Colonel Branson that day in the HoBo Woods. He was present on that fateful, futile day when I had become the temporary Battalion Commander-in-the-Field the very instant the Colonel was shot. Captain Davenport was merely grazed by a bullet and was back at his desk within days.

Captain Davenport had been following this Lieutenant's exploits and had read all the reports on the ne'er-do-well Lieutenant that had been accumulating in my official records. On realizing he was actually speaking to such a renegade trouble maker...receiving such blatant disrespect from the sonofabitch...the Captain grinned inwardly even though his face reddened in anger due to the insolence and the indifference this young Lieutenant so casually dished out. "You do that Lieutenant Lumbert. You look into it," he said as his driver lurched the jeep back out onto the roadway and sped on out to the Base Camp.

For some reason, I found myself making up another "last straw" joke in my mind as the Captain sped off: the last bale of straw, squashing the camel's legs out sideways like a cartoon when it was placed atop a pyramid-sized load, the final block at the top. It was an oddly appropriate, though humorous, metaphor.

That evening Strings was looking at me in a newly amused manner so I asked, "so what's up? You're looking at me kind of funny."

"Ooooyeah," Strings said, breaking into a grin. "I found out what a seriously funny guy you are, L T. You got a record, man...a fuckin' list of transgressions as long as a water buffalo dick. You been fightin' a lot of wars along the way, lieutenant...you got a lot of reports and shit in your file."

"Why do you think I was sent to this fuckin' garden spot, huh, meritorious service? HA! I punched out a Korean gook at the dump in Cu Chi is about all I can think of."

"Well that Captain who came in here today is going to write up a report on you allowing your men to drink beer on duty," he began explaining, but I interrupted.

"A REPORT!...on me allowing my men to drink beer?...when we both know that the Colonel and the whole Battalion Command section have their own beer and booze shipped out and delivered right to the CP? Shee-it."

"My point exactly in telling you, L T. I got a plan, see. We take a couple of snapshots of the colonel's trash cans and the dump, ya see, show how much beer drinking is done at his own, uh, discretion, you know."

This wary Lieutenant caught on quickly. "Yeah! We'll arrange a special shot of the trash cans out by the fence, with the Battalion Command Bunker right there in the background...heehee. I'll show that to the Colonel as a preview to my defense when the whole thing comes before a Court Martial."

"Goddamn, lieutenant. I don't think anything like that is going to happen. But it might be wise to have evidence that beer drinking is generally accepted as a fact of life anytime the troops sit anywhere for long enough to get resupplied. There's almost always beer involved in resupply if you look for it, right?" And that's the way it was in that part of the Country in early 1970...and everybody knew it. *Kolo my friend, wherever you are, I'll be coming along shortly. The rotten sonsabitches are out to get me...they're wiping me out, man.*

It was not unfounded paranoia that prompted such thoughts of conducting a defense at a Court Martial. Plans were in motion toward that possibility and the latest on a very long list of irregularities was being discussed by my "superiors" at that very moment while Strings and I smoked a very adequate bowl of Thai weed. The next morning, before heading out with the Recon Platoon, one of the HQ Company clerks came over and said, "Colonel wants to see you sir," giving me that look of amusement and secret respect that a bad boy gets from the good boys...the ones who behave the way their mommy told them to. I picked up the Polaroid photos Strings and I had already taken at first light and walked nonchalantly toward the Battalion CP.

Lt. Col Cargill was a serious military man and a good judge of character. He did not like certain attitudes he had seen in the young Officer during his first few weeks of duty; but he was always willing to give a man the benefit of a doubt. However there were just too many negative signs and tendencies in Lumbert to ignore. He recounted the various times he had observed the insolent Lieutenant failing to show even the most common forms of courtesy and respect towards the other Officers in his command. The man definitely had a huge chip on his shoulder from day one in his unit and he simply could not ignore it any longer.

"Lieutenant Lumbert reporting as ordered," the man said, not saluting, saying "sir" or showing any token of respect whatsoever, the Colonel observed with irritation. He indicated a chair. The intention of giving Lumbert a chance to explain the beer drinking incident and his insolent behavior toward Captain Davenport the previous day evaporated in the internal steam of anger ignited by the rebellious posture, the direct eye contact, and the confrontational tone. He took a direct shift to the bottom line – no question about it.

"I'll come right to the point, Lieutenant Lumbert. You were assigned to my command in order to be evaluated for elimination from the Service." He paused, looking for a reaction and saw only mute rebellion, then continued, "Since you have been in my command I have seen you showing nothing but disrespect, even contempt, towards other Officers you encounter and you have performed the meager role of Recon Platoon Leader in a barely acceptable manner. You have less than two months left in your tour, Lieutenant Lumbert, but you seem determined to end your career with a disciplinary action."

I replied in a tone quite like that of Corporal Quarles back at Ft. Hood when that troublemaker had said exactly the same thing. "I do my job and I do it right. If this is concerning the report that I allow my men to drink beer on duty, I can only point out that the Colonel evidently <u>allows</u> a lot of beer drinking here at his command post." I tossed the photos on the desk. "I cannot control what my men do every minute, colonel, neither can you. If I find evidence of drunken behavior that affects the tactical situation, I'll deal with it at that time."

Colonel Cargill was taken aback by the brash mannerisms of this miscreant. He had never been spoken to in that way by a younger Officer and he had certainly never seen such blatant extortion tactics tossed on his desk like a pack of playing cards. "Are you saying I condone beer drinking, Lieutenant? No one here drinks while on duty..." He stopped, caught himself explaining his actions to this insolent young pup, and he fumed at the utter nerve of the irreverent Lieutenant, then said, "Lieutenant Lumbert, perhaps since you are so unhappy with the Army, you would like to just resign your commission and save Captain Davenport the trouble of filing Court Martial proceedings against you."

Having no idea of exactly what the Colonel was referring to when he said the word "resign" and thinking only of expressing rebellion – the consequences be damned – I replied curtly, "resign my commission Colonel? Just show me the dotted line and hand me a goddamn pen." With that fate sealing response, I turned without a word and left the bunker to lead my men out on road sweep, another hot dusty day ahead. I felt a cheeky sort of overconfidence in my devious avoidance of consequences due to this latest evidence that the Army was out to have my ass one way or another. *Court Martialed for supposedly allowing my men to drink beer...what a crock of shit! I'll frag the bastards.*

Pushed to the wall by this unexpected level of insolence, the Colonel had no alternative but to initiate elimination proceedings. Although it might have seemed harsh, he was still able to give Lumbert a large measure of the benefit of the doubt by the manner and the wording of his report. He recommended an Honorable Discharge be issued and the Lieutenant be allowed to "resign for the good of the Service" and forego all reserve time under a seldom used regulation. In all his twenty-some years in the Army, Cargill had never heard of a combat Officer resigning during a combat deployment and receiving and Honorable Discharge; but the regulations did allow for the possibility, so he decided to pursue the matter on that course.

He offered the mitigating factors of the wounding by friendly fire at Diamond II and the fact that Lumbert had received the Bronze Star with "V" device for his actions that night. He emphasized that Lumbert had nothing but positive efficiency ratings before the wounding and had volunteered for a second tour in Vietnam. First Lieutenant (O2) Lumbert had been assigned as a Company Executive Officer and Battalion S-4 Officer and had remained at Fire Support Base Diamond II as a matter of personal choice, refusing to return to Cu Chi Base Camp on the last supply helicopter. Lumbert had taken on the role of Forward Observer and was assisting the Artillery FO at the time of the firing of "beehive" rounds by the Artillery Battery within the perimeter due to complete penetration by the enemy. Diamond II was overrun.

Completely unaware of the monstrously large straw I had just shoved up the camel's ass, this ignorant, doomed Lieutenant found Sgt. Davis and the men and prepared to head out for the day. Davis indicated an ARVN soldier nearby and said, "that's Louie, sir, a good scout from the local Arvins. He'll be riding along with us for a few days if that's all right."

"Fine by me sarge, you know the territory better than I do," I replied as we loaded up the jeep, checked the radios, and prepared to head down the dusty road. Our scout, Louie, looked alert and well-armed, his weapon clean, his manner serious and respectful. He introduced himself with a thin grin and seemed happy to get his hands on our .50 cal. machine gun. Looked like a capable soldier, unlike a lot of the South Vietnamese in uniform I had observed. This wayward Lieutenant was glad to have him along later that day, as Louie proudly showed us the ancient city of Tay Ninh.

A fascinating blend of influences from Thailand, Laos, Cambodia, and the brief French Colonial occupation, Tay Ninh exuded ancient-kingdom opulence dating back centuries among the Royal Families of Vietnam. The Buddhists had provided spiritual and secular guidance for two thousand years and were still a strong presence in and around the city. As I observed these people conduct themselves and their affairs during an ordinary day, I developed a deeper and deeper respect for the culture of Vietnam. This respect broadened to open-mouthed amazement later that afternoon when I noticed the work being performed by three old peasants out in a field about fifty meters from the road.

When we had driven by that morning, I was practicing my conscious awareness training, taking internal notes of specifics in my surroundings. I saw two old women working in unison, dipping a long, two-handled woven basket into a flooded field, hefting it over a low dike, and dumping the water into the adjacent higher field. Perfectly the two bodies moved: scoop, swing, dump...scoop, swing, dump...rhythmically moving two or three gallons of water at a time. A pool of muddy water had grown to about ten feet in diameter in the upper field as I watched, passing slowly along in the jeep. Nobody else seemed to notice. We posted guards as usual and drove on.

I also saw a third somber, aged worker slowly dipping a large, flat, woven bowl into the lower field, then flinging the contents upward over the dike, not even rising from his typical squat in the process. An old, old man was hypnotically making a scoop and a toss...scoop and toss. There was a pitifully small pool of water on the other side of the dike from the old papasan. *Jeez, they'll never flood that field...look at them scooping away like that...amazing. Better pray for rain.*

But late that afternoon there they were. The two old mamasans still synchronized perfectly and the very old papasan still scooping and tossing. The upper field, about half the size of a football field, was almost half flooded, the water seeming to creep toward the far dike even as I watched. The two mamasans never looked up, not in the morning nor in the afternoon; but the ancient man paused, his bowl floating, and he held up one thin hand while looking directly at me. He did not wave or smile or move...he just held up that thin hand and stared like an unblinking statue.

I was transfixed, ears roaring, eyes misting, chest expanding, as I looked at that ancient man focusing on me...looking right into my eyes as if we were sitting at a small table. It seemed I telescopically beamed in on the old man's eyes for an instant and saw massive ancient intelligence as he retrieved his bowl while still boring into my consciousness, deliberately scooped up one more bowlful of water, and tossed it over the dike. Then he just stopped, the bowl floating at his feet with his right hand loosely holding it, and he absolutely never moved again. I watched him until we were down the road and out of sight. The old man never took his eyes and his consciousness off me. He never blinked. He never readjusted his posture or squat. He remains in my mind today.

Only Louie noticed the Lieutenant watching the peasants. He leaned forward and said, "They move water, for the rice. If no rains, they <u>move</u> water." And that is what I watched for the next few days in stunned amazement. The people gradually flooded fields three and four tiers up from a small river, working day after day, secure in the knowledge that they had already seen it done in years past by their fathers and their grandmothers, so they simply worked at it because it had not rained enough that year. Some of the .peasants blamed the bombing and some of them blamed the desecration of ancient graveyards by the most recent foreign invaders; but all of them accepted the work as a part of the ebb and flow of life and all of them worked in the rice fields at times. Whatever it took to cultivate the rice must be undertaken and accomplished. They had developed methods for coping with anything: drought, bombs, and foreign invaders included.

The more I thought about it, the more amazement turned into embarrassment. I could not have done the days' work of the two old grandmothers. Could not have done it because I would not have stayed at it for a steady day just to see how much could be accomplished. Something about this realization left me feeling mystified and very small. Left me with an urge to develop and learn and grow to be more than a small confused man riding along in a jeep looking at farmers.

I was tremendously humbled by the two old mamasans and was absolutely mesmerized by the ancient papasan.

Watching the people reverently planting little handfuls of rice shoots in neat rows in the flooded fields for the next few days, I was further humbled and amazed. Being a city boy, I had never seriously considered, nor seen firsthand, the immense amount of physical work involved in farming, even in my own country. Then to see rice cultivation accomplished so rhythmically, so reverently, and so effectively in the midst of what I considered to be a war...simply filled me with an indescribable awe. There was something about the ancient, respectful, implacable rhythm of the rice planting that struck me speechless. I beheld the Buddha smiling, Vishnu preserving, the Tao unfolding, Nature being natural. The People simply worked, surviving as they always had.

I survived easily, being a mere tourist. Louie led us to a jewelry store one day in Tay Ninh city that specialized in making solid gold ID bracelets, chains, and dog tags – all made of 24K pure gold. I selected a heavy, ornate ring and paid a surprisingly low $30.00 in US greenbacks, which I always carried now on Mac's advice. The ring, which weighed about half an ounce, would have to be enlarged and we would pick it up the next day. *Yeah, the kind of thing a tourist would do. Also maybe making an investment on Mac's advice.*

Nothing happened day after day on the road clearing operation. The men discovered one buried mine and safely blew it in place. One of the resupply trucks broke down right in the middle of the road amid several roadside food stands and my trusty Platoon Sergeant sent three or four men to maintain security and probably indulge in local cuisine. *Oh well, everybody's got to make a living, even in a war zone.*

I admired the reddish glint of my 24k ring as we cruised the road, ostensibly doing a job, unaware that I had been given the innocuous assignment because it was thought I could no longer be trusted leading men in combat, what with my attitude and all. I was a known trouble-maker, bad for morale, and under investigation even though it was for unfounded allegations and speculations. This irrepressible young jerk even had the nerve to endorse an official letter of Intention of Elimination Proceedings sent out by, who else but Captain Davenport, with a caustic reply suggesting that if the Army proceeds with its usual bureaucratic bullshit, then the process will not take effect within the final five weeks of my enlistment anyway, so proceed, proceed. But the Army could move rather quickly at times, and the whole process took only two weeks.

The incorrigible Lieutenant was short – shorter than I thought – and I felt satisfied at having behaved with honor. I had done my part to the best of my ability. There was nothing wrong with placing the welfare of the men high on the list of priorities when the overall situation was confused and unpredictable. The missions were accomplished and we had always been at our ambush sites, regardless of Dudley's suspicions. That evening I got stoned with Strings and several of the Command Post RTO's. Whether a man was short or not, the main topic of discussion was often about plans when we got "home" - back to The World.

I spoke confidently of pursuing a career in aviation, a profession my father would have been proud to see his son achieve if he were still alive. "I'll tell you one thing for goddam sure, Strings, the first day I'm back, I'm going to get my Sportster out of storage, crank 'er up, and flat out haul ass for a day and a night...drive that sucker 'til my teeth are loose from the vibrations."

"Cool, man. No shit...have some fun, you know," Strings naturally encouraged, neither of us having the slightest idea of what lay in store for many returning veterans: depression and a sense of isolation, a strong tendency toward lawlessness and risk-taking behavior, the paradox of seeming old for our age yet naive socially due to having missed so much. Maybe this was especially true for the veterans who were at war during the late Sixties and early Seventies.

We smoked weed and dreamed. We survived our daily job and routines. There was really nothing else to do with only a few weeks left in Vietnam. Move slow and stay low, discuss plans for the future when we were free from the Army and the War. It seemed most of the Recon Platoon was short and only Louie, our trusted scout, was there for the duration of whatever was going on in that little corner of Southeast Asia. I isolated myself from the other Officers and held to the mantra day in and day out.

With the help of Strings, this not-quite-officially Resigned Lieutenant scored ten pounds of pure, manicured Thai weed and carefully packaged it in the plastic bags that PRC-25 radio batteries were shipped in. We repackaged a whole case, burning incense inside the box several times to mask the smell. Then I arranged to have the whole box shipped home in my "Hold Baggage" and delivered right to my home address. The term "hold baggage" was used when personal items shipped home from a war zone were carried in the hold of a ship and passed through customs on a blank check. My friend Strings and the covert supply system definitely served this unscrupulous

Lieutenant well, and I thanked anyone within the underground network I could personally contact.

The box was received by my brother before I got home and he opened it because it was labeled "boy's clothing". He flipped out at the discovery of the pot and wisely hid the whole box, less some smoking stash, deep in the woods outside San Antonio just as I thought he would.

The fateful day came when Colonel Cargill summoned me to the Command post to serve the official papers for my signature. Whether I fully realized it or not, First Lieutenant Jeffrey A. Lumbert was legally and officially a civilian right there in Tay Ninh Base Camp the minute I signed those forms. I was relieved from active duty and resigned my Commission in the US Army under Sections XI & XIV Chapter III AR635-100 SPN 611. Three days later in Cu Chi, I signed a second DD214 and was discharged under Chapter IV AR635-120 SPN 509. Character of Service: Honorable. I possessed two DD214's and two Honorable Discharge certificates. The dates were 7Feb70 and 10Feb70. I was so not-nice they discharged me twice.

The next day I caught a chopper out of Cu Chi and flew to Long Binh. The same range of feelings absorbed my consciousness as had occurred at the end of the first tour. I was mute with fatigue and relief...numb and somehow disappointed. I felt like a stone sitting there awaiting The Flight. Spoke to nobody. Looked at nothing. There was a vague sense of satisfaction in thinking I had pushed to the limit against stupidity and chaos; and had remained firm in the resolve to keep my men alive and with all their parts attached. I gave a silent thanks to all the men who had helped me survive, and took some solace in knowing I had helped others to survive.

Looking back one last time from the top of the stairway before boarding the Freedom Bird, I said one last time with extreme feeling, "OH HELL NO!" Not an eloquent expression of separation, but definitely heartfelt.

When this Resigned Lieutenant reached Oakland eighteen or twenty-some hours later at about 0300 local time, I removed my Class "A" uniform with all the medals and patches and insignias and stuffed it all into a trash can in an airport restroom. I donned a pair of black Levi's and a black T-shirt and went out to find The World I had left three years and seven months before. At twenty-one years and nine months of age, I was a graduate of a University called War.

CHAPTER V

A Resigned Lieutenant
Home from the War

"And, BAM, I smacked that fucker flush on the jaw and saw his eyes flip back, only the whites showing, as he sailed off this slope, man...it was just beautiful. He sailed right out there." This resigned Lieutenant described punching out the Korean at the dump while sitting with my younger brother on the roof of the trusty '65 Fairlane smoking hash, the car chugging along in third gear at 8mph, nobody at the wheel. The Ford was like that. At highway speeds, you could take your hands off the wheel for miles at a time and the car would go straight down the road, even following slight turns if the banking was right.

We were out in a planned subdivision in north Bexar County where the streets were completed, but no houses had been built yet. Phil and his high school friends, not being able to smoke at home, had taken to cruising around on the back roads and country highways north of San Antonio, smoking weed and listening to music. In my first week back in The World I became like a younger brother to my actual younger brother, relearning what in the world was going on because it was all so different. The beer drinking and hell raising of my high school years had been replaced by pot smoking and peace signs...kids giving each other the "V" sign for peace instead of a middle finger for "fuck you." I still thought the hand sign meant "V" for Victory, like in WWII. I was that out of place. I felt extremely uncomfortable most of the time.

...the returned veteran could not understand the hippy world...

I told a few stories to Phil and his friends – the funny ones – and added a few lies to demonstrate certain situations. I honestly and confidently answered "no" to my brother's one-time question of whether I had killed anyone. I never had, not personally. I had called in artillery strikes more than once, and a napalm strike, and I had definitely expended some ammo personally a couple of times; but I had never aimed at Charlie clearly in my gun sights, one-on-one, and seen him fall. Furthermore, none of my men had ever shot any innocent villagers or done anything like what the American public assumed all Vietnam Veterans had done.

It was shocking to realize the effect of a few horror stories and atrocious incidents that had been widely denounced in the news media. We had almost no access to national news while in Vietnam. I had no idea of the extent of the riots and demonstrations against the War. The general public knew nothing of the realities of the sweat, the courage, the frustrations, and the moments of sheer ass-clenching terror that soldiers were experiencing each nerve-wracking day and every long wakeful night. Soldiers were not recognized. Atrocities sold air-time on the networks. Disgust and rejection of the war was turned into negative emotions towards the returned Veterans.

It was frustrating to realize that I could not communicate my true feelings to anyone, especially to these young innocent kids. Based on a few instances of questions and the responses to my answers, I decided it was best to say nothing. I asked my brother to stop even mentioning anything about me having been in Vietnam. It was embarrassing when the best, most well intentioned responses I heard bordered on wondering how I could have been so stupid to have volunteered for God's sakes to go over there in the first place. It was quickly obvious that nobody could understand any part of the real story, so I buried it. I buried it deep.

The problem was: my emotional experiences did not remain buried for long. Instant reactions of raving anger to everyday problems; hopelessness when faced with any type of bureaucratic bullshit or authoritarian regulations; or feelings of helplessness when faced with familial or marital strife, would suddenly overwhelm me and I acted way out of character. I could surprise anyone, even myself. Many combat veterans did not cope well, to say the least. Often the best response we could muster was to just leave the situation, whatever it was. Just go off alone. And that was no help at all. Isolation led to more problems socializing and regaining some sense of self-esteem and positive direction and expectations towards the future.

I smoldered in resentment at being unable to find the means to tell these young jerks and jerkettes that I had done a lot more to stop the war than they ever had. *I was there, goddamnit...and I actually resisted the war...and I made life-or-death decisions...and nobody could be more against the war than I am you ignorant shitheads.* I fumed about more than just the general misconceptions of the American public. I hated all authority figures...they reminded me of fucking Dudley, who I held responsible for Pete's death. Internal rage fumed against the President and all politicians who were casually lying about the War and still sending more guys over there. I vowed to never vote because that would indicate acceptance of the entire crooked system. Worst of all, I blamed myself, however mistakenly, for not having done enough somehow.

No one ever clearly told me I had done a good job or that the Country as a whole appreciated the fact that I had served in the Military. It was years and years later before I ever heard any word of respect that I had "served" when called upon. It would be decades later, when many returned veterans were already in an early grave, before the American public awoke to the awesome sacrifices we had made. This realization, when it finally did come, was too late for most of us, who were already well along on a path of self-destruction, dope and lawlessness, in prison, dead, or "E" all of the above.

The damage done to the returning Vietnam Veterans was one of the darkest, most despicable episodes ever perpetrated by any society towards its soldiers, and it will never, <u>never</u> be adequately recompensed. It will never be erased nor eased in the hearts and minds of those of us who survived the apathy, the character assassinations, the negative stereotyping, and the lies and denials of every American citizen who supported the war protesters and the draft dodgers; but did not help the ruined, incomprehensible Veterans who returned to their own families and neighborhoods.

In the opinions of some surviving Veterans, now near to sixty years old, there should be another Wall built. There should be another Vietnam Veterans War Memorial dedicated to those who survived the war but did not survive long in the society they did not recognize...in a Country that did not recognize us nor honor us with any respect whatsoever. But at that time, a few weeks after coming "home", I just wanted to forget. I sought neither approval nor understanding, for I was resigned that there would be none. I thought I could forget.

My brother and several friends had been dealing grass in San Antonio and had even made a few runs to Mexico to bring back small amounts of marijuana in the spare tire or under the back seat. Phil knew many "heads" and I received an accelerated education in recreational drug use while driving around San Antonio avoiding the law. At that time in Texas, young people were being sent to prison for twenty or thirty years for possession of a single joint. Young kids were sent to do hard time with murderers, rapists, and assorted psychopaths. They became convicted felons, ruined for life. For one fucking joint.

Chris L., one of Phil's boyhood friends, was absolutely flabbergasted when he saw the ten pounds of Thai weed we had retrieved from the woods shortly after my return. Marijuana at that time was going for about $90.00 a pound, at least on the north side, and the quality was generally fair to good – nothing spectacular. When people began sampling the Thai weed at parties, though, they could not believe how strong it was. Several puked in astonishment, it was so unexpectedly good. I was used to it, as happens with any type of pot after a while and I just laughed at the reactions of the young smokers. I hesitatingly experimented with peyote and "magic" mushrooms when available, seeking a higher understanding of life...a deeper reality, like the experiences in the books written by Carlos Castenada. I tried dropping LSD one time and was glad I only took what was considered half a dose, because I was fearful of having a "bad trip". I was very leery of losing all sense of perspective and vigilance. There was nothing to be gained from the psychedelics.

I began thinking about writing a book on my experiences in Vietnam. Sentences and phrases sometimes floated through my mind as I imagined explaining my part in the War.

...the young Lieutenant, a known tough guy in high school, began to realize he was not so tough after all. He began to regret his fighting and injuring of others and was embarrassed to find himself feeling regret at destroying villages and...

My brother and I gradually doled out short ounces of the Thai weed for a staggering $15.00 when the going price for a lid was $10.00. We partied from San Antonio to Austin, went to a few rock concerts as I grew my hair and beard, and just had fun. I cranked my Sportster for all it was worth on occasion – like every time the weather and traffic would permit. Sometimes Phil was on the back; but that bike was not built for two. My younger brother had never had a motorcycle, was weak and sickly as a child, and had no nerve for the way I drove. I preferred riding solo anyway, and riding that Harley at 100mph while stoned on marijuana was just about the closest I could come to the thrills of Vietnam. But it did not take long for me to become bored with such a pointless existence.

I wanted to do something in life and was accustomed to the structure and pursuit of goals that the Military had provided for almost four years of my life. I was 21 years old when I resigned from the War in February of 1970. Being mature for my age due to my responsibilities and training in the Army, I was living in a different world internally than the 18 and 19 year old kids I was hanging out with. However in many respects I was still a somewhat shy 17 year old, having had no chance for a normal emotional development during my years in the Army. I did not know how to be a happy hippy and I did not discover where all that "free love" was located.

...the isolated veteran began to resent the hippy boys who were getting laid and felt hot anger rising...

Several close brushes with the Law while driving around smoking joints and dealing weed led me to the decision to move to California and get a fresh start. Maybe take little brother along to help him get out of the hometown rut he was in, too. I intended to learn to meditate in California so I could be happy without drugs, like the Buddhist monks...like Pete had been happy even as a draftee in a war zone. *Such a small hole...a good man dead...I will do what I told you I would do and change my mantra and meet the Maharishi, Pete.*

I could not collect myself to deal with the culture shock during those first few months. Feelings of rage, confusion, and deep, deep sorrow lingered at the edge of my consciousness at all times. I could not sleep sometimes and was afraid of what dreams I might have. I could not find love nor even a casual fuck. *What the hell's so wrong with me? I did not have any trouble dating in high school even though I was a known badass. What is so different?*

There was nothing that could have prepared me for the immense culture shock of moving to California in the Summer of

1970. I had a plan to go to a flight school outside Ventura, a random choice made by just looking at maps. I had about as much chance of fitting into the California scene as I would have had settling down in Tay Ninh City with Louie's relatives as neighbors. It had only been a few weeks before that I was cruising around as a wartime "tourist" with Louie and Sgt. Davis, fully armed and ready for anything. I was a complete stranger in my own home town and I would be stranger still in California. But I could not know that beforehand. I had to go and find out.

Spring was blooming in south Texas though, and I enjoyed just driving around getting stoned with Phil and his friends. Phil had not done well in school, being totally stoned every day of his senior year. Now it was almost a year later and he had no plans, and probably no capability, of attending college. Maybe he had what came to be known as "attention deficit disorder". All I knew is he might get busted and be sent to prison the way he was headed. He always smoked more pot, took more acid, and smoked cigarettes, even though he had been plagued with asthma since childhood. I had been healthy and athletic while he could not even attend gym class in high school. I felt sorry for him and realized maybe losing our Father had been harder on him that it was on me.

It felt wonderful to walk out in nature and not have to worry about booby-traps and snipers; but I still automatically and habitually scanned the woods and watched where I placed each foot. At times, hauling ass on my Sportster, I would imagine flying in a helicopter and would hear the chattering of the M60's and the clop-clop of the rotor blades. I was not concerned by these memories though, and had not experienced vivid flashbacks yet – these would come later. I was just reliving the excitement and adventure of it all in my mind, playing with the memory tapes and photographic images. When the really gruesome internal photos came up, I was usually successful at pushing them out of mind. When this was not possible, I would go off on my own to settle down. I never discussed the vivid experiences of the photographically explicit memories with anyone, and did not know to what extent other Veterans were having similar problems. There was no conscious recognition that I had any problems from the war.

There was no urge to join any of the Veterans' organizations. I could not have even named the principle groups such as the VFW, the DAV, etc. There was no inclination to attempt a connection with anyone from high school and I had no real friendships whatsoever. I did not realize how much my intensity and anger was immediately apparent to the young civilians I was cavorting with. They were just plain scared shitless of me.

Phil and his friend Chris decided to take me to Mexico to celebrate my 22nd birthday on May 5th. They wanted to demonstrate how knowledgeable and sneaky they could be in going across the border to score some weed or pharmaceuticals. They intended to buy some "black mollies" and Seconal, both of which could be easily purchased at any Mexican pharmacy in Nuevo Laredo. Cinco de Mayo was celebrated by the fun-loving Mexicans as one of two Independence Days and their revelry and fireworks could surpass most American Fourth of July parties. I had been nicknamed "Lunny" by these youngsters since we were children, which was a shortening of "loony Lumbert" due to my wild and pugnacious personality compared to young non-athletic Phil. Chris was none too reckless either and they were both somewhat in awe of my reputation in high school as a fighter and rebel.

I had often driven to Nuevo Laredo with my high school buddies and in my senior year, 1966, had one of my wildest birthday parties ever with the raucous Mexicans and drunken Texas "cowboys" in the red-light district of Nuevo Laredo, aptly known as "boys' town". Boys could definitely "be boys" in Boys' Town. *Some things never change...everybody's got to make a living, even when there was no* war *going on.*

After crossing the International Bridge, I initially perceived with honest appreciation that everything seemed the same as when I had first gone there with my father at about age ten to buy arts and crafts and curios. I already knew a few words of Spanish even at that young age and had later studied the language for two years in junior high school. I could understand some of the conversations by the Mexican people, even though they slurred the words and did not make certain proper conjugations of verbs. Being a combat veteran though, I certainly had a different perspective than on previous visits.

I quickly realized that everything was <u>not</u> the same when we were almost immediately asked whether we wanted to buy any marijuana. Every little street urchin who used to sell Chicklets chewing gum or trinkets now said, "you want la marijuana senor?" And each one claimed he had "the best – lo mejor" with the same certainty that the pimps formerly assured potential buyers that "my seester ees a virgen, but not theese time". I was cynically amused; but not interested.

Having seen the bars of Saigon, the roadside boom-boom girls so cute and petite, and the truly dire straits of the Vietnamese people, I now had a more jaded perspective towards the Mexican whores and the young street hustlers of Boystown. No sympathy arose for them and I was not attracted to the garish, disgusting women. I had come along for the fun of it and to maybe score some cheap speed, which relieved the sense of oppression in my chest and helped me get over my difficulty in talking to people at parties. I gave nothing to the beggars and was not in the least bit intimidated by the heavy stares of the badass Mexican hombres. *You give me any shit I'll take away your knife and cut your head off...completely <u>off</u> you muthafuckas. You want to find sympathy (a Marine expression) look in the dictionary between shit and syphilis you lying punks.* My internal dialogues and combat readiness served us well in the filthy streets of Nuevo Laredo. Nobody gave us any problems.

...the returned veteran of combat paced the old neighborhood always ready; but he was   prepared to kill, not just punch...

The possibility of writing a book floated through my mind on a daily basis, subtle yet persistent. The idea of writing about a known cover-up of "friendly fire" gradually became an inescapable duty. The absurdity of that most moronic of oxymorons demanded an explanation.

The training and experiences in the military prompted me to automatically survey the International Bridge as we had crossed, scoping everything out according to military tactics and possibilities. Late that afternoon, when we were getting off on the speed of the black mollies and drinking tepid beer at one of the better-looking bars in Boystown, I told Phil and Chris, "man, you guys are crazy to ever try to drive across the bridge with grass in the car. Sooner of later they'll search you and you're fucked." I calmly proceeded to lay out the tactical realities to them in the same manner I would have talked to my men, my soldiers, a few months before.

"Do you realize how many men it would take to patrol the whole river? I guarantee you it would require hundreds of trained men, every night, to guard the river from here to, say Del Rio, only about a hundred miles away. Shit, the thing to do is just wade across like a thousand Mexicans do in the early morning each day to come to work. You want to smuggle some grass, that's how I would do it."

"But, Jesus man, at night? What about snakes and shit? How are you going to see?" Chris asked, never having been trained in any way to navigate in the woods at night. We were city boys, all of us, and had not come from families who hunted or even went fishing. I had received some of the best training the Army provided and knew I could easily walk across, no sweat. It was nothing compared to leading an ambush patrol out in the dark to find a precise spot in the jungles of Vietnam. *Nuttin' to it.* I laid out a plan as a Platoon Leader, my gut tightening at the prospect of doing something exciting. I relished the idea of using my acquired skills to smuggle a little grass, and was well suited to the role of Head Smuggler.

...actions that might have seemed risky before Vietnam, now appeared simple and obvious...

The subtle undercurrent of possibly writing a book crept through my mind as we continued to drink Mexican beer and plan the escapade. We were young and speeding like hell on the black mollies, so there was no hurry. We'd be wide awake all night no matter how much beer we drank.

I did not have any real perspective on the possible dangers involved in smuggling a few pounds of weed across the Rio Grande in the middle of the night. I judged the situation as a calculated risk; but had no fear at all, having graduated from a school where "danger" meant instant death and/or dismemberment. Knowing clearly what danger felt like, this seemed fun...a prank.

At about 11pm we all three drove back across the border to the US and cruised the back streets of Laredo until we found a dirt lane that went right down to the river. I carefully judged the distance to the International Bridge, about a mile distant, and explained, "I'll have the Mexicans bring me down to the river right over there on the other side, then I'll cross and meet you here. You make damn sure you can find this exact spot again, that's all you two have to do." *Piece of cake.*

"How are you going to find us again, wait until dawn?" Phil asked, the lane being almost completely dark.

I laughed. "Oh I'll find you all right. You just worry about finding this little street and be here waiting in this clearing at three o'clock." I calculated that should give us enough time.

We returned to Mexico and headed back to Boystown on the west side of the city. Within minutes, a young hustler led us around to the back of one of the cantinas and a little while later a swarthy Mexican came out and introduced himself in a husky whispered voice, "I'm Rudy...what you want, senor?"

"Yo quiero dos o tres kilos de la marijuana, Rudy, y yo tengo quarenta dolares a kilo," I replied, using my junior high school Spanish more than adequately to order two or three kilos at forty dollars each. I fearlessly pulled out a roll of about $200 in twenties to show Rudy I had the money, no problemo.

"Si senor. Lo tengo. Vamanos amigos," Rudy responded immediately, giving me a compliment by using Spanish to show he appreciated my being able to speak his language. Very few

"Anglo" Texans could speak or understand a word of Spanish even though they lived among millions of bi-lingual Hispanic Americans whose primary language was used throughout the State. I had negotiated a deal which would bring a substantial profit as well as supply us with smoking stash for months. I sent Phil and Chris back across the river and told them to go to a restaurant or something while they waited...no more beer. They seemed uncertain about the deal and expressed concern about my safety, all alone in Mexico with what they considered to be lots of money. I laughed. I thought I could count on them to be at the rendezvous though, if for no other reason than worrying about me. Very touching. High as we were on the mollies, they would be awake all night, so they nervously took off for the bridge.

...the man began to use his military skills in civilian life...in criminal enterprises...

This fearless ex-lieutenant left with Rudy in a smoking hulk of a '55 Pontiac that was probably held together with mechanical contrivances known only to Mexicans, certain secrets of shade-tree mechanics passed down only to family members. I had a real appreciation of their skills in keeping old cars and trucks on the road. We headed south and west through town, Rudy finally pulling up at a deserted looking little house on a dark dirt lane in the barrios of west Nuevo Laredo. A couple of men approached the car immediately and Rudy placed the order in a word or two as casually as if ordering take-out pizza.

While we waited, I casually talked with Rudy like I would talk to anyone, practicing Spanish   even though we both knew he could speak English well enough for this type of transaction. It was what he did. He transacted...no translator necessary. Since I showed no fear, nor even nervousness, Rudy became slightly disconcerted as he listened to my hyped-up speedy speech and was uncomfortably aware of my rapid movements as I gestured with my hands. The tranquillo Mexicano saw that this "gringo" was not acting the way they usually did. They were usually pretty scared doing this sort of thing.

Rudy had been doing this for years and had any number of tricks and double-crosses he could put over on the average gringo who was crazy enough to try to score directly in Mexico when grass was cheap and safe to buy just over the river. Any notions he might have had about ripping me off faded as he contemplated this combat veteran. I could feel it. Maybe he respected me as a man and would do an honest deal. He was a businessman, after all, and he was as honest as could be most of the time. If given a chance though, or if the norteamericano was a disrespectful condescending jerk, Rudy and his muchachos could easily arrange any number of surprises and wind up with all the money and all the dope, and have fun doing so. As far as Rudy was concerned, it just depended on how things felt to him as they proceeded.

He felt that this "Loony" guy was possibly just a bit nuts, and I was pretty big and athletic looking besides, so he lapsed into genuine Mexican hospitality and interest in me. I had introduced myself as "Lunny"; but Rudy pronounced it "Loony" and was aware that the word meant "crazy". He liked me from the start and returned the simple courtesy and respect I offered to him.

I chuckled at the Mexican pronunciation and decided to adopt the new and expanded characterization indicated by that slight alteration of my nickname. Automatically checking the position and phase of the moon, I thought, *yep, that's me...one loonatic motherfucker all right.* When the three kilo bricks arrived, Rudy thought to impress me by flicking out a slender little switchblade knife to cut the newspaper wrappings for the usual inspection, but he was surprised when I had already whipped out a razor-sharp seven-inch Buck Hunter from a sheath beneath my shirt and paused with it held at eye level for a moment then said politely, "yo tengo"- I got it.

I zipped the blade across one of the bricks, then grinned at Rudy with a direct stare, pupils dilated due to speed...not trying to intimidate the guy, just having some fun myownself and showing some dramatic flair...just fucking around. I pried out a pinch, sniffed it, and said, "Si. Esta bien. Por favor rudy, lleveme al rio." That really blew his mind. I intended to cross the Rio Bravo with my weed all by my lonesome.

It was not done that way. For an extra ten or twenty bucks, Rudy could have a chico (boy) take it across and meet me on the other side. But here was this loony guy, wanting to cross a mere three kilos myself. Any other person would have been taken aback to the point of just wanting to get away from this crazy wide-eyed American; but the Mexicans, at least those engaged in this kind of dealings, seemed born and bred to be outlaws and they loved seeing in anyone else the qualities they encouraged in each other. Rudy laughed and joked as he took me down to the river.

With lights out, creeping along through alleys and side streets, Rudy negotiated the Pontiac to a spot about a mile west of the Bridge as instructed. He knew it was usually a simple thing to wade across the river in the summertime – he had done it hundreds of times. He was surprised to find this gringo acting so cool about it, though, actually looking eager to go on a very dark night. He had his money, so he had nothing to lose regardless of what happened. He wondered if the guy would chicken out at the last minute and ask him to do it. It would mean an extra fifty bucks or so, he thought, as he watched Lunny tie the bricks in a plastic garbage bag.

But without pausing any longer than to be sure my night vision had developed, I slipped out of the car, quietly closed the door, said "adios amigo," and crept right on down the bank and through the weeds, not even looking back. Rudy nodded in appreciation. Yeah, he decided, he would watch for this "Loony" guy again. He was real. He was fun.

This former Infantry Lieutenant, who had slogged a hundred miles of jungle during combat operations, waded easily across the Rio Grande. It was about hip deep and fast-moving in places, but had sand bars, vegetation, and ankle-deep water for most of the two hundred yards separating the two starkly different Countries. It had been a dry spring and the water was low as the river spread out on its way to the Gulf of Mexico.

Reaching the other side, it only took a couple of minutes to orient myself, then I crouched down in some thick bushes to wait silently. In about thirty minutes I heard Phil and Chris quietly close their car doors a short distance up the block and watched in amusement as they tried to creep down the lane. It was a rough section of Laredo and anything was possible. *Good job, right on time.* I crept noiselessly up on them as they stumbled around blindly, not knowing to wait until their night vision had developed after parking the car. "You guys sure make a lot of noise," I whispered, walking out of the brush about ten feet from them.

They both jumped about a foot in the air. "Goddamn," Phil said too loudly. "You scared the shit out of me...you got the grass?"

"Hell yeah I got the grass," I replied with a grin, "Nuttin' to it." A memory flashed of big Edwards saying that while he was cleaning that beautiful M60 machine gun right before my first ambush patrol as Three-Six. Then I saw every face of the Third Herd, my one and only line Platoon. I heard Pete's calm reassuring voice and felt his presence...then the photographic images started flowing...*a neat black hole Pete why don't you say something don't leave me goddamn you Dudley you sonofabitch I hate you a foot flopping an arm without a torso I wonder who that man had been when he still had all his color...*

"Well come on, man what are we waiting for?" Phil was saying as I recovered my sense of the present and reached down for my weapon...but there was no weapon. *I'm in Texas there is no war I still wish I had a fuckin' gun so I could shoot Major Stinson and Major Tantrum and all the Colonels behind all the desks just shoot them all goddamnit.* I found myself wishing for a gun of some type while creeping around in the middle of a dark night. It was only natural. Even my standard Springfield .45 semi-auto would be comforting. Three pounds of mayhem on my hip would have been nice. A phrase for my future book drifted through my mind.

...the young Lieutenant had left the Army on a sour note but the Army had not left him...

I had not grown up around guns and there was never a firearm in our house. My Father did not hunt, contrary to what most people thought about everybody who lived in Texas. I had a BB gun to play with in the backyard, but that had been the only "gun" I had ever handled until the US Army had issued me various weapons. I flashed on the thrill of a Mad Minute, just letting it rip on full automatic, burning up the ammo like there's no tomorrow. A memory of the Hobo Woods came to mind and I saw myself half out of my mind, standing up in plain sight as I jammed magazines through my M16 until Sergeant Thompson grabbed my arm and pulled me down. I really did want to carry a gun again.

We stashed the grass under the back seat and headed up the highway to San Antonio. There was always a checkpoint on the highway about twenty miles north of Laredo; but it was just the Immigration cops looking for illegals. We all looked like Americans, especially Chris who was a pale, clean-cut blond. We were waved on through with barely a glance by the Officer, who was seeing a steady stream of revelers returning from the Cinco de Mayo celebrations in Mexico.

Back in San Antonio we split each kilo brick into thirty "lids" of about an ounce. We had no scale. We made a profit of about $260.00 per kilo, while laying aside a smoking stash that would last a month. The grass business would never be so good again. I had saved about three pounds of the Thai weed for personal stash and after distributing the three kilos of Mexican lids, Phil and I had well over $4000.00 between us. It seemed like a fortune.

I had researched the flight school in Ventura, California with the FAA and talked with Jack Roper, my former flight instructor and my Dad's business partner. He recommended going. I was told the GI Bill would pay for the schooling and that clinched the deal. I had been flying airplanes since childhood and had legally logged over 200 hours of dual time (with a licensed pilot) when I had worked for three summers as a hangar-boy in my Father's aviation investment company. There would be no problem qualifying for my Private Pilot's License. It was a natural profession for me, and I thought it would help in coming to grips with my Father's early unexpected demise.

This Resigned Lieutenant did not complain about my experiences in the war to anyone. I did not obsessively dwell on the eight missing molars or the small scars that remained from was actually an incredibly light amount of damage and discomfort sustained from the wounding of the beehive fleshettes. I did gripe and complain however, both inwardly and vociferously vocally, about the mistakes and lies that I knew were being made on a daily basis in Vietnam. It was obvious the news media were printing and broadcasting outright lies; and I definitely knew that honest and innocent young Americans were scared shitless that very moment in Vietnam. They were still expecting a mortar round to drop on them or a sniper to be lining them up in his sights.

Each time I gave in to the urge to rant about the war, the memories would wash over me like a tidal wave and I would lapse into silent recriminations of myself and my actions. Then I would often take a joint and go off alone to think things over; but that was no help because there was no way to reach any decision or conclusion regarding any aspect of the War or my part in it. I went off by myself to watch the images swirling and whirling through the lens of a marijuana high. It did not help. I probably spent too much time alone, but was unable to sustain a conversation, much less a friendship or intimate relationship with a woman.

...the man was <u>in</u> the world but not <u>of</u> the world. An alien being...

The only conclusion I could reach was that there was nothing to be done about the War. I told myself that I was lucky to be alive with almost all my body parts still functional, so I might as well get on with it. Get Phil out of all the influences of San Antonio and maybe help the kid grow up. It seemed a damn good plan to go out to California and go to flight school. It was the obvious thing to do – the course of action I had been discussing over and over with "Strings" and the men just a few months back in Tay Ninh while we occasionally ducked rockets and got fucked up on the bunker line...vigilant soldiers at work.

Accustomed to the military way of doing things, I was always ready to pack up and leave at a moment's notice. The destination was irrelevant. I remained Ranger ready. It only took a couple of days to rent a U-Haul truck, put the Sportster and my stereo, and our bedroom furniture in the back, hook up the Ford with a tow bar, and we were ready to go. Our poor Mother was more bewildered than ever, but there was nothing she could do as she watched her only two boys prepare to leave her. She was left alone with only promises of regular phone calls. Her husband was dead...her daughter had moved to Dallas...and now her boys were gone. I could not understand her grief nor ameliorate her pain; but I felt it acutely. Her face and posture, and even her professional life had deteriorated so much during the past three years that she was barely recognizable as the same person she was three years before. My being in Vietnam had possibly been tougher on my Mother than on me, I thought sorrowfully.

I did not yet realized the extent of my injuries, the depth of my wounds, and the immense chasm that already separated me from the college kids and hippies my age. We drove the U-Haul truck to California, stoned as shit, without incident.

...the man did not equate being homeless with being lost. He left his former life...

We had no trouble finding an apartment in Ventura and rejoiced in the sights the way anyone does on first seeing the Pacific and the whole California beach-hippy-surfer scene. Ventura had a lot going on for a small town, and for the first few weeks we just cruised around in the Ford or on the Sportster together, enjoying each day. We rode up and down Highway 101 on the Harley, some vaguely remembered song from the Fifties going through this stoned Veteran's mind. We cruised through the mountains and wilderness areas to the east and north and looked at the miles of citrus orchards along beautiful roads bordered by eucalyptus trees and Australian pines. It was amazing to see pine trees, palm trees, cactus plants, and fruits and vegetables growing side by side in some residential yards.

I enrolled in the flight school with expectations based on many years of experiences flying around in small airplanes with my Father. My Father and two of my Jewish uncles from my

Mother's side of the family had all owned and flown small single-engine airplanes since the early Fifties. My Mother's only younger brother, Jacob, had been killed as a fighter pilot in WWII, one of the few Jewish airmen in the US Armed Forces. He was shot down while enjoying what was undoubtedly his ultimate revenge when he was escorting bombers over Nazi Germany. This familial background led me to feel quite confident in my future as a commercial pilot. I could not even remember the first time I had flown in a small airplane as an infant. I played clear memories of being five years old and flying in a Cessna 140 from Mansfield, Ohio to Niagara Falls. My Dad as pilot, Mom co-pilot, and the three of us kids in the back seat. I had some unusual experiences as a child.

In my high school years, my Father had tried his hand at an aviation investment company and during the summers I had been the designated hangar-boy, washing and polishing airplanes and taking instructions in a variety of aircraft from my Dad's partner Jack Roper. Jack had been a flight instructor during WWII and Korea and very much enjoyed teaching a youngster to fly. I had flown "dual time" in over 25 different aircraft by age seventeen and had illegally soloed in a Piper Comanche 180 when I was just fifteen years old. I had flown a familiar route from Stinson Field in south San Antonio to the International Airport on the north side to ferry my Father back over to the hangar where we had the business. That had been a very proud and memorable experience for both of us and I still had clear mental images of my one and only first flight by myself – my "solo".

So it was with a great deal of confidence that I approached the prospect of a career in aviation. When speaking enthusiastically to the instructor about my background as a youth, my excitement and natural energy led me to overplay my background without knowing it. The instructor decided to give this smart guy the kind of first ride that was sometimes given as an initiation rite – a wild flight that the experienced pilots would later laugh about in the pilot's lounge. For some reason, he overplayed his hand that particular day as well though, and in his desire to give a memorable first lesson to a would-be student he instead dashed the hopes of a young man unintentionally.

As we approached the aircraft, I was reflecting on the last flight with my Father in a Mooney 150, from Shreveport to San Antonio after basic training at Ft. Polk. My Dad had attended the graduation ceremony, an apparently healthy 49 year old, totally unaware that he had only two months to live. The proud pair had flown back to San Antonio where I spent my two week leave prior to reporting in at Ft. Sill, Oklahoma for advanced training in the Artillery. Before owning the Mooney we had flown in a Piper Comanche, both low-wing, retractable landing gear aircraft. My first post-Vietnam flight was to be in a Cessna 180, a popular easy-to-fly airplane with an overhead wing and fixed landing gear.

I felt comfortably familiar during the pre-flight checks and taxi procedures. As we took off I had my hands and feet lightly on the controls, as instructed, feeling good. Then my stomach lurched as the instructor took us into a tight climbing turn, leveled off momentarily, then banked hard the other way and kicked low rudder, pressing us down in the seats. I was looking almost straight down out the side window when a film of sweat break out on my upper lip. I was astonished to find myself struggling with the onset of airsickness for one of the few times in my life.

As the instructor abruptly leveled the wings into a long climb, this would-be student realized with embarrassment that I was definitely going to be sick. Then my recently perforated sinus cavities popped and cracked from the pressure differential and the exact pathways of the darts became evident once again, bringing vivid memories swirling into my consciousness. I saw myself being thrown through the air by the blast of the Howitzer shell, felt shattered teeth and blood in the back of my throat, and I got stuck on one mental image even though deliberately repeating to myself *I am in a Cessna 180 over California.* I saw the hundreds of strewn bodies in and around Diamond II that I had glimpsed when medically evacuated in a Huey that early April dawn just over a year before...*death and destruction body parts smoky stinking ruination loss loss loss.*

...the veteran began to have flashbacks at the most inopportune moments...

My stomach erupted, heaving itself inside out as I had never before experienced in my life. The diaphragm spasmed, my rib cage convulsed, and I spewed. I aspirated a small amount of vomit gasping for a breath and convulsed again when the stomach acids hit lung tissue. I began to cough to the point of near unconsciousness. I had just enough awareness to push my seat all the way back in order to collapse forward and not interfere with the controls of the aircraft as I gasped and spasmed and heaved, barely conscious.

Somewhere in the back of the mind I wondered calmly, in an intellectual manner, why this should be happening and whether this was a sign that aviation was not for me – like the Army had turned out to be not for me. Something inside clicked to fast-forward and seemed to indicate future outcomes that were to be a let-down...futures that ended in failure. And I gave up on aviation then and there because I had seen all too clearly that no matter how much you cared and how good you were at your job, you got fucked in the end anyway. I resigned myself to the inevitable, however prematurely in this instance.

...the stress-fractured young Vet began to realize how much his entire future was...

I was so sick I could not relate to the experience at all. I was barely able to walk away from the airplane after the pilot immediately landed. He was loathe to help me very much since I had just puked all over the instrument panel, the floor, and the seat. Cleaning the disgusting mess of his airplane was his first priority. I walked weakly away from my "first" flight lesson in abject misery, not looking back. Finding my way to the side of the hangar where the Sportster, was parked, I found a hose and sat down in the shade of the building drinking from the hose like a child. I sat there coughing up phlegm, blowing snot, and trembling with weakness. It was an hour or more before I had the strength to crank up the bike and nobody came over to help me in any way. I sat there alone with the photos flipping through my mind and gut-wrenching sadness in my heart. Tears streamed down my face and my ribs and diaphragm seemed stuck in spasm. Each miserable breath required conscious effort and part of me just wanted to pass out and never wake up. *You're no good no good you can't do anything right why the fuck did you live when good men died whywhywhy.*

I drove back to the apartment barely able to work the clutch and looking at each passing bridge abutment as a possible way to end it all in a fiery high-speed crash. I could not explain anything – not to my brother nor even to myself. I went to bed for a day and a night thinking about death...wondering about life...gazing in sadness at the images parading through my consciousness like extravagant floats in a parade of gore with blood dripping and severed limbs dragging along and torsos without heads. I could not stop the images... just could not. Whether my eyes were open or closed made no difference. Whether awake or asleep made no difference. I thought of death in its many forms and the myriad possibilities for death in an average day, even in sunny, gloriously carefree California on a peaceful flowery day in the Summer of 1970.

This resigned Lieutenant was more acquainted with death than with life. Death had affected me more in my twenty-two years than had life. I knew more about life in the Army than life in California in the summertime and more about an M16 rifle than a lawnmower or a surf board. I could direct Artillery bombardments; but could not direct my civilian life. Without a career in aviation to look forward to, there was no way to know what to do. I felt crushed, disappointed in myself and pissed off at everyone else who evidently had a life and a future plan. There seemed to be no resolution to the miasma of indecision. There was deep anger at the military, rage over the accidental wounding that nobody had ever taken responsibility for, and grief over the death of Pete. All these unresolved, unfinished internal conflicts combined to put me into a deplorable depression.

The full effect of having "resigned" as a method of release from the Army was skewed in my mind to read "in disgrace" instead of "for the good of the Service" as the actual clause read. Although I had received an honorable discharge there was no sense of being honorable. There was nobody to tell me otherwise. *Loser you fucked up you should have died that night might as well end it all.* Fortunately I had my two principle anti-depressants: Thai weed and a Harley Davidson. These two factors were just about all that kept me alive during the first few weeks in California after giving up on aviation. My younger brother was no help. He could not possibly understand.

I cranked up the Sportster and headed into the hills of Los Padres National Forest with half a dozen joints in the back of a pack of Marlboros. I blasted that bike to the limit, laying low through the turns, downshifting and accelerating, braking, leaning, cranking and power-shifting, then leaning into the next turn at twice the posted recommended speed, using the whole road and the hell with any possible oncoming traffic. Then I would pull over, gaze at the scenery, smoke a joint then a cigarette, take a long pull at my canteen, then blast off again, roaring down the road with no place to go but in a big hurry to get there. Thoughts of the War whirled through my mind like dust devils in the desert. Uncertainties about the future loomed like dark thunderous clouds. I was totally alone and adrift...twenty-two without a clue.

...negativity became a constant state of mind...

Somehow a clue did enter my mind like a meager ray of sunlight peeking through the clouds on a cold and windy day. I had to learn to meditate and gain some measure of inner peace. It seemed possible to imitate Pete and the Buddhist monks if I could find out where Transcendental Meditation was being taught. I resolved to stop smoking pot and carry out my promise to Pete. There had to be a scintilla of light in the darkness of depression or I would just veer off the road and over one of the cliffs that I was passing way too fast. I was barely in control and not sure I wanted to try to control what seemed beyond all reason or understanding: my life. A desperate need to end the suffering one way or another arose from within like the need for a breath after swimming the length of a pool under water.

The positive plan to learn to meditate was one side of a coin flipping randomly in my mind. The other side of the coin was joining some anti-government, anti-war protest group and blowing up some buildings like what had recently occurred at the Bank of America in Goleta, just up the road by Santa Barbara. I felt justifiably qualified to lead some type of raid against a bank or power station, or whatever; but fortunately for myself and America I did not know how to make contact with any of the existing radical groups. I knew there were many coordinated anarchists in the area.

...the man realized he had no connection with any type of group...

I stopped in at a couple of biker bars where some of the tough-looking men were also probably Vietnam Veterans; but I did not "look the part" and could tell that someone would give me a hard time if I hung around and asked too many questions. It seemed highly unlikely that I would be accepted into that crowd of thugs and outlaws. Even if they believed my stories of rebellion against the Army and my troubles with authority figures my whole life, the bikers of southern California were not open or friendly to me. Nobody was sure of my identity or background. They had doubts and could not categorize me as possibly one of their kind. Perhaps they were wary of a man who represented all thirty dots on the five dice – all possibilities. I might be just a wild Harley rider or maybe some type of narc or informer. I might be someone to kill or someone who had come to kill. They could not be sure and did make any attempt to find out. From my perspective I just felt rejection from all levels of society and I could not imagine ever making a social connection of any type with anyone. I could not find my group of outlaws. And I could not find or join the fun-loving hippies. I just did not fit in anywhere.

There also seemed to be a dead end in my search for meditation and enlightenment. I was having trouble focusing and believing in a surcease of suffering. Our savings were dwindling so we had to find some way to make an honest living. Our combined qualifications, my brother and myself, were dealing dope or leading a Recon Platoon. However, my family had lived in several houses, Mother having been a Real Estate broker, and my Father and I had done minor repairs and repainting on each house before my Mother had put the houses back on the market. So I put an ad in the local paper as a house painter and within a few days had my first job. Phil helped out a little and we found it quite easy to make a basic living. I ripped out the back seat of the Ford so we had more room for a ladder and various equipment. This alteration would prove to be our undoing when we crossed back over to Mexico a few months later for one last dope run.

This ex-Lieutenant found it impossible to settle into a life of house painting, though. I craved some excitement and danger. A natural dislike of all authority figures transferred to the Police, who were a constant threat to all drug users. Possession of even a single joint brought a penalty of years and years of hard time in Texas. Disrespect broadened to outright contempt after an incident with a stolen Plymouth Road Runner that two of Phil's friends drove out to Ventura for a visit. My chronic rebellious behavior, well practiced during the second tour in 'Nam, spilled out into civilian life where I was a total newby and did not know it. I was a rule breaker and a risk taker, having resigned a lot more than my commission as an officer in the Army. I had resigned from being bound to all rules and regulations...resigned from society as it was. I became a loner, an outlaw, a deceptive participant in society at times, but a man who made his own rules.

Chris L. and another kid, my brother's boyhood friends, showed up in Ventura in a racy '69 Plymouth that they claimed had been given to them by some guy driving through Texas who picked them up hitchhiking. It was such a ridiculous story from these two young thieves that it might have been true. Not having anything else going on in their misdirected stoned lives, they had driven to California for a visit. The two of them, along with my brother, had been pulling stunts and high-jinx together since grade school and had practically never been caught at anything, especially Chris, who was a nervous, self-centered double

Scorpio. After a few days in Ventura we all became paranoid about the probably stolen Plymouth so on my advice they abandoned it in a light industrial area and the two visitors took a bus back to San Antonio.

Phil and I watched the car surreptitiously for about a week and nothing happened, so we decided to have some fun with it. What the hell. It might have been due to the influence of some heady Afgani hash we had been smoking continuously for a week or it might have been just general rebellion, but we decided to take the Road Runner up into the hills of Los Padres National Forest and totally trash it. Why not?

We blasted around in the hills performing stunts worthy of the Dukes of Hazard...or worse. One of us followed in a Ford Bronco pickup I had bought while the other crashed and trashed the Plymouth. I went off the road at about 60mph and flattened a whole row of little reflectors on three foot posts, then slammed repeatedly into the side of a tunnel, bouncing all over the highway and laughing like a demon. Then Phil took over and, not to be outdone, he careened off the road in the middle of a curve, blasted right up the side of a hill at about 65mph, and skidded sideways to a stop right on the edge of a 200 foot cliff. I could barely make it up the slope on foot. I did not think the four-wheel drive little Bronco could have made the ascent. I was laughing like hell while Phil tried to appear nonchalant about barely stopping on the edge of a cliff that he had not known existed a moment before.

We smoked another bowl of good Afgani hash and decided to light the car on fire and get it to roll off the cliff. It was an automatic transmission so it was easy to douse it with gasoline, put it in gear, then jump back and flick a burning wad of paper at it. WHOOSH! It burned really well but got hung up on the edge of the cliff and did not go over as expected. We appreciated the way it burned in the natural updraft anyway though, standing nearby taking hits off the hash pipe. Then we went on our way as if nothing had happened out of the ordinary.

We almost herniated ourselves trying not to laugh, however, when we drove by the scene the next day and saw two County Deputy Sheriffs standing up by the Plymouth, literally scratching their heads in an attempt to figure out what had happened. We innocently approached the scene on foot, as might be natural, just out of curiosity. After a few minutes of casual conversation, one of the Deputies theorized that it must have "been drug up there with a bulldozer or something." He did not believe anybody could have driven it up that slope.

"Oh yeah? You think so?" I replied, trying to maintain the sarcasm to a minimum as I indicated to Phil with a nod at the obvious tire marks on the slope and the dirt plowed up where he had slid sideways to a halt on the edge of the cliff. We had to haul ass back down to the Bronco before we got arrested for criminal hilarity or something. "Oh shrewd guess Sherlock. A fuckin' bulldozer for sure," my brother commented. I was too hysterical to respond with anything coherent.

Seeing this level of Police "intelligence" at work fanned the flames of piracy and adventure already kindled in us and it was not a great leap of imagination to decide to go back to Texas and make a few smuggling runs with our remaining cash reserves. We had no illusions of getting rich and planned to stop when we each had $5000.00 free and clear. It was not a grandiose plan and was certainly attainable based on our previous experiences and contacts. I locked the Sportster in a storage area provided by the apartment complex, paid for two months in advance, and returned the slightly beat up Bronco to the dealer without explanation...the first of several "repos" in my life. Then we made the long stoned drive back to the old stomping grounds.

...the recently returned veteran could not settle into boring civilian life...

We easily arranged several potential buyers and started making runs in the same manner as the first spontaneous crossing. I waded across from Mexico to Phil on the other side. As an experienced and suspicious renegade, I changed the Mexican contact man and altered the times and locations of the operation in order to develop what was hoped to be a long-term game plan. We ferried bricks of mediocre Mexican weed to known associates in San Antonio and Austin, netting about $200.00 per kilo. Our cash built up quickly. Along the way we attended pot parties, rock concerts, and generally had a damn good time. We were instantly popular and greatly admired for our courage and subterfuge. There were no other youngsters capable of planning or executing anything like what we were so casually and successfully achieving. We did not know the ripped out back seat in the Ford clearly marked us for increased surveillance and suspicion of being smugglers.

All was going well until for some reason, my Mexican contact snitched us out on about the eighth attempt. I had waded across as usual and waited for thirty minutes silently in the brush by the river, as per SOP. I surveyed the scene using all my Ranger capabilities and did not see anything amiss. Phil came coasting down the block in the Ford and I got in with a large trash bag full of marijuana – 27 pounds – our largest haul. When Phil clutch-started the car and turned the first corner in the quiet neighborhood, police cars came roaring at us from all directions. We whipped down an alley and I tossed the bag out amid some other identical bags containing trash. Too late. The cops had seen me throw out the bag and they recovered it. We were busted.

My first impulse was to fight them and die in the effort. The thought crossed my mind to go for the nearest cop's gun and have it out with them and damn the consequences. As I got out of the passenger side door a Police car skidded to a stop right behind us and a fat little (American) Mexican cop got out with his pistol drawn and stumbled as he ran up to me with the gun pointed at my chest, the hammer cocked and ready to fire. *Oh fuck. I survived the 'Nam and now I'm about to be shot with a .38 due to obese clumsiness.* We tried to assume an innocent posture until one of the other Police cars pulled up with our bag of weed. We knew we were clearly fucked.

We spent three days in the Webb County jail before our Mother somehow arranged for our bail. I cannot express the dark thought processes that went through my mind while incarcerated. I hated everyone with a raging passion. There was no way anyone could have been gathering statistics at that time; but later studies would show that a disconcerting percentage of combat veterans of the war in Vietnam were in jail within one year of returning to the US. And an initial period of incarceration was just the start of a lifetime of lawless behavior for some of us. I probably became one of the few exceptions as I later turned my life around to some degree and never got caught at anything illegal again.

I immediately broke bail and hitchhiked back out to Ventura to liquidate our belongings and salvage what I could. I was broke, unstoned, and as unhappy as a living being could be as I caught rides across the great wide Southwest. *Just keep going get a gun and start robbing banks fuck this shit why try to straighten out go on and do it do some real crime I am going to be locked up like an animal don't ever go back.* Out near Casa Grande, Arizona I found myself stranded on Interstate 10 at dusk and was unable to catch another ride. I crawled up under a highway overpass to what was called the "hobo hotel" - the three feet of flat concrete at the top of the slope right under the intersecting roadway.

In the middle of the night, at about 0300 not surprisingly, I had a dream occurrence that I never could explain which unnerved me to the point that I was wide awake for the rest of that night. I dreamed I was lying on a battlefield during the Civil War, wounded and suffering. A Confederate Officer rode up on a pale white horse, leaned over holding a long-barreled pistol in his left hand, and shot me in the middle of the chest. POW! I instantly awoke in a sweat with crushing pain in my chest, thinking I had been shot by someone who had leaned over the railing above me. Heart pounding and ears seemingly still ringing from the report of the pistol, I raced up to the highway above and looked around expecting to see someone fleeing the scene. But there was nobody there. I stood panting and sweating in the middle of the desert, still certain someone had shot me even though I could see it was not so. I was surrounded by the immense quiet desert – nothing more. *A neat black hole in the sternum he never suffered.* I had never had such a starkly real dream and awakening and I clearly remembered the incident for the rest of my life. It did occur to me that it would not be a bad way to go, having seen a good man die that way.

I really came close to going completely berserk on arriving to Ventura and discovering that our apartment had been broken into, my Sportster had been stolen from the locked storage shed, and the landlord could offer neither explanations nor condolences. I could not even report the crime to the Police since I was not supposed to have left Bexar County while on bond. I cried and raged in grief but there was not a thing to be done about it. I hocked my Rolex Oyster Pearl for $50 to have enough money for a bus ticket and something to eat during the long depressing ride back to San Antonio. I boarded a Greyhound empty-handed, more angry and depressed than ever.

Even years later, the loss I still mourn with a continual ache in my heart was a baseball given to me by Whitey Ford, the great pitcher for the Yankees, after I had pitched a no-hitter in Little League when I was twelve years old. The ball had been signed by the entire 1960 New York Yankees Team: Mantle and Maris, Casey Stengle, Yogi Berra, and all of them. It came about because my Father had become acquainted with Ryne Duran, a relief pitcher for the Yankees who had grown up and played semi-pro ball in San Antonio. Whitey Ford had been good buddies with Ryne and they sometimes came to San Antonio during a break in their schedules or during the off-seasons. I had played catch with Whitey Ford when I was twelve years old in our backyard while my Father cooked barbecued steaks for everybody. I had just pitched a no-hitter in Little League Baseball. The gift of a baseball signed by all the Yankees meant more to me than the motorcycle and it was utterly irreplaceable. It was gone. Stolen by a burglar.

...the returned veteran suffered unusual calamities in the civilian world...

I have a hard spot in my heart for all thieves to this day. Stealing form ordinary folks is one of the lowest crimes possible.

I can understand robbing banks, beating up people during a passionate argument, even killing someone if they deserved it; but can not countenance stealing and I will hate thieves with a dark raging passion for the rest of my life.

I was practically paralyzed with anger and depression while we awaited trial. I got a temporary job with a construction crew and showed up with a common household hammer to learn framing. Everybody laughed at me. My Mother gave me ten dollars to buy a real framing hammer and I returned to the job site the next day amid blatant ridicule from the experienced men. Once again a green newby in a different scenario. Totally embarrassed and small. Again.

Our lawyer, J. Gillespie, advised us to plead guilty to one of the several charges and assured us we would get probation or a light sentence since neither of us had ever been arrested before. This calculating ex-lieutenant watched the Judge pass out lengthy sentences all morning and realized the glinting scimitar of Damocles was hanging over my head. We were on the chopping block for sure.

Judge Connolly kept a .357 magnum pistol on the dais next to his right hand as he presided over two types of cases: either smuggling illegal aliens or smuggling a wide variety of drugs, from ten pounds of pure heroin to possession of a few "roaches" - marijuana butts – in an ashtray. I astutely observed each case and also considered the possibility of charging the Bailiff when I went through the gate before the Judge, wrestling the Bailiff's gun from him, and shooting anyone and everyone related to the judicial process. *Shoot the fuckin' Judge first,* I fantasized on hearing sentences of at least ten years being passed out for non-violent offenses. My already dwindling sense of patriotism reached an all-time low while waiting for my Country to send me to prison.

I watched in stunned amazement as at least twenty defendants made the same mistake when asked if they had anything to say before sentencing. They started by saying, "I'm sorry," and the Judge banged down the gavel and replied, "you're not sorry you did it. You're just sorry you got caught." Then he passed out a long sentence. I could not understand why they all made the same mistake and resolved to not say those words when my time came.

I was embarrassed that my knees were quivering uncontrollably when Judge Connolly asked me if I had anything to say before sentencing. "Your honor, I know I did wrong and the only thing I can figure is that I just got back from the jungles of Vietnam where I started smoking pot and I guess I needed something like this to happen to get me to stop. I must have been confused and seeking excitement and did not realize how serious my actions were. I ask for leniency in the case of my younger brother, who just went along for the ride. I accept full responsibility."

At the last second I considered giving only my name, rank, and service number and playing the rest of my tour as a prisoner of war captured by the North Vietnamese Army...*and let them figure this shit out the muthafuckas I'll wreck the joint I could have that fat Bailiff's gun in a split second ME jeffreyalumbert first lieutenant 05347994 and not a fuckin' thing more goddamnit overandout for fucking ever!* Fortunately common sense prevailed and such a profane and useless thought did not make it out of my mouth.

...the errant lieutenant caused unusual problems whenever he opened his mouth...

The Judge was temporarily stunned because my terse yet relevant speech was so different from what every other defendant had said. He took a few minutes reviewing the pre-trial investigations by Court social workers, then handed down the lightest sentence of the day: three years in Federal Prison, with only six months to serve and the remaining two and a half years suspended for five years probation. *Fuck this shit...nothing to it.*

When we got back to the Webb County jail the other inmates congratulated me on my masterful speech. I replied that I had just spoken the truth and did not say the words that had provoked the Judge's anger and immediate sentencing. I added, "nobody can tell the truth, the whole truth and nothing but the truth, so why not bend the story for my benefit." Several other inmates cursed themselves for making what they now knew was a mistake by saying, "I'm sorry."

Phrases and thoughts often entered my mind and the idea of writing a book on the Vietnam War occurred often, regardless of circumstances.

...the young returned veteran accepted six months incarceration as a learning opportunity in the same manner as a he accepted a rigorous school in the Army...

I began a serious search for truth and enlightenment as a part on my incarceration and learned to read with total concentration. Having been a lifelong reader, I always made decent grades in school without serious study. Now I applied the level of concentration learned while looking for booby traps, while studying a map in Vietnam, when calling in an almost deadly close artillery bombardment during a firefight. There were few students of my age who had the type of training in concentration that a surviving combat veteran had received. I discovered an almost perfect recall and a photographic memory of information in a book in the same way I had maintained photographically explicit memories of the gory details of combat. There was pride in discovering a capability to learn and remember almost anything written. Having already become somewhat of a loner, I read a mountain of books in the coming years, starting right there in the County jail in Laredo, Texas. I began a very serious lifelong search for reality, self-awareness, and spiritual enlightenment while in prison.

Imitating meditation, trying to recall what my Judo instructor said when I was only ten years old, I thought any attempt would help when I finally learned Transcendental Meditation. That goal was now of paramount importance. Thinking of how Pete's face had looked when he meditated, my mind switched to that neat black hole in his sternum. Experimenting with using the word "mantra" as a focus, I kept slipping into the more familiar mantra, "oh hell no!" Then I just sat and counted my breaths to ten over and over again when I remembered that was the method taught by my Judo teacher so very long ago. That method seemed to work the best. My body relaxed deeply and the furrow in my brow disappeared. The other inmates were intrigued and a little scared of me. I made no attempt to form any friendships and said very little to anyone, not even to my younger brother.

After a month in the County Jail we were transferred to El Reno Federal Prison in Oklahoma. At that time it housed short-term nonviolent offenders such as drug smugglers caught at the border; car thieves who had crossed a state lines; and local Indians who had strayed from their outdoor prison – the reservation – and committed some petty crime or misdemeanor. It was barracks style living much like in the Army. I fell into the routine easily enough; but anger and depression increased daily and my contempt for authorities deepened.

I had been back from the War almost exactly one year when sentenced to prison. Obviously there had to be some serious changes made. Firm in a resolution to forget about the War, I concentrated on living one day at a time and increased the amount of time spent meditating or reading. A natural self awareness formed within and brought about a feeling of refuge and seclusion from the external world. I very seldom spoke and did not look anyone in the eye. Simple survival was sought and attained.

Mere breath awareness did not help however, on the day my work crew had to slaughter two cows in a hot, foul-smelling shed. We watched as one of the guards shot a cow in the head then smacked it with a sledge hammer to kill it. I had an overwhelming flashback watching the cow hung upside down and slit wide open by another inmate, its stinky entrails slopping out and completely filling a 55 gallon drum. I tried to maintain a steady breath while slicing around the hooves as instructed, but the smell and the very sound of the knives slicing through the connective tissues deeply affected me and I began to feel dizzy and nauseous. I hated being the weak member of any group and struggled against total revulsion; but the photographic memories began flipping through my mind showing charred little bodies and unidentifiable limbs laying about in smoky gray soil. I suddenly threw up all over the bloody slaughterhouse floor.

I barely maintained consciousness, kneeling there on my hands and knees listening to the ridicule and taunts of the other inmates and trying not to fall over and lie down in the gore. I hated feeling weak and so affected by the War, hated the other men who were unfazed and a deep resentment arose because they had not gone to the War. *You fuckin' pussies couldn't have walked ten steps in Vietnam.* Then I criticized myself and strengthened my resolve to do everything possible to get strong again. There <u>was</u> a path to enlightenment and happiness and I <u>would</u> discover it. I became a vegetarian for quite a few years after the slaughterhouse experience. Jeez, who wouldn't.

Fortunately the prison had a surprisingly well-stocked library. I studied Buddhism for several weeks while reading <u>The Teachings of the Compassionate Buddha</u> and wrote the publisher explaining my predicament without embarrassment and asked for whatever help they could provide. To my surprise, someone at the publishing house apparently practiced Transcendental Meditation and sent me two books by the Maharishi Mahesh Yogi: <u>The Science of Being and Art of Living,</u> and the first six chapters of the Indian epic, <u>The Bhagavad – Gita.</u> Vegetarianism was confirmed, though it greatly limited the diet in prison. I studied those two books as if my life depended on it. A promise to Pete to learn meditation became an absolute oath. Surviving a brief incarceration became easier with the knowledge that there was light at the end of the tunnel.

El Reno had its own farm system and complete repair and construction crews operated by us inmates. My crew strung barbed wire fencing, replaced windows, repainted rooms, and performed other jobs. It was not forced labor and the guards were generally easy going as long as some work got done. I read and studied for many hours each day, investigating ancient philosophies and classical literature from many cultures and times. A serious study began of all the major religions of the world in an attempt to piece together a personal world view...a philosophy of life.

The asceticism and renunciation of life, inherent in some of the teachings of Asia were very appealing. Perhaps this was a path to the alleviation of suffering by eliminating the desire for worldly things. My combat – ready sleep patterns kept me awake long into the night, practicing my conscious breathing technique, counting ten breaths over and over, drifting deeply where there was no sorrow. Enlightenment could be achieved through discipline and practice. I hoped to end the deep feelings of personal insignificance and depression. It was just a matter of using the right technique for long enough, or meeting an enlightened master, or studying enough metaphysical books.

My brother and myself managed to stay out of trouble at El Reno and were released on schedule on July 2, 1971. This date was to become my personal Independence Day for the rest of my life. This felonious Lieutenant resolved to never allow another arrest and played mental fantasies of shooting it out with the cops and dying a good death rather suffer the indignity of imprisonment. In replaying the memory tapes of the whole prison scenario during the bus ride back to San Antonio I realized the positive benefits of being briefly locked up. I could read with intensity and now had a definite plan. Maybe now I could settle down enough to start college or some type of professional training.

These sober and mature reflections did not deter me from retrieving an ounce of the good Thai weed hidden in a suitcase in the back of a closet at Mother's apartment though, and within thirty minutes of arriving "home" we two incorrigible brothers were cruising the unfinished suburbs north of town in Mom's Oldsmobile getting totally stoned. Right back into it. How quickly some plans could evaporate.

The idea of renunciation of worldly material things was helpful since I had lost everything except the search for enlightenment and personal harmony. That ideal would not evaporate. I fought through a fog of depression with the expectation that once I learned to meditate, inner peace would enfold me like a warm breeze on a cold day. I conjured up images of the smiling Buddhist monks in Tay Ninh; but intrusive memories of body parts crept and leaped into focus, destroying any positive visualizations. When thinking of Pete's face when he was meditating, the memory changed into the face of incredulity as he lay dying without saying a word. I read, went for solitary walks, exercised, practiced yoga postures, ate very little and slept very little. There was no sense of accomplishment. Everything seemed to end at a wall of disappointment. But a stubborn will to succeed remained.

This Federal felon-for-life prepared to enter San Antonio College in the fall of 1971, a well read 23 year-old freshman with a serious social adjustment problem. It seemed impossible to hold an everyday casual conversation and anxiety paralyzed me when realizing I was not making a good impression on the youngsters, especially women. I was trying too hard. They saw only anger and tension. Although I tried as often as seemed polite or reasonable, in almost two years of being back in "The World" I had not yet been laid. The last time had been when Mac and I had gone to Saigon the second time. Frustrated did not even approach my feelings in this area of failure. There were other failures as well: like close friendship or possible camaraderie with other Vietnam veterans.

The sexually liberated young women of the time playfully rejected me. They stalled and avoided my advances with such phrases as: "we should get to know each other for a while," or "let's just be friends." Then they immediately jumped into bed with other guys who were soft-voiced, happy hippy boys. I knew that for a fact and they did too. I was unworthy of consideration. The girls carefully worded their more serious objections with criticisms of my personality, character, tension, anger, and "E" all of the above. Certainly I seemed too needy and scary compared to the mild college boys with whom they were accustomed to having sexual relationships and friendships. I seldom even had a chance to hold an extended conversation without causing discomfort with the gentle flower girls. I did not even mention I was a Vietnam veteran. They just knew there was something different and wrong with me. They were right. I was wrong, so wrong.

I spent most of my time feeling unloved and what's worse, unlovable. The hippy girls had no love nor understanding for this semi-ruined war veteran. I suffered. Smoking weed for depression and drinking strong Chinese tea and reading and studying occupied all my time.

After reading an inscrutable book entitled <u>All and Everything: Beelzebub's Tales to His Grandson</u> written by a man named Georges Gurdjieff, I joined a Gurdjieff and Ouspensky "discussion group" at a local bookstore near the College. The explanation of the universe by the mathematician turned mystic P.D. Ouspensky was especially enlightening to me. He wrote a very obscure book entitled <u>The Strange Life of Ivan Osokin</u> which I read and reread many times. The main character lived and relived the same life over and over until he altered one circumstance. Somehow this gave me hope. I just listened and seldom said much in the discussion group.

Over the next year, in addition to attending twelve semester hours of college, I studied such literature as William James' <u>The Varieties of Religious Experience</u>, Madame H.P. Blavatsly's <u>Isis Unveiled</u>, and various authors including Carlos Castenada, Vivikenanda, the Persian Rumi, Attar the Chemist, and Edward Cayce, among others too many to enumerate. I read major portions of the Thirteen Principle Upanishads along with some of the lengthy epic Rig Veda. In Philosophy class we studied Kant, Nietzsche, Locke, and other famous modern-day mystics and deep thinkers. I rejoiced in the gloriously illustrated translation of the <u>Bhagavad Gita</u> by A.C. Bhaktivedanta and loved the barbed wit of Krishnamurti. I discovered the tremendous Arabic treasures of teaching tales, Sufi stories, and Mulla Nasrudin jokes, and I read Sir Richard Burton's complete compilation of <u>The Arabian Nights Entertainments: A Thousand Nights And A Night.</u>

I finally learned Transcendental Meditation in the Fall of 1971 right there in San Antonio. The Student's International Meditation Society posted a sign at the college for a free lecture so I signed up to be "initiated" in the long-sought practice of TM. The would-be teacher was a pale, etheric young woman who told me "Maharishi says" that aspirants had to be free from all drugs, including marijuana, for at least a month before learning Transcendental Meditation. While reading, taking solitary walks in nature, and practicing breathing exercises for the next thirty days, I did not realize that maybe I was placing too much expectation towards one particular practice. Having seen Pete meditate and seeing the monks walking calmly in the middle of a war, my mind recalled the memorable old man panning water in a rice paddy. That old man knew something or had some quality I wanted to experience. I wanted to be as powerful and serene as that old papasan who was flipping water from one field to another because it was just his job for the day. There was a strong desire to meditate like Pete had practiced regardless of external circumstances. I left a full ounce of good grass on top of the dresser for the whole month and did not smoke a single joint.

The initiation ceremony – a "puja"- was conducted by smiling calm Americans who parroted an ancient Hindu ceremony as if they really understood the words and the meanings of one of the oldest and most complex of all recorded religions. The initiators also placed great emphasis that this was a "scientific" technique, having nothing to do with Hinduism. The cost for students was $35.00. I submitted to the slightly ludicrous trappings of disguised Hinduism because I was convinced that TM would be my vehicle to happiness, my path to enlightenment, and I had no serious religious affiliation or preference whatsoever, so a little Hinduism was fine by me. Any skepticism I had was eclipsed by memories of Pete.

Accepting my ancient/sacred yet scientifically-derived and tailored exactly for me...my mantra: Ah ---, --- I repeated softly, "Ah --- --...Ah --- --." Beginning in a whisper then falling to silent repetition, following the instructor. It seemed too simple. Holding skepticism in check, I began the practice of twice daily meditation of twenty minutes, regardless of circumstances – just like Pete. I latched on to daily meditation with all the tenacity of a drowning man clutching a life preserver. Although I still smoked grass, I usually waited until after my evening meditation before getting high.

This misfit freshman finally met a woman in Philosophy class who took me to bed. Somehow, in the middle of a discussion of Plato, I suddenly looked at her and she grinned and nodded. I grinned in surprise then engorged in pulsing expectation. We had lunch then she suggested we go back to my place for a little "afternoon delight." Patricia was a beautiful, tall San Antonio native Mexican/American girl with ample breasts, slender hips, and almost no body hair whatsoever. She put it on me every which way but loose. Oh I was in love! I had always admired the dark-eyed, copper-skinned Latinas of south Texas when growing up and several times had barely avoided serious consequences from passionately protective brothers and cousins. I was in heaven touching her and being loved by her.

Patricia was a normal sexually-experienced nineteen year-old and I was totally inexperienced in dating and mating, so the relationship meant a lot more to a returned veteran than the playful woman could have understood. She did not realize how much a sexual experience might mean to a man who spent four years in the military while she was running free in high school, dating, making out at drive-ins, dry humping quietly in back bedrooms, and having a normal American sexual development. In Vietnam, we would often talk and fantasize about wanting a big-breasted "round-eyed" woman, the kind of woman we had known back in the States...back in "The World." After waiting for almost two years, I finally had a woman to sleep with. Wow.

Much to my discomfort and embarrassment however, I discovered it was impossible to fall asleep with Patricia hugging me or even snuggling up against me. She had a way of snuggling up under my arm and cradling my balls in her hand. Jeez, I did not know what to do about that. Allowing her to lie however she wanted to and trying not to disturb her, I grew increasingly tense and wanted to move. I could not fall asleep. I lay and meditated until my body became uncomfortable, then would shift around trying to lie without touching her even though I loved to touch and caress her wonderful smooth skin and marvelous breasts. I just could not fall asleep with any kind of physical contact and when I did finally sleep, the slightest noise or movement from my woman would startle me into being instantly fully awake. I still had the sleep patterns of a Lieutenant responsible for an ambush patrol. Not good.

...the returned veteran slept like a nervous alley cat...

My Patricia could not understand when I tried to explain. She would subconsciously seek me out during sleep for hugs and snuggling. I heavily criticized myself but the harder I tried, the less I could sleep. I was in love and sexually fulfilled and indescribably happy; but was getting very little sleep. Therefore there arose problems coping with any type of stress.

This became apparent when I received a surprise from Uncle Sam that should have boosted my morale a bit; but instead, due to internal rage and sleep deprivation, almost led to real tragedy and serious consequences. I got a letter from the Veterans' Administration officially informing me that I had been "awarded" a ten percent service-connected disability due to facial scars. The repressed anger over being shot through the face by a 105mm Howitzer erupted in full force. The wording of the letter seemed completely ludicrous...as if it represented some type of door prize or having a winning lottery number. I had refused a Purple Heart Medal for the incident and did not want the measly $25.00 a month "award" for having survived the injuries. The initial check was for $400.00 as back payment to February of 1970 when I was released from the Service. Even though the incident still pissed me off royally, the practical considerations ultimately overrode the disgust over the fiasco of Diamond II and I went out to try to cash the check.

At the time, and still today, a conviction for a felony cancels any and all veteran's benefits. I guess the information system was not coordinated at the time, and I wonder if today, when the VA finds out I am a convicted felon, they will cancel my payments and demand I repay everything previously received. I will take the risk to tell my story.

I went to three different banks where the teller cheerfully explained that they would not cash a check – even a certified U.S. Treasury check for a service-connected Veterans Disability compensation – unless I opened an account in their bank. I had no wish to interact with the banking system in any manner. The thought crossed my mind that I wanted to deposit a 500lb. bomb in one of their vaults as a means of creating general havoc and expressing rebellion towards the society that was still sending its young men and women to that War. When the third teller turned me down I became enraged and started making a scene. Screaming profanities and describing what I had gone through to get that check quickly attracted a manager and the bank security guard.

The armed guard approached thinking to calm things down by his mere presence but he blanched in fear when I turned to him, serious as a heart attack and close enough to fight for the gun if he tried to pull it, and screamed, "Go ahead and **shoot** me you sonofabitch...take one shot and let's see what will happen. I have already faced real soldiers you fuckin' wimp...come on and shoot me!" I showed neither fear nor respect for the armed guard and truly had none. This was obvious and more than a little disconcerting to all civilians present. I stomped out of that bank and resolved to tear up the check each month rather than submit to what I considered to be an unfair and ridiculous rule in an established institution. They took no risk whatsoever in cashing a Treasury check if a person produced any form of identification. I later relented and opened an account somewhere and resolved to use the money to buy marijuana each month as a token of disrespect.

I enrolled in Philosophy, English, Math, and various freshman classes. I found the courses to be very easy and breezed through the first semester. After enrolling in a speed reading class and demonstrating I could read with comprehension at a rate of over 1200 words per minute, the instructor gave me instant credit and did not require me to attend any more classes. The college algebra course was exactly the same as the one I had passed in the tenth grade of high school. Freshman English covered grammar and writing rules I remembered from the fifth grade. There was not much challenge to junior college for me.

Making friends did not seem so easy. In fact, month after month, I made no real friendships. Everyone seemed so stupid and childish. Wondering about the future, I took to roaming the streets and parks long into the night, depressed and lonely. My one and only Patricia had moved to Austin still having no clear idea how much she had meant to this friendless, now chickless veteran. Everyone around me seemed so happy and relaxed; but I was so depressed at times that a reply to a cashier at a store when asked if there was anything else was met with a slight head shake. *If there was anything else I would have brought it to the check out, idiot.* At times a slight nod of recognition was possible when someone greeted me but I was mute with unease and probably looked mean and angry. There was a horrendous inner dialogue constantly in my mind in response to the photographic images that occasionally pranced and drifted through my sleep-deprived mind. There did not appear to be any answer or means of relief. There was a feeling that TM would not work for me as it appeared to help others.

This veteran was not an attractive man, despite the fact that I was not ugly, was well built physically, and quite sensitive and intelligent. In hindsight, emotional sensitivity was definitely not an advantage when dealing with the after effects of wartime trauma. I could not be any other way. Women usually avoided me as too angry, too complicated, too strange, too something. There were much easier men to love. I had to learn to live without love...without sex...without companionship or friendship and came to believe that I simply did not deserve these human enjoyments. I tried to resign myself to asceticism, but was not cut out for a life of renunciation and could not subdue my natural desires.

The idea that social skills could be learned and acquired through guided practice did not occur. Nobody told me I was simply a few years behind in certain aspects of communication relationships and was still a worthwhile human being. Immense importance was placed on the issue of sex and simply dating, which seemed so easy for everyone else around me. There was no counseling center for combat veterans at that time. It never occurred to me to seek help other than learning meditation and studying books on spiritual growth. A broken mind cannot mend itself.

A job of any kind was impossible to find because I had let my beard and hair grow out. I was even turned down by the Texaco gas station where they had known me since I was a kid. I heard that even Disneyland in California was banning anyone with long hair from entering the premises. What a sad joke when they had people dressed as cartoon characters and fantasy attractions aplenty.

One day I sat next to some other students with beards and asked them what they were studying and whether they had been able to find jobs of any type. They said they had transferred to a program of Respiratory Therapy and they were already accepted into an intern program at the county hospital. They were allowed to have neatly trimmed beards because many of the medical students and young doctors had beards and even long hair. I sought admission to the school of Respiratory Therapy through a program established by President Nixon. They even offered a payment of $65.00 a week while in training. I was accepted and felt hopeful at finding a profession.

A portion of the program included training as a nursing assistant. I read the textbook overnight and passed an exam in that part of Respiratory Therapy school the next day. The instructor was surprised. The program was designed for students to spend six months studying theory, then serve three months as an intern at the Bexar County hospital under the supervision of a licensed therapist. I challenged the theoretical part of the program after one month and passed the exam easily, the instructor already impressed by my rapid learning capabilities. I entered the intern portion and began working in the hospital before the other students had even finished studying the first few chapters of one of two textbooks.

...a veteran sometimes possessed concentration skills far above an average student...

I was well suited to the roll of helping others and enjoyed participating in hospital work. It was the only real social contact this reclusive veteran had. I realized that at the time. There were memories of a boyhood dream of becoming a doctor after watching the family doctor set a broken wrist when I was about ten years old. *I could have done that.* When making rounds in the hospital giving breathing treatments with a forced air delivery system called Intermittent Positive Pressure Breathing (IPPB) my natural curiosity and desire to interact in a positive manner took over and I was a capable respiratory therapist practically from the first day on the job.

By the time I was formally graduated from the course ten months later I already had a good job on the night shift at the county hospital paying a staggering $4.75 and hour – about twice the minimum wage. When I passed the National Board exams a few months later I got a raise to $5.25, a decent wage at the time. Living a simple life, with rent on a garage apartment of $65.00 a month and not smoking or drinking at all, except very moderate marijuana use, I found saving money was natural. I quickly saved enough for a down payment and with Mother as co-signer financed another motorcycle and was able to quit riding city buses, which I detested.

I bought a slightly used 1972 BMW R60/5, a bike reflecting a self image as an intellectual, a student of mysticism and a regular meditator. It was a quiet smooth ride, in stark contrast to the Sportster, and having only a 600cc engine it seemed to just crawl up the acceleration scale, but I loved that BMW and rode rain or shine, summer or winter. It also came to be the best vehicular investment ever, since the German money system changed and the price of new BMW's almost doubled between '72 and '74. I paid $1525.00 for the bike when it had only 1600 miles on the odometer and sold it for $1600.00 four years later when it had over 40,000 miles on it. That marvelous bike had required no maintenance other than oil changes – a fine machine.

By 1974, three years after returning from the War, I gave little thought to my combat experiences and when reminded of a particular memory I was usually able to focus on something else and not dwell on the photographic images which still drifted through my mind. I did not watch television and did not even have a TV at any time for years and years. I read and studied, exercised and meditated, went for long walks, and took my hospital work very seriously. The entire time in the Army was "compartmentalized" and I guess I was in a state of denial over the whole mess. The search for enlightenment and a constant desire to gain medical knowledge occupied all my time. Perhaps a psychologist who observed me at the time would have taken steps to draw me out socially, but I never considered any type of therapy or counseling. There was no chance to talk about Vietnam because I seldom conversed with anyone about myself. There was no clear idea of the fact that I was a walking time bomb, set to explode at the least provocation, like at the bank when first trying to cash my disability check. The word "disability" was repugnant and not in my vocabulary. Depression was easily assuaged with mild doses of marijuana and strong black tea.

...the returned veteran refused to admit any weakness or after effects from the War...

Then came a day when I had to admit to some problems coping with adversity. Hearing the usual rejection by one of the nurses after haltingly asking for a date, I took off from the hospital and went for a drive to sort things out, as usual. Again. Parking the bike near a small river, I walked down the bank muttering to myself, pissed off again...as usual. *What's wrong with me? Why do women treat me this way? When will I ever be accepted?* After smoking a joint then a cigarette I should have been feeling a little better, but was still depressed and angry. It was the wrong day for anybody to give me any shit. However, some people fail to heed the warning signs...see the sizzling fuse...hear the ticking of the time bomb.

A carload of native Texas "Mexicans" (I call them what they called themselves at the time) pulled off the highway and parked just beyond where I had parked my bike, making it necessary to walk almost right beside their car in order to leave. *These punks will just have to say something smart. I know they will.* And sure enough, in keeping with their cultural heritage of hatred towards "gringos" (how they referred to all non-Mexicans) the two boys and two girls in the immaculate low-rider Chevy stared at me menacingly as I walked up the path. Probably came from a family where a common expression was "the pinche (damn) gringos stole our land." An expression showing total ignorance of the historical fact that many Hispanic families in the 1800's joined the American settlers (Texans) in the revolution against the totalitarian Mexican government in the war for Texas independence. Even though the two young men were both smaller than I was, they pumped up their machismo and began laughing and making comments in Spanish, all four of them staring at me. *Fuckin' punks. This is the wrong day to give me any shit.*

I walked past the car not looking at them, not trying to start any type of confrontation, and simply taking the only possible route back to my motorcycle. I steadily did <u>not</u> look at them the way I had to do while in prison and resenting it just like in prison. The driver tossed out an empty beer can as I walked past, almost hitting me. When this did not draw a response, he got out of the car and started taking a piss, eyeballing me continuously and giving me that flat dull look they practiced so well. As I got on my BMW and looked up, the driver tenderly shook his dick, still staring at me, and said, "whatchu looking at maricon? You want some of this?" Then he said something in rapid idiomatic Spanish to his girlfriend I did not understand but I knew what the word "maricon" meant. It was a slang expression for a homosexual or a sissy. As he turned his back and got in the car, something snapped in this depressed and lonely combat veteran.

I ran up to the side of the car and smashed a left hand into the side of the guy's face then pulled the door open and dragged him out and slammed his head against the edge of the roof. As the boy in the back seat started to get out I jammed the door on him when he had one foot on the ground and his head above the top of the door, then pulled back and let the guy have a vicious punch right in the mouth. I flung the door open and literally threw the kid halfway down the slope towards the river. By that time the driver was starting to get up so I kicked him in the ribs and he rolled down the slope groaning and bleeding.

I jumped in the front seat, snatched the keys out of the ignition and threw them in the river in the blink of an eye. Both girls were screaming and hitting at me so I dragged one of them out and threw her down the slope and completely into the river. I turned to the now terrified girl in the back seat and screamed, "you think something is funny now, you fuckin' puta (whore)?" This rampaging ex-lieutenant then picked up a baseball sized rock and hurled it through the windshield. Satisfied with the result, I picked up a bigger rock and started pounding on every surface of the car, growling and cursing, totally out of control. Within about thirty seconds I had smashed all the windows, dented the hood, the roof, and the trunk lid. Then I rammed one front door open so violently that it ended up shoved against the front fender, all the while screaming at the top of my voice. It is amazing what a man can do under an intense adrenaline rush, especially when gifted with speed and strength to begin with.

...the returned combat veteran could summon adrenal responses that were off the chart...

Then I turned away, got on my motorcycle and drove off, trembling so much I could barely work the controls. Once the bike was up to about eighty, I started laughing so hard I had to stop and pull off the road and wait until clear sight returned in my contorted watery eyes. I laughed and laughed. *Hey, maybe I just discovered the cure for depression. Beat up a couple of punks and wreck their fuckin' car.* Feeling definitely better, there was initially no remorse at all. *Fuck 'em. If they can't take the heat, don't call in napalm goddamnit.*

But after consideration, there was no pride in what I had done. Surprise turned to deep disappointment which became shame. *What would the Maharishi have done? Laughed at them? He certainly would not have destroyed that beautiful automobile and smashed faces...fuck me.* The incident certainly did not elevate my self esteem in the long run, that's for sure.

Evidently TM was not working for me the way it apparently did for others. They were mellow, smiling flower children and did not need much help in finding happiness. I imagined they would achieve enlightenment – the state of internal bliss and spontaneous right action – and I would not. Why did I have to suffer so much? Depression always turned to anger and anger was directed toward myself. Years of social solitude were wearing on me and I still did not have a steady girl friend *like every skinny overconfident goddamned prick hippy. I'm just no good nobody will ever love me it will never be any different fuckthisshit I don't want to live any more.*

I often sat beside a railroad track smoking grass and sometimes thought about darting out in front of a roaring freight train; but did not want to cause any emotional trauma to the engineer. I blasted around on my mild-mannered BMW taking unnecessary risks and breaking all the known traffic laws. Many of my habitual walks occurred in cemeteries. Gradually the realization came that I had to seek another form of self-development, but no idea came to mind as to where it might be found. There was nobody to ask. Sometimes self-pity reduced me to tears. But embarrassment quickly overcame self-pity and resolution took hold again. I would survive. I could endure.

Surprisingly though, when at work in the hospital I could lay personal grief aside and enjoy helping others. Then yet another possible pitfall occurred. What might have been considered a minor setback became a reason for resigning from an endeavor...once again. I could have resigned and given up on a positive identity, just like resigning from the Army. Just like giving up on aviation. I almost cast myself into the void of unknowing, becoming a pariah...a man living on the fringe of society...on the brink of chaos and mayhem. Fortunately a wise nurse saved me.

It happened on a Saturday night at the County hospital. I was the only respiratory therapist working and had to respond to an urgent call to the emergency room, a part of the job usually carried out by one of the more experienced personnel. I entered the ER to find a young man bleeding and screaming, having understandable difficulty breathing due to 26 stab wounds in the chest, arms, and back. An anesthesiologist was trying to place a plastic tube down the patient's throat and into the trachea without success and the patient was fading fast. When the doctor removed the tube in order to prepare to try again, it was my job to fit a mask over the man's face and pump oxygenated air into his lungs by squeezing a rubberized bag.

The procedure required strength and coordination and, unfortunately, also required a certain amount of detachment...of professionalism not affected by blood, by screaming and thrashing, by imminent death. I suffered another episode of overwhelming mental imagery looking at the knife slits seeping blood and smelling that peculiar coppery odor of bloody mortal injuries. I passed out cold in the middle of a crucial situation. When coming to a few minutes later with one of the assistant nurses holding an ampule of amyl-nitrate under my nose, I was confused and had no idea where I was. I initially thought I was in the hospital at Cu Chi being attended to for facial wounds after being shot by the beehive round at Diamond II.

"Feeling okay now?" a concerned nurse asked as she mopped my forehead with a cool cloth.

"Yes. I guess. What happened?"

"You fainted. Do you know where you are?"

"Yeah. Bexar county hospital. I really messed up, huh?"

"Hey, it happens. Most of us have had the same feeling at times. Didn't you just start here?"

"A couple of months ago. That was the first time I had to do that."

"I remember my first time. You want some water? Can you get up? Let's go over to that break room for a while, okay?"

"Alright."

I still felt shaky as she led me into a nearby nurses' break room. I was beginning to get the whole incident clear in my mind. *Shit, I'm not cut out for this job.*

Her name was Janet Russel. She said she was in the ER as a substitute because someone did not show up that night. Her normal position was in the nearby recovery room, a job she preferred because she was also adversely affected in a situation like we had just seen.

Janet was understanding and supportive. I guess she intuitively knew how important an initial experience could be to a beginner and she began to explain that it happens to the best of us and one must not put too much emphasis on it. "Have you ever been seasick? I used to get carsick when I was a kid, but of course I got over it. Same thing with seasickness. My Father had a fishing boat and the first few times I went out with him I hated it and once got terribly sick and threw up all over everything. But later I got used to it and now I love being out on the water and it has never happened again. Believe me."

I believed her. I had been on hundreds of airplane rides and never had been sick. That time in California had been the only time and I had let it affect me too much. We decided to go out for breakfast when we got off in the morning and, fortunately for me, struck up a solid friendship. We never dated because she was about 40 years old and had a kid almost my age, but we became good friends and I could visit her in the Recovery Room so we could go on breaks together. Janet helped me through my difficulty and she was responsible for my continuing in Respiratory Therapy. I owe her a lot because I became a very competent therapist and in the coming years functioned well in many similar situations in my career.

Janet helped me realize the fact that the young man we had been treating that fateful night had gradually recovered and once or twice I had seen him in the hospital afterwards. I had to check on his supplemental oxygen delivery system and began to feel more confident in myself. I also began to realize the tendency of giving up too soon and resolved to be more tenacious towards my goals. That resolution transferred to the practice of meditation and the process of dating, smoothing the future social integration process for me. I had more confidence in myself.

After taking a more active part in the TM movement and attending meetings and group meditations at the TM center at the college, I decided to become a teacher of Transcendental Meditation. This led to a month long seminar in the piney woods of east Texas where we did yoga, meditated for several hours a day, and watched the Maharishi on video tapes giving marvelous, happy, profound lectures on the nature of the universe and the natural growth of all things, animal, vegetable, and human. That month changed me forever.

My Mother had moved to the Dallas area to join my sister there and my brother and I followed. My Mother was without a doubt the smartest person I have ever known. She was the first woman to become one of the vice presidents of Dallas Title Company and ran on office in nearby Arlington. She rented a large two bedroom apartment in north Arlington so we could all get a fresh start in new surroundings. This was important for Phil too, since he had been arrested again in a dope raid at a house he had been staying in. He got off with only probation.

I gained employment at Parkland Hospital in Dallas and commuted on my trusty BMW motorcycle rain or shine, summer and winter. We joined a Kung Fu school and started working out with Sifu Biff Painter, who named his style Tao Chi Chuan. The focus was on self development, meditation, and exercise – not fighting. Sifu Biff became an important influence for both my brother and myself. He had an extensive library at the school, covering many ancient practices and principles from China, leading me toward the study of Acupuncture. A turning point.

I transferred from Parkland hospital to a Dallas Osteopathic hospital because it was smaller and did not treat many serious trauma patients. I did not even know what a Doctor of Osteopathy was. Of course the definition of the term was apparent: doctor of bones and joints. Assigned to the evening shift where it was usually not very busy, I had plenty of time to read charts, gossip with nurses, and continue my studies. One evening I was studying a book on acupressure written by a Japanese practitioner and one of the nurses commented that one of the Doctors practiced acupuncture. Maybe I could meet him and get some advice on finding a school of acupuncture. I was already known for giving competent acupressure treatments at the Kung Fu school and realized the importance of learning to locate all of the 365 principle acupuncture points.

I rented a decent apartment near the hospital in an area known as "lower Greenville" (avenue) which was undergoing a minor urban renewal. The neighborhood was becoming a center for artsy restaurants and upscale galleries. I liked it. There were plenty of parks and quiet areas for my habitual walks when not on duty at the hospital.

Work at Dallas Osteopathic Hospital was leisurely compared to Parkland. At Parkland I often was required to give as many as twenty IPPB treatments in an eight hour shift. Using three machines to treat two or three patients at the same time did not allow any time to give much attention to any one patient. At the Osteopathic hospital I usually had only three or four patients to treat and was able to provide much more personal care and could talk to the patients and get to know them. I enjoyed the social interaction. I even had time to meditate in the evenings in the chapel. Transcendental Meditation was as natural a part of my daily routine as brushing my teeth. Just like Pete.

One evening as I was strolling the hallways between treatments I passed a room where a Doctor was doing acupuncture. The patient was lying on her side and already had several needles protruding from the leg. The Doc was inserting a three or four inch hair-fine needle into her hip at a point I knew was called (in English) gall bladder 29. It was used for treatment of lower back and hip problems. I could see he had already put a needle into gall bladder 34, just below the knee. He was saying, "tell me when you feel this connect and go down your leg." The patient's leg gave a slight jerk and she replied, "yes. I feel electricity going down to my knee." "That's good, now just rest for a while and I'll be back in a few minutes," the Doctor replied. I was transfixed. Another turning point in my life.

Doctor McC. was well into his sixties, calm, polite and very widely educated. He told me he had learned acupuncture in France in the 1930's and practiced Osteopathy instead of regular "traditional" Medicine because he was allowed a wider range of options in the care of patients. At that time acupuncture was not at all respected by the AMA or the regular M.D. establishment. This was the first time I realized the misuse of the term "traditional medicine" when applied to the modern western approach. Acupuncture was "traditional." Modern practices were entirely experimental. Dr. McC. was way ahead of his time. He encouraged me to continue studying acupuncture and said he hoped eventually the U.S. medical establishment would catch up to the Europeans and the rest of the world. Interestingly, he had attended lectures in France given by a Vietnamese Doctor.

I began to actively search for an acupuncture school in the U.S. There was apparently a school in Boston and several in California. There was also a home study course offered by the Occidental Institute of Chinese Studies in Quebec, Canada. I ordered that course and began a systematic study. Already on the right track by learning all the points, I began absorbing the indications for the use of the points and more thoroughly understood the finer aspects of physiology and the flow of energy (chi) in the human body. Some of the ideas regarding the visualizations during Kung Fu exercises began to make more sense. I accepted the laws of acupuncture without question. Two thousand continuous years of explanations and observations by learned Chinese Physicians could not possibly be wrong.

I began incorporating acupressure treatments into my work with patients and learned how to explain some of the principles of Chinese physiology. Patients were more accepting than M.D.s. The American Medical Association dismissed acupuncture and reasoned that by eliminating pain, acupuncture might mask the symptoms of an underlying serious disorder. Even at that time, early in my studies, I countered that erroneous presumption by stating that the use of almost all the over the counter medications and most of the prescribed experimental medications given out by M.D.s were doing exactly what they objected to regarding acupuncture...alleviating symptoms without healing the underlying cause. An obvious example is habitual use of antacids for digestive symptoms instead of a change in diet. Another obvious ignorant mistake is blocking the pores with antiperspirants which leads to congestion of the lymph system and probably the formation of cysts and tumors. Maybe I was also becoming ahead of the times.

When I completed the acupuncture course and received a diploma from Occidental Institute they recommended I enroll in an intern program with one of their graduates. It was suggested I contact Michael Conneley in Santa Fe, N.M. and study with him for six months, then take their Master's Course, which would qualify me to practice acupuncture (in Canada). Researching Santa Fe, I discovered that a well respected Naturopath, Dr. J. Victor Scherer ran a massage school there and the idea of becoming a Naturopath first occurred to me. It seemed I might be headed to Santa Fe. I figured I could get a job as a respiratory therapist to support myself while continuing my studies.

A move to Santa Fe was postponed due to an opportunity to enroll at Maharishi International University in Fairfield, Iowa. It was a surprise that one of the teachers at the meditation center recognized my potential and suggested I would be a good teacher. Most of the teachers had gone to India to study with Maharishi and become certified teachers and the school in Iowa had just opened. The cost was $1500.00 for a three month course and included room and board. I decided to go. Living a simple life, I had saved up enough money.

So in late January of 1975, five years after the War and four years after prison, I decided to ride my motorcycle to Iowa. Crazy. After purchasing the best snowsuit available, dressed like a polar explorer, I headed out and arrived during a cold snap in the most severe conditions I had ever endured – twelve degrees with stiff gusty wind, patches of snow on the ground, and ice on the roadways.

Rather than see the icy beginning as an ill omen, this disciplined veteran practiced deep breathing techniques learned from a book on Tibetan Mysticism written by an Englishman renamed Chogyam Trungpa as I chugged into the parking lot in front of the registration building of what had been Parson's College. To the astonishment of many of the soft, pliant, sheltered TM'ers, a man had driven all the way from south Texas on a motorcycle to attend MIU. Their amazement immediately set me apart as an enigma...not of their kind. I made them nervous. This aspiring seeker of enlightenment, of surcease from suffering and depression did not exactly feel welcomed. I only felt different.

The practice of mantra meditation has been proven to be an effective method, used for millennia in India. In the Upanishads and other guides to enlightenment the aspirant is warned of dangers, often presented vividly as wildly accoutered demons. A student is repeatedly admonished to use certain powerful techniques only as directed by a master yogi. In other words, there are certain meditation practices that are considered to be as strong a stimulus as modern prescription psychotropic drugs or illegal psychedelics. "Side effects" could be recognized and corrected by one's Master, a yogi, whose advice could prevent madness, demons, and suicide. Meditation has always been considered to be a very serious undertaking when practiced in concentrated centers such as monasteries and temples and even mild forms of mantra-type practices should be done in a protected, secluded environment. It was for this reason that Maharishi International University had been situated in the quiet little city of Fairfield, Iowa, on the staid and respectable grounds of Parson's College.

I was a very serious aspirant and scrupulously adhered to the program of meditation, breathing practices and yoga postures. We practiced six to ten hours a day, interspersed with delicious vegetarian meals and delightful lectures by the Maharishi on videotape. During the first two months of the teacher training course I felt more wretchedly alone and isolated than ever. I did not sleep well, to put it mildly, and had vivid unsightly memories in my dreams that, even while still asleep, resolved to forget when I awoke. Trying to keep the box closed, nevertheless some photos would not stay in the box and some memories lingered on the edge of consciousness. Everyone around me was so calm and happy. I felt I was the only one suffering. Not one of the other 200 aspirants had served in the military. In fact, many of them were war protesters who had spit on and cursed the returning Vietnam veterans. The war was still occasionally in the news.

Within the TM movement, the ancient admonishments concerning the incursions of demons were re-explained under theories of "unstressing."- the release of tensions and negative experiences. The theory was that stress caused people to live in darkness and ignorance of our true nature which was pure bliss consciousness. Picture a baby laughing and taking ecstatic joy in the simplest things. Once one had released all the stresses one would live in Cosmic Consciousness and be as happy as a newborn child. It sounded too simplified and a bit phony to me. Maybe such a theory applied to ancient people living a very simple life. We were told that when we released certain stresses we might re-experience the emotions which occurred at the time of the stressful event. Great. Just when I thought I could forget.

Residents at the course were encouraged to seek counseling if we felt overwhelmed in any way. Though I doubted the validity of the theory of unstressing, I had read numerous accounts of similar explanations in ancient scriptures. So I bolstered my confidence in TM and tried to continue in a practice that seemed to help so many others. I only sought counseling once and was told that I would not feel so alone if I would just join in more and participate instead of hanging out alone. How simplistic. The counselor was a mild-mannered rich kid, younger that I was, whose main stress was probably being bullied in school or targeted during dodgeball. Maybe he had incurred immense stress at losing a volleyball game. That is how he impressed me. I doubted he was prepared to hear about my dreams or memories of combat. I am certain he had never been arrested smuggling pot or gone to prison. I did not mention my first powerful mantra "Oh **hell** no."

It was in this setting, with these doubts, that news of the fall of Saigon first fell on the ears of this Resigned Lieutenant. During the course it was emphasized that all worldly contacts be suspended: no reading of newspapers or magazines; definitely no watching television; and all residents were instructed to stay on the campus of Parson's College, the little town of Fairfield being considered too stressful for a meditator when engaged in the many hours a day of intensive practices. Deep personal relationships between participants were discouraged and even married couples were told to maintain separate quarters and refrain from sex during the 90 day teachers' training. "Maharishi says" that emotional sensitivities and vulnerabilities are acutely enhanced during the intense unstressing of the course. Rumors of strange, erratic, even suicidal behavior had occurred in previous courses.

Near the end of the course we were told that teacher training had been extended to require another three month course after we had interned at a TM center somewhere in the country. I was shocked and disappointed. I felt it was all a scam to make more money. The second three month course would cost $2500 – not $1500. Someone asked if the Maharishi would be coming to

Fairfield for the second part of teacher training. I for one had been hoping for a personal audience with him. The answer was somewhat vague and the smiling administrator suggested that we should try to go to India and meet him in the future. Another disappointment arose within me. Another lie and false expectation was revealed. Another failure to reach a satisfactory result in an endeavor. Shit.

I was returning from lunch one afternoon when I heard the familiarly strident voice of a television newscaster coming from one of the staff offices. Even before distinguishing the words it was obvious something very important had happened. Hushed silences were broken by cheering and applauding. I slipped into a doorway and beheld the memorable film clip of the last helicopter lifting off the roof of the American Embassy in Saigon, a sea of reaching hands and pained pleading faces surging around and under the aircraft. I saw the swarms of humanity on the grounds of the Embassy and in the streets of Saigon. This Resigned Lieutenant, who had resisted the war to the utmost of my ability, who had known the war was a lie when ranting to Jake and the other photographers in the Saigon Hilton on my last visit to that war-torn city, felt a grenade explode in my chest. I briefly wondered if I was going to die of a one-time fatal heart attack like my Father.

Fucking Dudley I hope you burn in hell...a foot flopping the stench that awful stench a neat round hole right through the chest a purple pumpkin for a face...Bert twitching spasmodically...   a   purple-tinged   Major   a   flat   black room...FUCKTHISSHIT! PAINT IT ALL BLACK AND DIE!

I stormed back to my room seeing red, hearing distant artillery, smelling blood and shit, and feeling blackness all around me. My eyes were streaming tears but I was not crying. My chest was heaving and straining but I could not draw a breath. *All for nothing we lost we lost...kill the Generals and fuck LBJ's beagle dog in the ass...it was all for nothing we lost.* After slamming my door with a tremendous BOOM I opened it and slammed it again even harder. I began pounding on a built-in desktop until it separated from the wall then used the desktop to smash a whole set of shelves. I grabbed one end of the bed and began slamming the whole bed on the floor until one leg was loose then snatched that leg off and started smashing out the window and bashing holes in the sheet rock walls. Within a minute or less I had demolished a newly-built dormitory room while neighboring students fled from the dorm in droves.

Finally I began crying so hard I could not inhale and flashed on the memory of willing myself to take a breath or die as I lay on the ground watching Bertocelli convulse limply nearby during the horrendous ground attack at Diamond II. When a deep breath became possible, I screamed so loud that it was heard in the Administration building a block away. I cried and ranted in my demolished quarters until I was paralyzed with exhaustion, then squatted in the corner watching all the photographic memories parade past my conscious mind.

When the campus police burst into the room I did not even notice. When they threw me on my face and handcuffed me I showed no resistance whatsoever and vaguely wished they would just shoot me and get it over with. I had no memory of being taken to the city jail. Completely separated from reality, I was living in an internal hell of anguish and pain. I demonstrated a completely new level of "unstressing" because I was uncovering stresses that were quite outside the normal civilian meditator. The curriculum was not designed to cope with combat veterans, a fact becoming increasingly obvious to the students and staff of MIU, the Fairfield police, and half the neighboring community on that troubling day.

This semi-insane resigned combat veteran regained my sense of the present when two guards entered my cell later that afternoon to escort me to some sort of examining room where a doctor asked me stupid questions and flashed lights in my eyes. I had no answers and hoped they would simply beat me instead of asking stupid questions. I had no answers anymore. I sat mute. I recited silently what could be remembered from the US Army Code of Combat regarding the priorities when captured by the enemy. "Escape" was the first demand I remembered. Escape as soon as possible and keep trying to escape at every opportunity. The chance would come soon, so I sat quietly ready. *Ranger style escape and evasion...oh yeah...chase me down you fat fuckin' cop. I dare you. Oh yeah...spring like a leopard and run like a deer.*

There were no further clauses or instructions I needed to remember. I sat still and I watched and listened. Sat like a cat in a cage, waiting, ready and single-minded. They had no idea of my capabilities.

I was initially diagnosed as schizoid/catatonic and the doctor said he did not think I posed any threat to myself or others and when I started coming back around to normal I would probably just want to talk and eat, not break any more furniture. He also diagnosed possible fractures in both hands, pending X-ray confirmation at the county hospital. Since I seemingly posed no further threat to the guards, they did not replace the handcuffs as they escorted me out of the clinic into the back parking lot. One deputy indicated an unmarked Ford Galaxy 500 and this wily prisoner stood limply waiting for the rear door to be opened, passing a "test" in the mind of the deputy who was trying to gauge the amount of vigilance required to keep this so-called dangerous Vietnam veteran in custody. So far the prisoner had been no trouble. He had no idea of the extent of that misconception.

We entered the county hospital and headed for a side corridor of the emergency room. As we passed an employee break room with numerous vending machines, one deputy decided to try out the doctor's theory and find out if the prisoner was hungry or would say he wanted anything. Any normal prisoner would ask for a coke or a candy bar at that point. Realizing the ruse, I relaxed and gazed out the window, across the parking lot towards a treeline about 300 meters away past a meadow. Beyond that there was nothing but rolling hills and clusters of trees becoming dim in the fading light of early evening – ideal for escape and evasion *if I can get that far without being shot.*

There was a fire exit about ten feet away and my heart started accelerating, but I remained outwardly calm as deputy number one came up munching on a muffin and eyeballing me. *You ignorant fat fucker, I could have your gun in a flash...you'd probably have to look for a place to set down your coffee and donut before drawing on me if I started running...shee-it.* Deputy number two chose that moment to indicate to his partner with a gesture that he was going to take a piss and he turned and walked down the short hallway and around a corner. Deputy number one indicated a chair to this prisoner and seated himself with a groan and a mouthful of muffin. This wily prisoner, of course, chose that moment to bolt. I sprang like a leopard across the hall and out the door in the blink of an eye. I was free, literally, before the cop had blinked twice.

I had once run a timed hundred yard dash in 9.8 seconds in high school and I had not slowed down very much in the nine years since then. I was out the door before the cop had put down his coffee cup and this leaping lieutenant was across the parking lot and into the meadow before the law had exited the building. By the time deputy one had reported the escape on the radio and deputy two had returned from a one-minute piss this exuberant escapee was approaching the treeline over 200 meters away without having slowed down or looked back in my headlong dash.

I paused and stepped behind a tree and looked back at the two uniformed officers of the law standing beside their vehicle literally scratching their heads, then their crotches alternately, and I laughed. I laughed and laughed then I got suddenly hungry. I got awfully hungry. But I proceeded with the mission immediately. *A ranger doesn't mind hunger...a ranger cannot be captured and held... a ranger survives, doing what must be done.*

I started moving in one direction in full view of the deputies and kept moving in that direction, which would have taken me out of the populated areas, then faded into the trees. Then I changed direction and sprinted back towards the town, soon chancing on a bike path that bordered a city park, which greatly accelerated and disguised my flight. I might have been a jogger out for a run before dinner. I focused on breathing evenly while traversing the park and found myself a block from the campus of MIU. Traveling about a mile and a half in less than ten minutes – no great athletic feat, but well beyond the expectations and response times of the local law since it would have taken that long to drive to the campus from where they were behind the hospital.

The police force had, by that time, mustered the only other squad car available and the four small town policemen were beginning to plan any actions they should take and which agencies they should contact at that point. As I approached my trusty BMW the two "responsible" deputies were still watching the treeline with binoculars and awaiting further instructions from their superiors.

Fortunately, this meticulous ex-officer had stored all my riding gear in the hard shell saddle bags, there being little storage space in the dorm room, and there was an extra key and a hundred dollar bill in the tool kit beneath the seat. I was suited up in jacket, gloves, boots and helmet within about a minute and the bike started faithfully at first the first touch of the button. *Fuckin' A. Smoothly cruisin'.*

It was not far to the State line on secondary highways where this exuberant escapee gassed up and bought some snacks, then immediately continued, driving smoothly within the speed limits and imagining I could become invisible through mental effort and secret techniques. When I stopped for gas the second time, this rapid ex-lieutenant was about to cross into Oklahoma. I called my one and only brother and tersely referred to the predicament. Phil gave the right co-sign and knew to prepare for an identity transfer...a TIP...Temporary Identity Transfer...a possibility we two brothers had plotted and planned while we were within the walls of El Reno Federal Prison in 1971.

We were about three years apart and bore a strong resemblance, depending on hair length, beard and mustache, etc. Phil was holding our "get away" bag containing duplicate current driver's licenses for each of us in which we had rehearsed giving the same expression for the photo. The bag also contained a few hundred dollar bills and some survival gear including an emergency medical kit and instruments that I had lifted during hospital work. As a combat veteran, I had also considered adding a gun, but had wisely deferred.

Back in Iowa, they had reached the conclusion that they could only watch the bus station, and that the airlines had been notified, and that "well, he would turn up." Since I held my motorcycle in high esteem, I had covered it soon after arriving on campus and had gradually shifted it around to an inconspicuous area of the parking lot. It would be four working days later before the Iowa State Police had my name and a description of the motorcycle. I was described as a Karate expert Vietnam veteran who had freaked out and no one could understand why. "Considered dangerous even when unarmed." I consider that a compliment.

Everybody wondered why a veteran could not be glad the war was over. The screening process for admission to MIU was altered as a result of my unarmed "mad minute," and many of the staff members expressed outright disbelief that any man could have destroyed so much furniture without any tools or anything in such a short time. Some of the students reported that they thought I was blowing up bombs or something, the booming and shaking of the neighboring rooms was so violent. It was so loud and violent they just could not believe it. It was completely outside their "box" of comprehension. Some said I seemed so quiet and so well-read; but they did not really get to know me. Few of them forgot me, that's for sure.

I might have been hard to forget, and was about to also be hard to locate and identify. This well read veteran/escapee possessed survival skills far beyond the average fugitive, not to mention the aforementioned look-alike brother. Phil had relocated into a rear garage apartment in Arlington, Texas and fortunately, had failed to notify his parole officer of his change of address. I parked the bike deep in the garage, entered the apartment behind my brother, lit up an immediately offered joint, sat down with a sigh, and said, "well man, the shit just got deeper."

"Time for the disappearing act, maestro?" Phil asked with a knowing grin.

"Time for the duplicitous duplication, my good-looking brother, ah yaas."

"Ah yaas," he replied, slipping as easily into his W.C. Fields imitation as I could. We plotted long into the night and proved that two stoned heads are better than one lately issued arrest warrant. The next day I rested, changed the oil on my bike, assembled my gear, and waited.. waited for an idea...for an influence or a sign. I breathed and waited, knowing full well that I could live in the world of unknowing until something came up and expecting it would not be long in coming. An avenue for an aspirant. I was a student waiting for a master to appear...a liberated man looking for a new rule book...looking for <u>my</u> group of outlaws.

Phil had continued his studies at the Kung Fu school and was increasingly impressed with Sifu Painter. I was not that interested in continuing with an American who claimed to be a great teacher of martial arts, however. I wanted to meet a Chinese Sifu and commit myself totally in the ancient manner, living each day immersed in exercises, meditation, medical training, and mysticism. I was ready to change my identity way beyond any previous plans, based on my disappointment with the TM movement coupled with a continuing thirst for personal enlightenment.

In the back pages of a martial arts magazine this earnest seeker read a vague reference to a real Taoist Master of Tai Chi and acupuncture in the Los Angeles area who had a school with the structure and priorities of true monastic living. I ordered a book written by this Master, Ni, Hua Ching, and recognized my path after reading Master Ni's translation of the <u>Tao Te Ching</u> which I found in a local bookstore. I ordered and received Master Ni, Hua Ching's two volume set entitled <u>8000 Years of Wisdom</u> and was committed to a plan to proceed. I would go to California again and study Tai Chi and acupuncture and maybe meet up with my band of outlaws...the ones who believed in making up their own rules...the name changers.

There were many miles of highway between Texas and California though, and many bridge abutments and high mountain passes to traverse along the way. I was well known, even to myself, as being a man who definitely had extreme ups and downs. I read a chapter in the Tao Te Ching before climbing aboard my heavily-laden motorcycle in the middle of that Year of Disappointment: 1975. The lesson randomly selected that day was clearly directed towards travelers and begins with: **A journey of a thousand miles begins with a single step.** The lesson ends with clear advice: **A man often gives up just before succeeding.** The Resigned One took heart from this ancient text and thought about an old, very old, Papasan out in a rice field panning water all day, and I stepped out smoothly on my way.

THE END   10 Feb. 1999

Author: Jeffrey Albert Lumbert, 1Lt. (resigned) 05347994

Thus ended my first effort at writing my story which I started in 1992 while a patient in the 90 day PTSD program in the psychiatric wing of the Miami VA Hospital. As mentioned, I had experienced many thoughts of writing my story throughout the years in the War and in the civilian world afterward. During a group counseling session in the PTSD ward the instructor suggested we write out a story about who we had been before enlistment, what happened in the War, and what we were like when we returned. It could be five sentences, five pages, or whatever. That night I wrote 50 pages, mainly concerning chapters I and II.

I expanded those notes in 1996 while living in a remote twelve-sided cabin near Alamo Lake, Arizona, designed and built by myself alone. The cabin is probably still located approximately 52 miles down a dirt track south of Yucca. I donated it to the Nature Conservancy Society when I left in '97. Though never having built a real bookshelf, I built that cabin alone and drove 82 miles to Kingman for supplies at the nearest hardware store. Making a list and not forgetting anything was obviously of paramount importance. The initial manuscript was typed on a manual portable typewriter bought in a pawn shop in Kingman. It came to about 120 pages.

Then I bought my first laptop and traveled to Costa Rica to transfer the typewritten pages to digital. That transfer brought the book to about 200 pages, roughly to the shape you have just read. I first transferred it to hard copy and copyrighted it when I returned in '99. While in Costa Rica and other countries in Central America I sought out and counseled other Vietnam veterans, most of whom were MIA from their families and the United States for years and years. I shamed a few of them to call home and arranged for a few to return and report in to a VA hospital. But that is a whole other book that may be in my future.

I allowed a few vets to read my story and the usual response was appreciation followed by the question: "Yeah, but what have you been doing since?" Okay. Here is what happened when I went to meet Master Ni, Hua Ching and a brief autobiography of the years 1975 – the present 2017.

Yeah, I certainly left this on the back burner for a long, long time. I have just spent a whole year editing and improving my mediocre writing style based on suggestions by several friends with much more knowledge of prose writing than I had. I hope it is a readable, honestly presented, and occasionally humorous presentation. Maybe it will be published and distributed.

CHAPTER VI

And Then What?

I left my brother in Arlington and drove very, very legally to California, not wanting to show my fake driver's license to law enforcement. For many reasons, among which the fact that Phil was on probation and was not supposed to be traveling, and also because I had no idea what possible situations he might get himself into day by day. I knew Master Ni was living somewhere in Santa Monica but did not have an exact address. A sudden desire arose to stop in Santa Fe, N.M. and meet a Naturopath, Dr. J. Victor Scherer.

Dr. Scherer was a seventy-something energetic, funny, and loving man who welcomed me and listened intently to my story. I told him of Vietnam, being wounded by a Howitzer, becoming a rebel, and resigning in disgust from the Army. He encouraged me to continue with TM and was very supportive of my desire to become an acupuncturist. He knew of Michael Connolly and said

I should definitely finish my internship with him. Legal licensing was about to be enacted in New Mexico so I should not waste any time completing my degree with Occidental Institute in Quebec. He instantly understood what I was trying to say before I even got the words out. I loved him immediately. He also encouraged me to go and meet Master Ni.

My journey continued with renewed joy and confidence. A person like Dr. Scherer had a naturally beneficial effect without trying. He was just himself...a highly advanced human being. He was a healer of more maladies and erroneous thinking than a person was even aware of. A saying from my studies of mysticism came to mind: when the student is ready, a Master appears. Just so.

I had an address in Santa Monica but had no idea how to negotiate the massive mess that is Los Angeles. Stopping at a "New Age" bookstore for no particular reason somewhere in the metropolis, I struck up a conversation with a feisty redheaded woman named Carolyn who worked in the store. She admired my BMW and made fun of the noisy Harley-Davidsons and called them "Hogly Davidsons" because that's what the guys riding them generally looked like. I told her of my quest and she was very interested and called a friend of hers who practiced Tai Chi.

After mentioning I was a Vietnam veteran presently practicing TM and working in health care in an effort to rehabilitate myself from wartime trauma she immediately went into a rant against the war protesters who were cursing and assaulting the returning veterans at the airport. She said they were giving the Peace Movement a bad name. Wow! How insightful, I thought. Amazingly enough, her friend knew of Master Ni and came right down to meet me and help out.

Following the young man's directions, who by the way also practiced TM but was seeking other methods, I eventually found the house in a rich neighborhood somewhere in what was called Santa Monica, although it all seemed the same to me – immense, confusing, and hectic. On entering the residence the atmosphere changed dramatically to serenity. The people there were happy, welcoming and beautiful. They seemed very calm yet focused. I was served a delicious lunch in a joyous dining area. Several of them understood my story like Dr. Scherer had – almost before I had completed three sentences. There had been other Vietnam veterans who had come to seek out Master Ni. No one in that household expressed any negativity towards me. One beautiful woman said that protesting the war was like fighting darkness... it is better to just be a source of light. Whew. How immediately reinforcing and encouraging they were! My chest expanded with light and it was hard not to cry with relief.

People came and went at internals during the afternoon. It was explained to me that Master Ni did not allow anyone to stay for long and did not permit "guru groupies." I was welcome to stay for three days and told that Master Ni would see me eventually and probably give me a "life reading" or an acupuncture treatment. One treatment. They showed me to a room I would share with three other young men, all of whom were seriously studying Chinese mysticism, Tai Chi, and meditation. We four got along marvelously without much conversation. There was simply acceptance and not a single negative word was spoken by anyone on any subject whatever. I was almost jealous of their apparent development and briefly wondered if I deserved to even be there.

Master Ni taught that every person was already perfect. Acupuncture, exercises and meditation just removed blocks in energy flow and spiritual growth was as natural and inevitable as the growth of a tree or the opening of a flower. One need not go anywhere but within.

The day came when Kwan Yin, one of the name-changed Americans, came to inform me that Master Ni would see me. Maybe three or four days had passed in that serene environment. I had lost track of time. She led me to a remote room in the back of the house I did not even know existed.

Master Ni, Hua Ching was seated in a normal chair behind a small desk. There was the scent of sandalwood in the room and a small candle was lit on the desk. There was also a treatment table and a shelf with acupuncture supplies. Master Ni smiled and indicated a chair. He looked at me with eyes that conveyed wisdom, love, and power. I had never seen such eyes. He asked, "tell me a story about your life."

I did not know where to begin. I told him about Vietnam, about being blown up, my attempts at TM, giving up on aviation, and I cannot remember what else. I stopped, stuttered, and felt lost in his powerful gaze. He said, "tell me about that scar on your head, young warrior." I began to explain the ground attack and what a Howitzer was and what beehive fleshettes were. He said, "it was a mistake, yes?" I had barely even begun to explain and probably was going into a rant about the whole thing, as usual; but realized he already knew. He knew me after two minutes. He understood more about me than anyone who had known me for years. His love, understanding, and total forgiveness washed over me and I began to cry. He gently touched my shoulder and I stopped. Then he indicated the table and I lay down on my back.

I breathed naturally and instantly relaxed. I might have been almost asleep within seconds when I felt his warm hands approach my face and a hot finger begin touching various places on my head. It seemed gentle warm hands were supporting my wrists and ankles though I had not heard anyone else enter the room. Master Ni began gently stimulating acupuncture needles in my head and face. I did not know he had inserted any needles at all. "Do you feel some electricity here?" I felt it all right. Then he touched needles he had somehow inserted in my wrists and ankles and neural pathways became energized with electrical charges that raced through my body. A deep meditative calmness enveloped me and I drifted in the indefinable brief gap between cognitive thoughts. I felt completely empty yet somehow whole. A fantastic light show was appearing behind my closed eyes. It was the most enjoyable experience I had ever imagined.

I think he touched the needles again in my head and face, then in my wrists and ankles but I could not be sure. I was just cruising in the infinite nothingness of the universe. When he told me to open my eyes it was amazing to realize that nobody had been cradling my wrists and ankles. The Master was placing about twenty or thirty used needles into a cotton ball. I never felt him insert a single needle.

I got off the table feeling not only lightheaded, but light bodied. Words fail me in expressing how different I felt. An immense surge of gratitude and love erupted in my chest and tears streamed down my face though I was not crying. Somehow Kwan Yin knew to enter and escort me back to my room where I lay down and enjoyed ecstatic relaxation such as I had never imagined could happen.

The next day I prepared to leave and thanked everyone I had briefly known. No one told me to leave, the situation had just developed to a natural conclusion. I did not fully realize the extent of the changes in my nervous system and perspective on life until years later. For about five years or so **I forgot** I was a Vietnam veteran! There were no dreams about the war, I never even thought to mention it, just forged ahead in my studies towards acupuncture and health care with new found confidence and purpose. Master Ni lifted memories and trauma from my being on a deep and profound level. Right now, forty years later, when I think of him my chest surges with love and appreciation and my eyes form tears. Any possible explanation falls far short of the effect of one acupuncture treatment from Master Ni, Hua Ching. And that was not the one and only time he would alter my life and future.

When motoring along on my BMW back to Santa Fe, N.M., I felt more happy, relaxed, and confident than ever in memory. There were no doubts towards a future in natural health care. A definite plan was not necessary. Cosmic intelligence would guide me to where ever was best and no more effort was needed than the effort a flower exerts to bloom. There was a natural awareness of each breath without conscious effort and everything seemed brighter and more in focus visually. It seemed even the bike ran smoother. I could express a thousand metaphors and still not explain adequately.

Dr Scherer was glad to see me and immediately said I looked completely different than a week before. He took me on as a personal student and assistant. The massage school he had established years before was filling up beyond all expectations and he had hired a couple from New York to come to Santa Fe and organize the school in a new location in a large house on the road up to the ski basin. He usually taught about a dozed students in a nine month course after which they could take the state licensing exam. In the fall of 1975 there were ninety students seeking admission. I met a recently graduated Chiropractor, Dr.

Bob C., who had been one of Dr. Scherer's massage therapy students a few years before and would be one of the instructors at the new location.

Dr. C. and I became immediate friends and he was very impressed when I gave him an acupressure treatment. He was known affectionately as "B.C." by Dr. Scherer and preferred the term instead of "Doctor." He did not mind the humorous hint that he looked like the comic strip character of the same name. B.C. would become everyone's favorite instructor and almost instantly had a busy Chiropractic practice. He invited me to join his practice as I continued my acupuncture internship with Michael C. in his quickly blossoming practice at his own office in downtown Santa Fe. I was already very involved in natural health care before the massage school even started.

Michael C. and several other acupuncturists were practicing without any form of licensing, based on a diploma from a recognized school and their own brazen initiative. Among them was a serene and loving man named Daniel S., also from California where he had learned about Chinese Herbal Medicine as well as acupuncture. He was aptly named (of the Saints in Spanish) and I greatly admired and respected him. It was expected that when the State licensing board organized the testing procedures they would be "grandfathered" in and granted automatic licenses. As it turned out, the test would not be conducted until almost two years later and they would have to take the exam like everybody else. I was not approved to take the test and had to join a local school recently opened by a man named Stuart W. who had graduated from a school in San Francisco, California.

When I first met Stuart W. I noticed he was carrying a copy of Mao Tse Tung's <u>Little Red Book</u> in his hip pocket. Jesus Christ, I thought, he's a fucking communist! That's what we were fighting against in Vietnam and in a general sense worldwide. I did not like him, to say the least. He was obese, filthy, had disgusting body odor, and long, unkempt scraggly hair and beard. Even more disturbing to me was the fact that all the women simply adored him. **UGH!** That was yet another part of the "hippy movement" that I had no part in whatsoever...personal filthiness and total disregard of decent clothing and polite manners. He was simply gross.

Dr. Scherer and B.C. assured me I did not have to attend the massage school and could practice under their auspices without my own massage therapy license. Dr. C. showed me how to do most of the spinal adjustments done in the practice of Chiropractic in about two afternoon sessions. He joked that ninety percent of Chiropractic school concerned how to promote one's business and make a lot of money. Michael C. taught me needling technique and said I had natural talent. Before long, I was giving acupuncture treatments and chiropractic adjustments to both B.C. and Dr. Scherer. I had a diploma "with honors" from Occidental Institute of Chinese Studies and completed their Master's Course in acupuncture when I was denied the "privilege" of taking the State of New Mexico acupuncture licensing exam. They said I had to graduate from a local recognized school. In other words, to my dismay, disgust, and extreme disappointment, I had to join the school started by Stuart W. Despite my recent apparent progress in personal spiritual development, I was still having trouble with goddamned authorities. Shit.

I worked really hard at forgiveness towards Stuart and joined his school as a first year student in the two year curriculum. He had no idea of my initial impressions of him. To his credit, he recognized my previous studies and reputation and allowed me to challenge the first year final exam. I passed easily. They were still trying to learn the names, indications, and locations of the points which I had learned years before. As soon as the second year final exam was constructed I challenged that and passed. Stuart appointed me as an instructor with a specialty in point location and needling technique. My total time in classroom studies at Southwest Acupuncture College was about two months. I took and passed the next State of New Mexico acupuncture exam and was formally licensed in 1982. My lack of certified classroom hours in a recognized school would become yet another blockade years later when I tried to obtain licensing in other states. Oh well.

I began practicing massage and acupressure out of a small house. I met a gay couple, Larry and Gene, who owned a ritzy furniture store and interior decorating service and they became my first reliable weekly clients for massage therapy. They helped me greatly by recommending me to many wealthy friends. I soon had a good practice, treating over twenty patients a week for an average of $25.00 each. Plenty of money since I still lived like a monk. I continued having lack of success dating or entering a serious relationship with women and still did not have a close friend of either sex.

I became popular among several wealthy Santa Fe restaurant owners and through their recommendations met quite a few famous Hollywood actors and movie personnel. Among them: Larry Hagman (J.R. from Dallas), the songwriter and performer Roger Miller, the comedian Buddy Hackett, and Kevin Klein, whom I did not recognize and had not seen any of his recent movies. One of my favorite students, Karina, was "sitting clinic" during her second year of school. (A student would spend a day at my clinic and sit quietly watching as I gave treatments). Karina was a vivacious fun-loving tri-athlete and my hiking buddy on many occasions. She came into my treatment room from the waiting area looking starry-eyed and told me my next patient was ready and that he was Kevin Klein.

The man said he was having lower back pain due to riding horses on a movie set near Santa Fe. I had him strip to his shorts and lie on the table. I had already worked on several members of the film crew during the making of the film Silverado, a comic western spoof. As I was poking around on his back determining which points were sore, I asked, "so, uh, what do you do in the movie?"

He raised up and turned his head to the side and replied humbly, "well, I'm sort of one of the stars. Have you seen Sophie's Choice?...A Fish Called Wanda?"

"No. I don't have much time for movies. Sorry. You're just another butt on the table to me." And I pulled down his shorts a bit and dug into his gluteal area. Karina could not hide a wide-eyed grin and I knew she would later report to fellow classmates that she had seen Kevin Klein's crack.

I also worked on many members of the Santa Fe Ballet and greatly appreciated seeing strong well developed legs. I could also see how much ballet dancers suffered at practicing their craft and how they literally deformed their feet. They are serious committed athletes, though, and as aerobically fit as any person in any sport. I enjoyed free tickets to several performances.

One day I answered the phone and a gruff voice announced, "this is Stanley Marcus. I understand you are the best acupressurist in Santa Fe. How about coming out to my little chateau this evening to give my wife and me a treatment?" I did not make the connection until he added, "ever been to my store in Dallas?" Oh yeah, Marcus of...Neiman and.

"Yes sir, I certainly know of your store and I have read your opinion column in the Dallas newspaper. What time do you want me to come up?"

I gave Mr. Marcus and his beautiful wife several acupressure treatments during the next week or so and he complimented my work and said he had a Chinese practitioner in Hong Kong and I was as good as he was. Then he gave me an even more impressive compliment by offering me a job on his yacht during a one month cruise in the Mediterranean. Like many wealthy Hollywood people, Stanley Marcus received a massage every day. I had to turn him down, though, because I was one of three instructors at the acupuncture school. Missed a big opportunity there, I'm sure. Mr. Marcus paid me three hundred dollars cash for each time I visited his "little" chateau on the mountain road to the ski basin above Santa Fe, which was twice my normal rate. He insisted.

I did finally meet a young woman who came to Santa Fe to further her massage training. She had already been practicing for several years. I became very serious with her and eventually even married her in a ceremonial manner – not legally. Almost right after becoming "married" and living together, she gained about thirty or forty pounds of weight and started exhibiting more sleep problems than I had. She seemed sweet and innocent. As I knew her better, she revealed that she had a serious cocaine habit and had lived with a mid-level dealer in Detroit. She said they used to engage in knock-down fistfights as often as they had raucous sex. She would awaken at night screaming about someone in the room, then immediately fall back asleep and not remember anything in the morning. Shit...I could not handle it.

She never cooked a single meal during our months together. We ate out. I usually made breakfast. We split up and she later came over to my house and attacked me viciously after attending a "women's support" group and telling a bunch of lies about me, saying that I had beat her, substituting me for her former boyfriend to gain sympathy. I found out she was on strong anti-depressant drugs when her psychiatrist (a woman of course) called me and told me it was all my fault and that I had been the reason my "ex" was suicidal. What the hell was I to do? There was nothing I could do about it.

Meanwhile, in the late '70's and into the 1980's, Santa Fe became a Mecca for "new age" mature hippies, lesbians from California and New York, and every conceivable variety of strange social experiments in mysticism, feminism, and weird pseudo gurus and inventors of special newly discovered methods of self-development: Crystal healing, Peruvian chakra whistles, fake Tibetan breathing and tantric sex practices, hot stone healing, and others too unbelievable and weird to mention. Traditional methods like I practiced became passé and obsolete. Everyone wanted the latest technique dreamed up in California. Then AIDS became apparent and rampant and everyone was afraid of needles. I did not belong in Santa Fe any longer. I had been there for about eight years and wondered where to go next.

I entered the food co-op one day and, while ducking the hostile stares from the thin-lipped lesbians and furious feminists who had taken over the place, I saw a poster on the wall advertising a weekend seminar given by Taoist Master Ni, Hua Ching in, where else but Taos, New Mexico. I signed up. This was in 1986, about eleven years after I had met him in California.

If I could recount, recall, or explain what Master Ni said during two days of lectures and responses to varied questions by a group of about thirty stunned listeners, I could explain every facet of human existence since the dawn of time and what the universe was before time began. There is no such "thing" as time anyway. Time is a human invention. Read Stephen Hawking's <u>A Brief History of Time</u> and if you can understand that the title is a triple entendre then you might understand Einstein and the universe. I do not. I understood how little I knew after listening to Master Ni, Hua Ching.

The sponsor of the seminar announced we could sign up for a "life reading" or an acupuncture treatment by Master Ni the next day. The cost was one hundred dollars. Cash. She further explained that we should have two or three questions in mind before we enter the small room to meet the Master because most people are too awestruck to think straight when meeting him face to face, one on one. She cautioned that if we just sit and smile at him he will simply sit and smile back. I paid the money and thought about three questions. When Master Ni had looked directly at me during the lecture I had the distinct impression he remembered me from years before. When I went before him the next day, I realized that ten years or ten days or ten minutes were the same to him and he remembered me clearly. I almost forgot my questions.

He was seated again in an ordinary chair behind a small desk with a candle burning and the scent of sandalwood in the room. He smiled and indicated a chair. He asked me almost the same question as last time. "Tell me a story about your life, young warrior. What have you been doing since we last spoke?" His English had improved. His memory was so absolute there was no room for improvement.

"I have been meditating and studying and practicing acupuncture, Master Ni. I have two questions. Do you think a person like me, a westerner, can ever learn how to understand taking pulses for diagnosis? And, Master Ni, what is the reason I have so much trouble finding a lasting relationship with a woman?"

"You should go elsewhere to find a woman. Women come here for fire and metal. You need to live where there is water and wood. (Referring to the Chinese theory of the five elements) You must continue to take pulses in every patient for many years and understanding will come."

"Go elsewhere?"

"Yes. Live where there is water and wood."

"Uh...but Master Ni, I have somehow become an instructor at an acupuncture school and classes will begin next month."

"Do you have family here?"

"No sir...but..."

"Do you have a car?"

"Yes sir...but..."

The Master leaned forward and his hypnotic eyes became stern. "Do you have a suitcase?"

"Master Ni, you are saying I should leave Santa Fe?"

"Yes. You should go. GO!"

He sat back and closed his eyes. I understood the life reading was over and left the room in a daze. I left Santa Fe within a week.

I had made several friends among the acupuncture students during the nearly two years of being an instructor. One very good female friend was Maggie B., from Ketchum, Idaho where she had practiced massage with a Chiropractor for many years. She was one of the few people I told of my departure from Santa Fe. I had no idea where to go. Maggie suggested I come to Idaho to attend her wedding and perhaps continue my practice there.

In Idaho I met one of Maggie's nieces, Kristi, who lived and practiced martial arts in Portland, Oregon with a well-known instructor, Al Dacascos. There was state licensing in Oregon so I followed Kristi and moved to Portland. Just like that. It does not take long to tell the story. I became the team "doctor" and traveled with Sifu Dacascos to several martial arts tournaments in the great Northwest. There was definitely a lot of water and woods out there and I applied to take the next licensing exam and practice in Oregon. However, the usual difficulties with authorities occurred and I was denied licensing because I had not attended enough certified classroom hours at a recognized school. Another disappointment!

I called another woman friend who had come to Santa Fe to study at the acupuncture school. Jan G. lived and practiced massage therapy in Tallahassee, Florida. I was certain Florida had a licensing program in place, so I moved. Just like that. Clear across the country. As bad luck would have it, the Florida Board of Professional Licensing had a lot of complaints about the poor quality of the previous exam in acupuncture and suspended all future tests until the National exam for acupuncture was formally adopted. That would take almost two years to accomplish. I hooked up with a Chiropractor again for a while, but other adventures intervened.

I lived in a tent outside Jan's house west of Tallahassee and became acquainted with many of the local rural neighbors, among whom was a famous marijuana grower known as "Leebo." I omit his real name for reasons which will become obvious. Leebo and I became expert partners at horse shoe pitching, a game popular with a wide variety of local residents, almost all of whom were weed smokers and occasional cultivators. This was towards the end of 1987.

One day, after we had known each other for months, Leebo approached me with a proposition. "I know a lady from Columbia who comes to the U. S. every now and then to ensure proper delivery of coke. I gave her a sample of my home-grown sensemilla weed and she wants me to come to Columbia and teach them to grow high quality pot. Want to come along? All expenses paid." (Sensemilla marijuana is accomplished by extirpating all the male plants, thereby causing the females to put all their energy and resin into the flowering buds instead of into seeds, thus the term "sensemilla" which means "without seeds" in Latin.)

I thought about it for about five seconds as Leebo continued his reasons for asking. "You speak Spanish, right? You're a 'Nam vet and have been in jungles, right? You got nothing really to do until next year when you get licensed."

"Yeah. Okay. Why not?" Leebo explained that he had close friends in Georgia who made two or three flights a year in a twin- engine Beechcraft airplane to bring back marijuana and if we grew a ton of pot they would bring it back for us. For half the load, carrying charges. These Georgia "good ole boys" were farmers who had pilot licenses and would file a flight plan for the Bahamas, then file an open flight plan for island hopping in the Caribbean. Then they would stop in at a reliable contact in Columbia, pick up a ton of weed, and fly back to Georgia. On the way, they would fly over a relative's large land holdings and kick out the weed, then have their own marijuana-sniffing dogs go out into the woods and find the pot. They had been doing it for years. Sounded reasonable to me.

I had to help Leebo obtain a Social Security card and a Passport. He had never had a real job and had grown and sold marijuana since the eighth grade in school. We were both about 40 years old at the time. So we went to Santa Marta, Columbia, on the north coast of the country, and were met by his friend, Beatrix L., at the airport in Barranquilla who escorted us to a luxurious apartment in the nearby party town of El Rodadero, which was like the Ft. Lauderdale of Columbia. Quite an eye opener!

Beatrix introduced us to her boss and associate, Jose A., who was a powerful mid-level transporter of goods in Columbia. What "goods?" We did not ask, of course. Jose was amicable, owned a large dairy farm on the northeast coast of Columbia near the border with Venezuela, was married to a school teacher from a rich influential family, and lived a respectable life. He and his relatives would be our protectors and guides in the endeavor. One of their jobs involved the securing of a remote airstrip which was "rented" out by various groups who thereby were confident in a safe transferring of money and goods. They were already rich on the cocaine trade and probably adopted Leebo and me as an amusing hobby. We were very well treated.

I showed up carrying a black doctor's bag full of acupuncture supplies and a left-handed Gibson guitar, and Leebo was a long-haired hippy farmer with a face all scarred up from a car accident years before. Suffice to say, we were not suspected of being DEA agents. We entered Columbia, South America carrying a six-cell flashlight full of Leebo's special hybrid marijuana seeds and another flashlight full of his high quality weed. We smuggled weed <u>into</u> Columbia. That was completely nuts, come to think of it in hindsight. But we did it.

One of the cousins of the family showed Leebo and me to an apartment where we would live during the month or so while a site was selected and secured for the weed growing operation. He led us upstairs to a two bedroom area and opened one of the unlocked doors. Inside were tables on which were about 160 kilo bricks of cocaine wrapped in plaster-of-paris and drying beneath heat lamps and fans. Carlos said, "aqui no entren," (here you do not enter) as he touched his revolver he habitually carried in his waistband with the barrel stuck down beside his dick.

Carlos then politely showed us the other spacious bedroom, casually opened a bottom dresser drawer, pulled out a kilo of coke, broke it open on the edge of the dresser, and said with a smile, "aqui duermen y pueden usar esta." (Here you sleep and you can use this). So we snorted pure Bolivian flake, played about a thousand games of backgammon, and shot a thousand games of pool across the street at a bar while drinking excellent Colombian beer which cost about seven cents each and came ice-cold in wide-mouthed eight ounce bottles. We did not mind waiting for the preparation of our farming situation. Shit, what a life! A maid came in every other day and cleaned up and another woman prepared breakfast and supper for us during the month or so in El Rodadero.

The day came when we met Victor, who would be our guide and protector in the coming months. If ever a person is traveling in a possibly dangerous foreign land, it is recommended that one chose a guide with a strong name like Victor. No worries, mate. Victor carried his pistol in his waistband in the back. They all carried guns. We proceeded to drive in a brand new Isuzu Trooper to the beautiful city of Bucaramanga, Columbia, a city I'm sure W.C. Fields would have loved to tell a story about. For the pronunciation. Victor checked us into the Hotel Balmoral. I did not see any money change hands. Then we drove up into the mountains to the east in the deluxe Isuzu Trooper and arrived at a small village where the dirt lanes were populated with more horses and burros than automobiles. Victor secured several horses and we set out up a mountain trail through a rain forest. Leebo and Victor rode, I walked.

It was possibly four or five miles up a winding trail to a settlement with very crude houses and barns, populated by farmer-peasants who greeted us like visiting royalty. It was embarrassing to be treated better than I thought we deserved. On the side of the steep mountain there were terraced former coffee tree plantings which had been cleared out for our endeavor. There were about a thousand newly dug holes about two feet wide and two feet deep where the soil had been fluffed up. Leebo and I examined the soil with his Ph and mineral test kit and he said they would need to burn some wood and put a shovelful of ashes in each hole to adjust the acidity and phosphorus levels...or

397

maybe it was nitrates. After issuing orders concerning this immense and meaningful task to the humble farmer, we went back down the hill to the hotel. Victor said he would return in about a week and we should just relax and enjoy. Meanwhile we ate meals in a very nice dining room and strolled the streets of Bucaramanga, called "city of parks." The staff of the hotel were respectful and it was difficult to convince them to even accept a tip for their services. I theorized that the Family, our sponsors, were feared in the manner one recognized in third world countries. I felt sympathy for the hotel employees and gave them tips and gratitude while I improved my language skills. It was great. Felt like a plan that was working.

Victor returned a week later and we proceeded up to the farm as before and Leebo said the soil was ideal. We placed three seeds in each plot, watered them, hoped for occasional rain, blessed the sunny hillside, and returned to Bucaramanga. The farmer would assure regular watering if it did not rain enough. That was all there was to it. My buddy Leebo was ecstatic. He had always dreamed of such an opportunity. Victor drove us back to El Rodadero on the coast and we resumed residence in the apartment. I peeked into the other bedroom and all the bricks of cocaine were gone. However, our own gift was still available in the bottom dresser drawer. More backgammon and pool, and strolls on the beach watching the locals enjoy fun and sun. Fantastic. We were growing a ton of pot in Columbia. Wow.

About three weeks passed before Victor took us back up to the farm. The seedlings had sprouted marvelously and were already about ten inches high. Leebo said he had never seen such rapid growth. We congratulated the peasant/farmer and, with the help of Victor as translator, I asked if there was anything I might bring up next time as a gift. The man humbly asked for a better radio so he could follow futbol games...that's soccer to us Americans. I bought a nice transistor radio in the city for him. He was so appreciative it was embarrassing.

Leebo had bought a house a month before we left and his girl friend, Jennifer, was living there. She was a tall, skinny barmaid who I did not trust at all. A cokehead for sure. A problem arose and my buddy had to go back to Florida to straighten out something concerning the house. He did not specify and I suspected she had run out of cocaine. We arranged for me to call him at a certain time at the bar where Jennifer worked. Meanwhile I arranged a ride up to the village from the city and hiked up to the plantation to check on the plants every week or so.

In order to call Leebo I had to catch a taxi in Bucaramanga and go to the one and only telephone center where you could make international calls. The Family had single side band radios they used to contact people in the U.S. but I thought it best not to use that pathway. Anyway, that would require a long bus trip back to Santa Marta, so I learned how to make phone calls from Bucaramanga. It was quite a process. I phoned him only at certain times, person-to-person, with a phony name. Jennifer would make it a point to answer the phone at the bar where she worked at five o'clock on a Wednesday, our specified time. A month went by and Leebo either was not there, or stalled when I asked when he would return.

Our marijuana had grown amazingly fast. It was about three feet high and I could begin to distinguish the male and female plants. It was important to eradicate the males as soon as they showed their genitals so they would not pollinate the whole crop. If pollination occurred, seeds would be produced and the whole crop was less powerful. Yes, there are some plants which have distinct sex organs. Look it up in High Times magazine. I educated the farmer and one of the cousins of the Family to recognize the males. They felt it was a waste to destroy some of the plants, but I convinced them.

It might be hard for young people nowadays to realize what it was like to make simple phone calls before cellular phones. When the plants were about seven weeks along and doing very well, I decided to go back to Santa Marta to reconnect with the head of the Family to issue a report. I called Leebo on our schedule and me gave me bad news. "The bird is dead. Come home."

I understood he was talking about the aircraft owned by his Georgia friends. "You cannot be serious. Everything here is fantastic. Fix it."

"There's no fixing it, man. I am wiring you five hundred to come home."

"Oh fuck no. I am staying. I will call again in one week. Fix it. Out."

After an anxious week I called again and Leebo repeated what he had said. "There is no way to fix the problem. Come home."

So I returned to the U.S. empty-handed and disappointed. The brothers from Georgia had made a run and encountered engine trouble and bad weather. They had performed an emergency landing in Nicaragua during their civil war. The plane was shot up by the Sandinistas and one of the brothers was killed. The guerillas then confiscated everything, fixed the engine, put the deceased in a body bag and told the surviving brother to get the hell out and feel lucky. That was the end of their enterprise. I had never even met them. We had no reliable way to transport our crop. Fuck a duck.

My buddy and I finally laughed about the whole thing and congratulated each other on our miraculous and bold attempt. We did teach the Colombians how to grow sensemilla marijuana. We did escape with our lives. We were not captured by the rebel forces in Columbia and held for ransom. We did not get arrested. We had a hell of a story to tell to select friends at a much later date. Amazingly enough, I was not even searched when I went through the Miami airport after spending five months in Columbia, South America, when even a casual check with the

FBI would have revealed my sordid and questionable past. Whew! Amazing. It would not happen today.

As my personal luck would have it, I arrived just in time to apply for licensing in Florida. They would use the test approved and administered by the National Board of Acupuncture which I had already passed years before. To insure I would be included in a "grandfather" clause for admission to the exam I sent in copies of over five thousand treatments I had given while in practice in Santa Fe for eight years. My application was over three inches thick. I passed the exam. The audacity of my application caught the eye of one Harvey K. who lived and practiced in the splendid city of Sarasota, Florida.

Harvey contacted me and asked if I would be interested in taking over his practice for a few weeks so he could get married and go on honeymoon. He was connected with an acupuncture school in Tampa and he had already cleared it with them for me to take over his classes there. So I had an automatic entrance to practice in Florida. Oh my lucky stars! I moved to Sarasota.

The students in Tampa were in their second year of training and, much to my astonishment, could not accurately locate the acupuncture points. They had memorized invisible dots on the skin but could not precisely needle a point. The points are not on the surface of the skin. They are down in the muscles amid the nerves and tendons. I taught them to press the points until their classmates winced, then release the pressure and visualize where the point was situated. They had not been taught this technique. We spent every class with me putting dots on skin and them pressing and visualizing. They learned where the points were located: how deep to penetrate, how to avoid blood vessels and tendons, and how to insert a needle painlessly and accurately. I completely changed their idea of what and where the acupuncture points were.

Meanwhile, as I gave treatments to Harvey's patients, they commented that my needling technique was much different that what they had been used to. They felt electric sensations and appropriate aching when I stimulated the needles. They told me they had seldom felt that from Harvey's treatments. Make a long story short: I succeeded in stealing a good many of his patients and was assisted in establishing my own practice. Harvey K. was completely beside himself and called me issuing curses and threats for weeks after his return. I laughed.

I began giving a combination massage, acupressure, and acupuncture treatments to several very wealthy people at their homes, which Harvey had refused to do. He disdained giving massage and hired others for massage at his clinic. Home visits became my main practice and, thanks to the example of Stanley Marcus, I charged much more than I was accustomed to in Santa Fe. In no time at all I had ten regular clients per week and charged a cool ninety dollars per visit. Naturally many chose to pay me in cash and gave me a hundred.

I joined a successful massage therapy business and was naturally given referrals. I quickly built up a steady practice at a well known location. I also began giving lectures at two local massage schools on the use of powerful Chinese Liniments, which not many people outside of martial arts knew about.

I lived and prospered in Sarasota and eventually rented a small apartment on Siesta Key. One of the students from the acupuncture school in Tampa, Marilee M., became attached to me since she lived in Sarasota and she decided to become an intern for me. She said the school in Tampa had not provided very much practical experience so she decided to watch me give treatments and provide whatever help she could. I did not ask her and had little to do with her decision. She was extremely smart and nobody told her what to do or not to do. I very much enjoyed her company and her contribution to the patient care environment. She was a natural healer and intended to become a midwife, among other goals. There was no doubt she would do whatever she set her brilliant mind to.

Marilee knew a psychologist in Miami who was starting a program giving acupuncture to inmates in Florida prisons to help them with drug addictions. For various reasons, I had become aware of being a veteran after almost forgetting for years due to the power of Master Ni. I had begun counseling at a local vet center because it was becoming obvious there were personality issues and sleep disorders still troubling me. I correctly surmised that some of the inmates in the Florida prison system were probably veterans, so I became interested in the possibility of providing help.

So when Marilee moved to Miami and told me the program was going to proceed, I followed and slept on a couch in an apartment she and Ian, her Irish husband, had rented. Ian was a fine man and was also very smart and interested in helping in the program.

The program was run by a thin-lipped angry feminist, however, who only wanted to start up a way of cashing in on a government subsidized endeavor. She did not give a damn about any men who were locked up and wanted to initially limit enrollment to female prisoners only. She was involved with an absolutely hateful lesbian who immediately disliked me. Whoa! I put the brakes on and wondered about returning to Sarasota.

It might seem I just drifted like a pinball without rational thought. My rational thinking was that I would be led by the forces of good if my intentions were correct and I continued in my several spiritual practices...Transcendental Meditation, breath awareness and visualizations according to Chinese traditions, and yoga and regular exercises. Therefore I made no intentional plans. I let the Universe decide for me. I was unafraid of the great void of unknowing and still had the survival skills taught by the US Army Rangers. I flowed with the river of life and trusted in unplanned outcomes.

Harvey K. contacted me one day to inform me that an acupuncture program at a small para-medical college in Ft. Lauderdale was suddenly without a director and he had recommended me to the owner of the school, Patricia W.

Perhaps he had gotten over his justifiable anger at my incursion into his practice or maybe he was insuring I had some place to go besides Sarasota. Either way, he did me a favor and we exchanged best wishes.

I contacted Ms. W. and we had an interview over lunch at a restaurant in Ft. Lauderdale. She was a dynamic, very intelligent and altruistic human being originally from Barcelona, Spain. The school was called Barna College. The people of Spain referred to Barcelona as "Barna." The school she operated catered to students needing loans and grants for their education and conducted courses in Nursing Assistant, X-ray technician, EKG tech, and most recently, Acupuncture. The gentleman who had designed and led the program became incapacitated due to medical issues and she needed someone to take over immediately. I got the job and moved to Ft. Lauderdale. What a gypsy, huh?

There were eleven students – seven women and four men. The course had just begun, so we all had a fresh start. The former instructor had not even organized a real plan and the students had only the most basic textbook. The course was not recognized by the National Board of Acupuncture and the innocent students did not know they would not be qualified for licensing after graduating. I set about teaching twenty hours a week, organizing a curriculum and applying for approval by the National Board and the Florida Board of Professional Licensing, and also began teaching basic Chi Kung exercises and demanded all students exercise and meditate daily. Some of the students were already massage therapists and began to recommend me to their clients. I was quickly occupied for sixty to seventy hours a week but felt up to it and enjoyed the entire endeavor.

After a year of hard work, I had established the first accredited program, approved by the traditional college agencies, that issued a two year associate degree in acupuncture and whose graduates were qualified to take the licensing exams. The first school in the nation, to my understanding, to offer a fully accredited two year associate degree in acupuncture. However, I worked myself into a state of exhaustion and became too well acquainted with the cocaine possibilities in Florida. I was also drinking every day and became depressed, irrationally angry, and lost sight of the importance of meditation and exercise. I needed help.

I had been seeing Dr. Henry L. at the Ft. Lauderdale Veteran's counseling center since first moving to Ft. Lauderdale and hid nothing from him, including my history with cocaine and my present reality. Doctor Henry was a rock-solid psychologist and a no bullshit counselor of veterans. He was the first person to hear my tales of Vietnam and he insisted I apply for disability. I resisted for months but Doctor Henry was one tough negotiator. He would not give up on me. My initial application for disability from the VA came back in forty days and awarded me for 30% disability for combat related PTSD, along with ratings of zero percent for shrapnel scars, sinus problems, knee problems, and combat related loss of teeth. Doc Henry said he had never seen an initial assessment come back so quickly. The VA usually automatically denied all first claims and veterans had to wait out a lengthy appeal process. He said if I got 30% so quickly it meant that several members of the judgment board probably recommended 50% or even 70% for PTSD.

Then the good Doctor pulled another ace from his sleeve and demanded I stop everything and enter the PTSD program at the Miami Veterans Hospital. If I refused he said he was done with me as a patient and the hell with me. Yeah, he said it just about like that. As mentioned, a tough negotiator. He added the incentive that I would also have to enter the drug and alcohol rehab program before the 90 day PTSD program and my combined time in the hospital would result in my receiving 100% payment for each month in the hospital since it was all for a service connected disability. At that time, 100% disability from the VA amounted to $1883.00 per month. That clinched the deal. I owe Dr. Henry Leon my life. He would not be denied. He was so right.

I entrusted my few belongings to a neighbor and entered the drug and alcohol rehab program in the Miami Veterans Hospital. I smoked one final joint on the drive down from Ft. Lauderdale. It so happened that another experienced acupuncturist had recently applied to become a teacher at Barna College, so Ms. W. was not left with no one to continue the program I had created. Once again, trust in the flow of life resulted in positive outcomes for all involved.

The rehab program usually involved 28 days. Patients were locked down for the first week on the fourth floor of the hospital, considered the Psychiatric wing. It proved to be quite the eye opener for me and pushed me toward my future avocation of helping homeless veterans. There were about thirty patients and what a diverse and motley crew they were! They represented every form and every level of drug and alcohol involvement, from hard core heroin users, crack addicts, alcohol abusers, marijuana aficionados, and combinations of all of the above. Every age group and race and background were represented. I fit right in. I was somewhat surprised that very few were combat veterans. Only two others were Vietnam veterans, both of whom had been homeless on the streets of Miami for years and years. They were also MIA from their families, without marketable skills and more or less completely useless to themselves and society. I learned a lot from them about the plight of Vietnam veterans who had returned from the war but could never find their place in the Country.

I realized with gratitude I had not sunk so low as I thought. When attending required AA and NA meetings and listening to stories of lives gone awry, the reality of "hitting bottom" was revealed to me. Any thoughts of self pity vanished as I gained insight into the fact that my "bottom" was nowhere near the depths of despair most of these men had sunk to. One "inmate" had used coke and alcohol combined with huge doses of prescribed anti-depressants to the point that he was confined to a wheelchair and suffered extreme atrophy of the musculature. He was truly a pathetic case and I truly felt sorry for him. There was little or no judgment among us. Everybody could understand the story of everybody else.

We attended music therapy, occupational therapy, exercise in a well equipped physical therapy department, and could amuse ourselves with card games, board games, model car assembly, artwork, and various activities. We were not allowed to be idle or isolate ourselves, as had been the general lifestyle for many of us. We also attended individual counseling and group counseling. When I first arrived, I was interviewed by the primary psychiatrist and the nursing staff. The Doctor seriously informed me that I had registered at the absolute top of the measurable scale of THC content. I replied honestly, "I'm not surprised sir. I smoked my last joint on the drive down here yesterday." He was not amused although I did see one of the nurses try to hide a smile. I was also called in and informed I had Hepatitis C, which was presented to me with all the seriousness as if I had terminal AIDS. The medical establishment had only recently isolated the virus called Hep C.

In the coming years I found out that almost every Vietnam veteran I met who had been "out in the bush" had been diagnosed with Hep C. It is my opinion that Hepatitis can be transferred by mosquitoes. There are many other blood-born viral infections transmitted by that pestiferous insect, so why not Hep C?

My contention was to tell the truth and they should be prepared to handle it. After the third weekly piss test, Nurse Ellen called me in for an interrogation. "Mr. Lumbert, you are still at the top of the scale. If your THC level is not down to at least a measurable level by next week, we are going to assume you are still somehow using marijuana. Either that or you must have been smoking some really good green bud."

"Yes ma'am. I had a friend who grew superb sensemilla. I am not still consuming in any way."

Nurse Ellen fixed me with a withering gaze. "Okay, smart guy. I have been doing this for sixteen years and you will not put anything over on me. We can dismiss you from the program if you are not measurable next week." She somewhat resembled Nurse Ratched from the movie One Flew Over The Cookoo's Nest when she put on her hard face, but she really loved us and had a hearty sense of humor in her own way. I liked her. The next week my THC level was down on the measurable scale. I had to remain in the rehab unit for seven weeks before my THC level dropped to zero. Nurse "Ratched" told me with a motherly smile I had set a new record. Only after testing clear of all drugs could a patient be admitted into the 90 day PTSD program.

The PTSD program was at the end of a hall on the fourth floor behind locked and guarded doors. A deliberate aura of incarceration was created. There were eighteen of us who all started together. We had all been diagnosed with combat-related Post Traumatic Stress Disorder. We were all about the same age. We had all had similar difficulties at remarkably similar times in our lives. During one of the first group sessions, the lead psychologist asked, "how many of you were in jail or prison within one year of returning from Vietnam?" Seventeen of us raised our hands. We all looked at the one who hadn't. He remarked with a sly grin, "well, for me it was almost two years." Everybody laughed. Shit, I had no idea so many others were having similar difficulties and experiences. Several of the men had also been homeless for years and years and had survived their own personal demons of drugs, crime, alcoholism, marital and family strife, and violent emotional explosions. I did not feel so alone after hearing their stories.

I worked the program and the program worked for me. It was a fact for most of us that we were substantiating our disability in order to increase our rating and monthly payment. There was no shame in this. We had gotten over whatever macho attitudes we might have had about being unaffected by the War. We freely divulged our histories of the adverse effects of the War and, for most of us, the way we were treated when we returned, not only by the protesters at the airport, but by the negative stereotyping by society in general and also by the lack of respect many of us witnessed from the Korean and WWII vets who populated the three major veteran's organizations: the DAV, VFW, and American Legion. I had never even considered joining any veteran's organizations and was shocked at some of the stories of rejection and belittling some of the men had suffered from these groups.

Those subjected to the curses, taunts, and assaults by the hippy war protesters all said that those experiences were more hurtful than whatever they had been through in Vietnam. I was lucky to have arrived at Oakland at 3AM when there were no demonstrators. One "exercise" we engaged in was to split up into pairs, and share the worst thing we had ever seen or done in the War. The instructor said, "everyone of you had that <u>one</u> thing you will never forget. The day you will never tell to your family or friends. The experience that changed you forever. Tell your partner, who you might never meet again outside this setting about the worst of the worst day of your life."

I related being blown up by the beehives fired by our own artillery and also about seeing Pete shot through the chest. My partner told of riding shotgun in a deuce-and-a half after being ambushed several times during the previous week and seeing a kid running up with something shiny in his hand and shooting the boy dead as an instant reflex. The kid had a can of coke he was trying to sell. My response was, "fuck, man. That's a rough one. Hey, you going to be at the poker game tonight in the day room?" That represents how much understanding we could give to one another. How little we judged each other. Every one of us got an immense load off our chest as a result of telling our worst story and having our buddy, one real person, understand and still be a friend.

I was the only person in the program not taking some sort of psychotropic medication so I was selected to undergo a sleep study of veterans with PTSD conducted by a psychiatrist from the University of Miami. I was not thrilled about the idea but decided to be a test dummy for a psychiatric study that I doubted would make much difference one way or another for most of us.

I was led to a claustrophobic room in the basement of the hospital and hooked up with about twenty electrodes on my head. Then I was supposed to sleep. Shit. I never liked anything against my skin and had always avoided wristwatches, rings, dog tags around my neck, etc. So I lay on a bed with several people watching me from behind a glass, monitoring my brain signals. I meditated to relax, had a few brief dreams, and lay there awake but immobile for a long uncomfortable night.

The investigator/psychology professor said he had been testing brain patterns in sleep clinics for years and had never seen anyone show the type of brain activity I had. He said I had not demonstrated any deep, undisturbed sleep at all. I had spent a lot of time in what was called "alpha" state, which was meditation; I briefly entered "REM" phase which indicated dreaming; but I had been awake yet relaxed for most of the night and had shown adrenaline surges throughout the night that he had never seen before. He was not sure I represented any indicators he could include in his study. I was too far off the norm. I told him I was a long-term practitioner of Transcendental Meditation and practiced ancient Chinese breath awareness exercises and that I thought I still had the sleep patterns of a responsible Lieutenant in charge of an ambush patrol in a combat situation. Understanding this, he replied that maybe he had collected some data that truly represented the disturbed sleep of veterans with PTSD. I declined to go through another night of testing.

During the program, I was aware of the probable notations being accumulated by the staff in my file. When asked how I felt, I never answered "fine." That would be what was written by a staff member: "the patient reported he felt fine." Instead I hinted or directly indicated that I was depressed, had not slept well, and was uncomfortable over some class or exercise we were required to perform. During private one-on-one counseling I would stare unblinking at the forehead of the psychologist and de-focus my eyes. If the lighting was correct, this was the technique I had learned to help recognize auras and energy patterns. It usually made the recipient nervous and my personal psychologist told me exactly that. I kept doing it to him. I did not especially like him.

One morning I experienced an especially deep meditation as I lay there after awakening. We were often required to have our blood pressure taken in the morning before coffee or breakfast. I maintained awareness of my breath and deliberately relaxed when I sat down for the blood pressure reading. Nurse Helen was on duty. She was a huge very black woman who stood about six feet tall and must have weighed well over 300 pounds.

Nurse Helen had the build and the brow of a gorilla but the heart and laugh of an immense angel. We all loved Nurse Helen and she could joke around with the worst and the best of us equally.

She read my blood pressure as 112/60. "Oh my gawd! Is you alive in deah?" She actually had normal well educated speech patterns, but would lapse into "negroese" and street dialect as a joke. She loved to laugh and loved to make us laugh with her.

I said, "Take it again, nurse, I think I'm coming back to life."

I deliberately tightened my anal sphincter, clenched my toes, and performed a Valsalva maneuver by swallowing then closing off the epiglottis and tightening the rib cage and diaphragm. My pressure shot up to 138/88 within about a minute, without making any outward changes.

Helen went through an exaggerated freak out. "Oh hell no! You cain't do dat. You a voodoo man! I ain't takin' no mo' blood pressure on no voodoo man. Don' you be lookin' at me dat way!"

We had a good laugh. When Nurse Helen politely asked one of us to calm down or "straighten your sorry ass up!" everyone complied. She could have swatted any of us like a fly.

So we did have our lighter moments during the three month course, and I personally gained great benefits. The plight of so many of us also became clear to me. I had no real idea of how many of the homeless were 'Nam vets and had not lived in a major metropolitan area where the situation was obvious on a day to day basis. A resolution formed deep in my mind and my heart to help anyone I saw in the future who appeared homeless or in otherwise dire straits. This later became a deliberate personal mission that I pursued throughout the United States, Mexico, and Central America. I found Vietnam veterans and took many literally by the hand or by the scruff of the neck to Veterans clinics or hospitals and got their names on the rolls when many of them had not even been counted on any census because they did not reside at any known address or household. Perhaps the particulars of that quest might be covered in another book. I am still trying to complete this one.

After being released from the hospital I joined the ranks of the truly homeless. I had no inclination to practice my level of health care on the general populace. There was no close friend or relative I could stay with comfortably. After staying a few nights on the sofa at my former friend's apartment, it became apparent that he had become immersed in crack use and had hocked or sold all my belongings I had entrusted to him six months before. I owned a very used Plymouth Volare, about two changes of clothes, and nothing else. I began sneaky-camping in and around Ft. Lauderdale, sleeping in my car in inconspicuous places, cooking simple meals on a propane camping stove in a city park, occasionally pitching a tent, and so on. I discovered that if I leaned a fishing pole against my car and parked where overnight fishermen parked, I could sleep undisturbed by law enforcement personnel. When I was rousted by the cops, I always treated them with respect and I had started wearing a "Vietnam Veteran" baseball cap that they all noticed and maybe led to my being given a break. I lived for four months on my 40% monthly disability check which was $383.00. It was more than some guys got under similar circumstances.

Ft. Lauderdale did not have a large homeless population; but now that I was aware of the situation and was essentially homeless myself, I met quite a few other displaced, semi-useless individuals and felt it was my duty to see if any were veterans. One such man was Larry, the dumpster diver. When I was still useful and working, I had seen Larry a few times behind the grocery store sorting through a dumpster...standing inside the thing and picking out edible vegetables and fruit. I dismissed the scene. Did not give the man a second thought. Now I did think about the homeless and stopped to talk to several people and find out about them. I knew his name from previous conversations and had given Larry five dollars a couple of times.

I saw Larry sitting in a small city park with a filthy rag wrapped around his hand one day. I had planned to cook some canned soup and intended to share. Larry did not look well. He was obviously in pain...said his hand was "all swoll up." I had him unwrap the cloth and saw that he was in serious trouble. He had a hugely swollen hand with pus leaking out and red streaks going up the forearm. It was a staff infection and if allowed to continue would lead to very severe complications. That day Larry had on a US Army ball cap so I asked if he was a veteran.

He was. I told him to get in my car and I would take him to the veteran's clinic just a few blocks away.

Larry told me he could not go to a veterans clinic because he was not in combat and had just been a jeep mechanic in Germany. I asked, "did you get an honorable discharge? Do you have any ID?" Yes and no. This was the first of many times I encountered veterans who were not aware of their right to seek medical help from the VA. Most thought it was only for those wounded in combat. So I took Larry to the outpatient clinic and his hand was so serious that they called a helicopter to evacuate him to the Miami Veterans Hospital. Saved his hand and maybe his life.

I found out that the VA has a rule to treat anyone claiming to be a veteran whether they have appropriate ID or not. The VA had to prove they were <u>not</u> a veteran before refusing treatment, especially in an emergency situation. Larry remembered his service number. I saw Larry the Dumpster Diver a week later and he said I had saved his life. The VA had verified his service and provided him with an appropriate ID card for future care. I realized a future avocation had appeared for me. I vowed to seek out homeless veterans and take them to a VA facility. This plan would become an ongoing endeavor for many years thereafter.

I did go back and check in with Dr. Henry Leon at the Ft. Lauderdale vet center. He had several suggestions like staying at a shelter or the Salvation Army, but I declined. He assured me that I would get an increase in my disability check and would receive something over $5000.00 as back payment of 100 percent service-connected disability for the almost six months in the hospital. I said I would wait it out. Sometimes I would set up a campsite way out on the western edge of Ft. Lauderdale and just sit alone swatting mosquitoes and wondering about the alligator population and how hungry they were.

My former neighbor had owned several boats and we had talked about living on boats – the advantages and disadvantages. Dr. Leon was restoring a Chris Craft motorboat and he also spoke about the joys of living aboard a small boat. Living in Florida it seemed a sensible choice. There were many people living on boats and otherwise conducting a normal day-to-day life in the city. The idea was very attractive to me. My family had never had a boat and I had almost no experience with boats at all; but it seemed like something new to try, so I fantasized a boat in my future.

The day came when I got a check from "Uncle Va" - my term for the Veterans Administration- for $5242.00. My rating of 40% disability remained the same. I immediately went to Dr. Leon to share the news and wanted help and advice. Doctor Henry literally pinned me against the wall and told me nose-to-nose, "you spend every dime on a good used boat to live on!" It was quite a dangerous situation and he had seen other veterans blow through such a sudden windfall and go down the tube with partying, drugs, etc. I had never had so much money at one time. There was no one in my life to party with anyway, and I was already used to living on the brink of poverty and seclusion, so buying a boat was not a difficult choice.

My vehicle at the time was a worn-out Plymouth Volare that I had neglected due to spending money on coke, superb weed, and high quality wine and beer. There were minor repairs needed: tires, brakes, oil change, etc. After another severe counseling session with Dr. Henry, I cruised down to the Florida Keys with about $4500 to spend on a boat. I wanted a sailboat. I had been sailing once with my former brother-in-law on a large lake in Texas and sailing a boat reminded me of flying an airplane. Traveling all the way to Key West and checking ads in local papers and on message boards at marinas, I found what I wanted.

I saw an ad for a used sailboat in Key Largo and called the owner, Doug Hum. The boat was still in a boatyard for final painting and restoring. It was an old 25 foot wooden boat that had been fiberglassed and partially refurbished as a year-long hobby and Doug had bought it and completed the job. The style was determined by the position of the sails and my boat was an old style known as a gaff-rigged cutter. That meant the mainsail had a spar on the top and opened up in a trapezoid shape, not a giant triangle, as most modern boats. It also had two jibs, the small sails at the front of the boat. Doug was a Korean War veteran and, whether he admitted it or not, also suffered certain aspects of PTSD. We got along great and I worked off part of the cost of the boat by helping him with painting the bottom and completing the interior. He was asking exactly $4500. I paid four thousand and worked for the remainder. It was a good learning experience.

Doug claimed an ancestral heritage of indigenous "Indians" of the Cherokee nation. He named the boat Crazy Horse in honor of that great chief of the Cheyenne/Sioux nation. I had read and studied the Indians of the Americas while living in Santa Fe, N.M. Some of the tribes were definitely the most advanced stone-age peoples ever encountered and demolished by the invading Europeans. I felt an affinity towards the native peoples and, of course, had built my profession by practicing ancient medical techniques instead of modern technologies. My boat was over ninety years old and had originally been used to transfer cargo from anchored ships to the docks of New England. It seemed fitting to name it with respect towards an ancient culture, because the boat was a relatively ancient design no longer in use. I loved it.

Crazy Horse was not an ideal boat for the Florida Keys, where the waters were shallow with many sand bars. My boat had a full keel and drew four and a half feet of water. Also the configuration of the sails was not easy to manage, especially for a beginner, but I learned and I sailed that boat up and down the Keys. I stayed on the north side of the Florida Keys for several months while gaining some experience before passing under the seven-mile bridge at Marathon and heading south toward Cuba. The first time I sailed out of sight of land and into the depths of the Florida Straits was a huge thrill. The water depth is suddenly three thousand feet and the color changes from pale blue to deep purple. Sailing alone into the deep purple ocean was as thrilling as the first time I had flown an airplane alone. There is nothing like it.

I lived aboard Crazy Horse for almost two years, never tying up to a dock or entering a marina. I lived "on the hook"-anchored off shore. I constructed several mooring buoys by using my dinghy to haul eight or ten concrete blocks stolen from construction sites, chaining them together, and tying a floating empty water jug on the surface. The Volvo Penta two-cylinder diesel engine was not dependable, the bilge pump was unreliable, and I was plagued with an infestation of small German cockroaches, though, so I eventually fulfilled my desire of living aboard a boat and sold Crazy Horse for $3500 and proceeded with other options.

I survived those two years on $383.00 a month, occasionally working for low wages at several marinas, usually painting; but sometimes struggling with the shitiest job in a boatyard – scraping and cleaning the bottom of boats. That particular job was not easy or pleasant, but I did it.

Then, in 1994, I was called in to the Ft. Lauderdale VA outpatient clinic for the first re-exam for my primary disability of combat- related, service-connected PTSD. I told the truth: that I no longer felt capable of practicing my profession of fifteen years, lived alone on a small sailboat, and had no plans for the future. I did not know it at the time, but there was a disagreement between Psychiatrists and Psychologists over the proper treatment of PTSD. Psychiatrists, who were Medical Doctors, favored the use of drugs and thought "talk therapy" conducted by Psychologists was useless.

Without realizing it at the time, I was an example, in the mind of the examining Psychiatrist, that talking about my problems and going through the ninety day PTSD course without medication had led to my becoming 100 percent disabled. This degeneration in my condition was especially disruptive because I had been involved in what was considered a "profession," not just a job. Therefore, I was given a huge boost in monthly payment – to 100% at $1883.00 a month. Furthermore, I received a payment of three months back pay covering the time between the exam and the approval of the new judgment and got a check for over four thousand dollars. After selling Crazy Horse, a new plan developed that greatly expanding my horizons.

I bought a used Volkswagen camper van for $4000 and spent another thousand bringing all the amenities up to working order. The plan was to travel the country rounding up homeless veterans and signing them in at a VA outpatient clinic or hospital. From 1994 to 1998 I traveled across the US locating and identifying veterans and doing whatever possible for them. I learned to locate homeless encampments and how to enter those dangerous environs and offer help without being robbed, beaten, stabbed or even killed. After watching suspected homeless people as they slipped off into a nearby wooded area, usually by a small stream and within walking distance of a grocery store, I would buy twenty dollars worth of canned goods and other non-perishables, park the van about a block away with my wallet hidden and locked inside, then enter a hobo jungle and say, "I am a Vietnam veteran and I have some help for other vets. Here are some groceries for anybody who needs them." I never had any trouble and rescued many vets in this manner, from Montana to Arizona and from New Mexico to Florida.

On many occasions, after stopping to help a person holding a sign indicating they were a veteran asking for help, a doubt arose as to whether they were a veteran or not. I asked, "What unit did you serve with. Give me your name, rank and service number. **Now!**" If they hesitated I told them, "if you are a veteran I will help you. If you are lying I will stab you. **Now speak up!**" Gripping the handle of a seven-inch sheathed Buck Hunter knife on my belt as I stared at them, more than one liar was frightened to the point of literally pissing in their pants. It is doubtful any of the liars were standing on that particular street corner again. This activity has now become known as "stolen valor" and I hate that more than almost any type of crime. I was not kidding. If there were no witnesses and a liar had challenged me, I probably would have stabbed him. Nobody issued a challenge. They apologized or offered excuses. There is no excuse I would accept and I told them exactly that.

While camping out near Alamo Lake, Arizona, I met some geologists from Nebraska who owned a continuously populated housing settlement on the north side of the lake. There were three brothers in their sixties and one nephew about thirty years old. Their land holding was officially BLM (Federally owned by the Bureau of Land Management) but was technically leased for 99 years by this group of three brothers, the Huffmans. I bought a corner of their claim under a clause called a "quit claim deed." It was here that I built a twelve-sided cabin and typed the first draft of the first five chapters of this book. This took place in 1997.

After several conversations in the coming months I realized these guys held the same views as the Nazis of Germany. They were absolute white supremacists; they believed the Jews should be exterminated; and that they and their kind were the only ones who understood the meaning and intentions of the Founding Fathers of this Country. (Substitute "The Fatherland" for "Founding Fathers"). They had pulp newspaper publications I had never heard of and possessed over thirty or forty firearms in their home. They also believed that the U. S. Government planned to hire mercenaries from Eastern Europe to confiscate all the guns in America and incarcerate "patriots" in concentration camps. They applauded Timothy McVea when he blew up the building in Oklahoma and said they were friends with his partner, Terry Nichols, who was from nearby Kingman, Az. They hinted at the fact (which I verified secretly) that they had twenty 55 gallon drums of bat guano of the type used by

McVea to make the explosive charge he used. I put two and two together.

We got into a spirited disagreement one day and the young nephew pulled a pistol on me and told me it would be easy to kill me and drop my body down an abandoned mine shaft. I disarmed him in a flash and tossed his gun through a large window in their living room. Then I somewhat calmed the situation down and apologized saying it was just a reflex. I packed my van that night and left forever at about 3AM.

I stayed with my sister for several months, bought my first computer, and began transferring my typewritten manuscript to digital. Meanwhile, I called the FBI and told them about the Huffmans, described the location of their compound, and indicated the shed where they had the barrels of bat guano. I also told the FBI about the number of firearms they possessed and that they were ready for an armed confrontation. I provided information on their attitude toward what McVea had done and that they claimed they were friends with Terry Nichols, McVea's partner. I left for Costa Rica soon afterwards and have no idea what happened regarding those Neo-Nazis, the Huffman brothers and their nephew. The FBI spoke to my brother after I had left the Country. More than one veteran had told me over the years that many ex-patriot vets were in Mexico and Central America, so I went. Caught a flight to Costa Rica as a start.

I landed in Liberia, Costa Rica on May 4, 1998 and proceeded to a little coastal village called Playa Cocos, a fishing town not often of the itinerary of the usual type of traveler. There was no rational reason to chose Playa Cocos. It was not a popular tourist spot listed in the travel guides. The next day a volcano called "Arenal" exploded about thirty miles to the east and I took that as an indication that I was in the right place at the right time. I met a young tough guy that day who was an illegal immigrant from Nicaragua and had been a Lieutenant in the losing side of their recent civil war and we became instant buddies when I explained I was also a Lieutenant in a losing war. We went on a good drunk on my birthday, the fifth of May. A great start to my time in Costa Rica.

I rented a decent apartment for about $150.00 a month from a nice German lady and began to type out my manuscript on my new IBM Thinkpad. Playa Cocos is in the State (departamento) of Guanacaste in the northwest corner of the Country by the border with Nicaragua. It did not take long for me to recognize that the light-skinned Spanish descendants living in Costa Rica detested the darker mixed-blood Nicaraguans and referred to them as savages and "monkey fuckers," if I may translate their slang term. Guanacaste had at times been a part of Nicaragua, and many of the people were a beautiful mixture of Spanish, Negro, and Native "Indios." At least I thought they were beautiful- tall, creamed coffee-colored, athletic, and smilingly happy. Racism exists everywhere. The light-skinned Spanish descendants have almost always ruled Mexico and all points south, and have always looked on the Indios and Mestizos (mixed blood peoples) with condescension, and the "blessed" Spanish Catholic Church built every one of their glorious cathedrals by enslaving the indigenous people, after saving their souls, of course. Historical fact.

The Fodor's travel guide on Costa Rica warns against the eastern coastal towns as being rife with drugs, crime, and dangerous elements. Naturally, I went to see for myself. Puerto Limon is the major city and was connected only by railroad until sometime in the 1970's. There was no highway from the capital of San Jose. The populace was largely descendants of African Negro slaves who had escaped captivity from islands in the Caribbean anytime within the past two or three hundred years. The country of Costa Rica had only granted them citizenship sometime in the 1960's, considering them "illegal African slaves" until then.

I very much enjoyed the eastern coast of Costa Rica and the city of Puerto Limon. I met several veterans there in the city and in the two or three small towns to the south toward the border with Panama. Most of the local people spoke excellent English with a delightful Jamaican lilting accent. I might have provided some help and advice to several vets. I still think of returning. None of the vets wanted to return to the United States. Some of them were MIA from their families for many, many years. But that is part of another book, maybe in the future.

At the villa where I took a room in Puerto Viejo, the cleaning girls were very cute little "Indios" who spoke a melodic language I had never heard before. They also spoke Spanish and I wanted to know more about them. They were from a tribe called "Bri Bri" and lived in a portion of the dense jungle that had never been found or conquered by the Spanish. They were shy and had not talked with many travelers. I tried to entertain them with tales of the Indian tribes in the United States, explaining that many of them maintained their language and traditions much as the Bri Bri had, perhaps exaggerating the positive and not dwelling on the negative aspects of the plight of "Indians" in our Country. I thought it somewhat interesting that their grandmother had never left the village, not even to see the road where they caught a bus to come to work, and grandma did not believe them when they tried to explain what a bus was and that twenty people rode in one mechanical contraption. How beautiful and innocent they were!

But the crack cocaine was consuming travelers in that area. Having already graduated from that destructive school of dire consequences, however, I had a unique and painful vantage point from which to try to rescue several doomed American veterans. I was not successful...a sad chapter in my efforts. A traveler was met at the bus depot, such as it was, with offers of a handful of rocks which would have been considered "twenties" in the US; but could be had for a mere two dollars each in Puerto Viejo. I was saddened at the disparity in the economies, but there was nothing to do about it. My own demons threatened to arise, so I did not tarry for long in that part of the country.

Another sad and surprising fact about the dope trade in Costa Rica was that the marijuana was not worth a shit, so I gave up on that drug as well. The rum, however, was fantastic and the best 12 year-old liter of Flor de Cana rum sold for about seven dollars. It would have been about fifty dollars or more in the US if you could find it. Oh well, there had to be something attractive and addictive. I did not get too carried away, though, and kept working on my book and looking for veterans I could help.

Then came hurricane Mitch, the single most destructive natural catastrophe in the known history of Central America. Mitch stalled over the mountains bordering Nicaragua and Honduras and poured torrential rains for over two weeks continuously. Entire mountains were flattened and valleys filled up. Villages and even small cities vanished from the face of the earth. The topographic map of the area had to be completely revised from satellite photos. Roads and highways had to be entirely rebuilt. In Puerto Viejo we had lots of rain but nobody worried until the highway to Puerto Limon became an impassable lake and the beer ran out. No problem, the fisherfolk organized an armada of small boats and went to the city for beer and other essentials for the village and us thirsty tourists.

At the beginning of each month, I traveled to Liberia where there was a bank with international possibilities so I could withdraw four or five hundred dollars for expenses. There was no place in the small villages a credit or debit card could be used. In Liberia I passed a storefront where the Red Cross had a collecting point for clothes, food, etc. I donated whatever clothes I had in a small bag and asked the Red Cross lady what else could be done and when would the items be delivered. She replied it was still too dangerous to get to the affected areas, and anyway guerrilla forces were operating and they would confiscate anything delivered, so the situation was stagnant until the Nicaraguan Army rebuilt the roads to the worst-hit territory.

A traveler in Costa Rica had to leave the country for three days every three months, then return to renew a visa. In the north of the country, most people went to the Nicaraguan coastal town of San Juan del Sur. I had been there and met several soldiers of the Nicaraguan Army and discussed their civil war as I explained the book I was writing about intervening in the civil war in Vietnam. There was a senior Sergeant who was especially interested in my story. I recalled him showing me on a map the pueblo of Ocotal, near the border with Honduras, his home town, and had an impulse to go and speak to him about the possibilities of delivering help to his family...and to find out if they had even survived. There was no communication with the destroyed areas. With this in mind, I asked the Red Cross representative if they would give some essentials to the Nicaraguan Army if I could arrange for a truck to come to Liberia.

Back in San Juan del Sur, Nicaragua, Sergeant Robles remembered me and we commandeered an Army two-ton flatbed truck and returned to Liberia, Costa Rica. The Red Cross filled the truck with barrels full of packages of beans, rice, and concentrated soups. We also carried soap and bleach with instructions on how to strain and purify water. I happened to have a Coleman dual-fuel camp stove that operated on regular gasoline, and that certainly came in handy. The Sergeant arranged to follow a road-clearing operation and we set out to Ocotal, high in the mountains of east Nicaragua. It was still raining.

We were on the road for ten days in order to travel less than a hundred miles. They were literally building the road in front of us as we proceeded. I became the cook, crouched beneath the truck boiling beans and cooking rice for ourselves and the starving refugees who immediately converged on us when we stopped. We passed out bottles of bleach and bars of soap and taught the people to strain water through a washed sheet, then add a tablespoon of bleach to each gallon in order to purify the water for drinking. Some of the children were chewing old shoe leather and the inner bark of trees in an attempt to survive. I had never witnessed such a heart-rending scene.

A few days into our journey we were joined by several SUV's carrying Doctors Without Borders personnel. They were the most daring, fearless, and totally selfless medical people I had ever imagined. Mere humble admiration does not even begin to indicate how I felt about them. True and absolute heroes, every one. We finally arrived at what used to be a village, but was now a mire of mud, unidentifiable debris, demolished former houses, and starving, suffering human survivors.

Doctors Without Borders set up a mobile clinic in what was left of a house and began treating patients and Sergeant Robles and I issued soap, bleach, and packets of beans and rice. I continued cooking with the Coleman because there was hardly any wood to be found that was dry enough for the people to cook anything. The Sergeant and another military man also tried to maintain some semblance of law and order. The former Mayor of the destroyed pueblo provided what help he could, but he was struck down into an emotional abyss, having lost his family and most of the populace.

Then an atrocious incident occurred which soured my outlook on Central America and caused a revision in any future plans Doctors Without Borders might have had. Armed thieving guerrilla forces entered the back of the makeshift clinic at night and stole almost all the medical supplies and all the personal luggage and belongings of the Doctors and Nurses. It was disheartening, to say the least, for the medical personnel, who were only there to help. I was really pissed. I pressed the Sergeant to follow them, but he had only a 9mm handgun and his Corporal had one AK-47 with three magazines of bullets. The guerrilla forces had plenty of guns and ammo, so no attempt could be made to recover the stolen items.

We returned to San Juan del Sur, passing out the remainder of the food and supplies on the way. Doctors Without Borders returned to Costa Rica and some of them vowed to never again enter certain parts of Central America. It was a sad reality for all of us.

I spent a few months in San Juan del Sur, Nicaragua and traveled to several other cities in that Country. An interesting caveat to tourists was explained to me by a taxi driver in the ancient city of Granada. At all the bus stops, one was accosted by hoards of taxi drivers as soon as you climbed down off the bus. I made it a habit to refuse these initial offers saying I needed to walk around a bit after the long bus ride. Then I would walk around until I spotted a cab with a mature driver whose car had no dents and decent tires.

This tactic was illustrated to me by a tourist at a bus station in Guatemala City, at the main bus terminal in that largest city in Central America. I spotted a rather obese probably American man in his sixties panting and sweating while sitting in the waiting area. I approached and asked if he needed any water or if I could help him. Yes, he needed water and I bought him a liter bottle. We talked for a while. He was from Houston, Texas and had been traveling in Central America for over two years. I asked where he was going, and after refreshing himself and resting for a while he said he would show me how he determined his destination.

We strolled past all the idling buses and he examined the tires and listened to the way the motors sounded and he explained. "This here bus has a smooth running engine and new

tires. That's the one I'll take. Where it's going ain't important."
The man had good instincts toward safe travel.

So I hired a taxi with good tires driven by a relaxed mature man. I told him I wanted to see the whole city of Granada and to just drive north, south, east, and west, then I would buy him lunch somewhere. He was delighted to proudly show me his city. As we cruised through a large park with a playground for kids, several amusement rides, and many refreshment stands and restaurants, he cautioned me: if you come down here in the evening, sir, you will find all the possibilities. (My Spanish was fluent enough by then and my accent and pronunciation led some to question whether I was Italian or French. A compliment towards an American). The man continued: and I mean <u>all</u> possibilities. You understand? If you go from one of the cantinas to the next, sir, you <u>must</u> take a taxi! Even if it is only one hundred meters! If you walk, young men will come out of the bushes with baseball bats and leave you naked and crying in the street. <u>Believe me!</u> Do you think you can hide money in your shoes? They will steal your shoes. You will be desnudo y llorando in la calle!" He repeated the naked and crying part. I believed him. I did not venture to the park after dark.

I enjoyed the city of Granada, the oldest major city in Central America. My driver told me I could buy a nice condo in a modern building for five thousand dollars American money. Interesting, but I was not tempted. I was tired of Central America by then, wary of Mexico, and wanted to return to the United

States. I had been down there for almost two years by then. It is interesting to learn what you miss after a while. Good wine, for one thing. Pizza, Texas barbeque, M&M candy, and being able to converse in my native English, to name a few more. Also good weed.

So I took a long, leisurely bus trip up through Guatemala, Belize, and the east coast of Mexico, stopping every day in mid-afternoon, finding a decent room, and enjoying a good meal and a night's rest. Sometimes staying for two or three days where ever I felt like it. There was no hurry. I used the old Hustonian's advice on choosing the next bus to board. Time and distance meant nothing. When I came up through the valley in south Texas, I decided to stop over in Corpus Christi and rented a little car. My family had visited the Texas coast many times when I was a kid and I wanted to see what was what. In the little town of Rockport, I recognized the bait shops by the harbor. They were exactly the same as in my memory of forty years before. I decided to live in Rockport, Texas. It was that easy and automatic.

After another bus ride to Dallas, where my brother and sister lived, I bought a motorcycle and piled camping gear on it and drove down to Goose Island State Park, east of Rockport. Within weeks I bought my first house, at age 52, using my benefits from the GI Bill. It was very pleasant to feel rooted after about ten years of drifting. I enclosed the carport into a garage, made some alterations to the interior, bought the first TV I had ever owned, and even signed up for internet access. I had two hard copies of my completed book made at a Kinko's store and sent one in to the Library of Congress to adhere to the copyright laws. Wow! It felt good to think I had completed the most difficult project I had ever undertaken. Summer of the year 2000.

I sent chapters two and three to a man in Austin who claimed to be an agent and got very little encouragement. He said he had a stack of manuscripts on his desk from veterans; most concerning the recent war in Iraq. He also discouraged me by saying that almost all the editorial readers at the major publishing houses were women, and my story had nothing a woman would be interested in. Also, he said that most habitual readers in America were women, and if I had been a woman who had a combat story I would almost certainly get published. I put the whole thing aside for years and years...probably gave up too soon after an initial disappointment.

I had no ambition for a while. Just lived, rode my motorcycle around, got acquainted with folks, joined a Unity Church, went for walks, sat on the beach, went to Port Aransas and Padre Island near Corpus, and enjoyed having a house and a garage and a refrigerator and a TV. Bought some tools to hang on a pegboard in the garage, bought a very used Mitsubishi Mirage for $500, and even met a nice woman to date for a while. That winter I ordered a put-together scale-model wooden dinghy, ordered from an ad in Wooden Boat magazine. A plan arose to build a little sailboat.

At the Unity Church I became friends with the minister, Alan Lee, from Perth, Australia. Alan was a lifelong musician and he induced me to join his keyboard and sometimes his vibraphone (which is an electrified Xylophone) and during the next year I learned to play guitar along with everything from Amazing Grace to Zip-Adee-Do-Da. Such was the music at that delightful Church. I became quite an accomplished guitarist under Alan's tutelage and influence.

I had decided, after fumbling with tiny balsa wood pieces trying to build a ten inch model of a ten foot dinghy, to build a real dinghy. I met a skilled woodworker named Jim Smith at the Church and we had both been reading Wooden Boat magazine and had both decided to build the exact same sailing dinghy, the plans of which were advertised in the magazine. So a thorough course in wood working ensued with an excellent teacher. When the student is ready, the Master appears. Again.

Jim was retired from an engineering job with the oil companies. He was a master craftsman with wood, having built splendid furniture and almost all the cabinets in his house. He was not just a carpenter – he was a master cabinet maker. I helped and observed Jim as he built an eleven foot wooden dinghy in his double garage which was full of every type of equipment invented for working with wood. Then I built an identical dinghy right there in his shop. It was a sleek little row boat with sailing capabilities. We built the boats from very detailed plans – not pre-cut kits. I promptly bought a trailer from Home Depot and launched my craft in Aransas Bay. Wonderful!

Then I ordered the plans for a ten foot dinghy of a different design and built that boat in my own garage. That dinghy immediately sold for $1200. It cost about $400 to construct and took me about 60 hours or so. So I built two more dinghys and with the profits ordered the plans for an eighteen foot sloop and over the next six months built a sleek beautiful sailboat. I built an 18 foot boat in a standard 20 foot garage. I hand-laid fiberglass over the entire boat and learned to expertly paint with marine quality paints so there was not a single brush mark. The surface was as smooth as glass. I named my sailboat SIMPLY because that is how I lived and sailed. People pointed at my boat from their $200,000 yachts and shouted admiration and asked me what kind of boat it was. I was more proud of that boat than they were of theirs, I think. SIMPLY cost about $6000 to build.

Meanwhile I continued to deliberately look for and meet veterans, especially anyone who seemed to be in dire straits. One of these was named Steve Brady, known as "Psycho Steve" in the local boatyards where he had worked, been fired, worked somewhere else, stabbed someone with a screwdriver, been fired, and so on. Steve and I became buddies. He had been with the 173rd Airborne during their ill-fated attempt at parachuting into the jungles of Vietnam. He had one eye almost poked out when he landed in a dense triple-canopy forest and hung there in his parachute straps for two days before he was pulled out. One eye still looked different and he could not see well. Steve had never applied for disability benefits. Like most of us macho guys, he just coped and did not complain. He did not realize that I recognized signs that maybe he was a speed freak. Meth.

I saw Psycho Steve one day barely able to walk along the road and stopped to help. He had lost thirty or forty pounds from his already slim physique. He was homeless, anemic, and when I took his pulse, I correctly diagnosed cardiac insufficiency. I immediately took Steve up to the San Antonio VA Hospital. While he was recuperating from triple bypass heart surgery a social worker had him sign up for disability. He was released after less than a week, given medications for a month, given an appointment for follow-up <u>six months later,</u> and told he could re-order his meds through the mail. He did not even have a mailing address in Rockport...had been staying with various low-life friends here and there for several years. He was a mess. Drank whiskey of any brand, somehow obtained dozens of asthma inhalers from the Austin VA outpatient clinic, and blew through his initial disability check in a few months. He was rated at 100 percent disabled and gave me credit for saving his life and helping him obtain benefits. I was not sure he would survive very long. He should have been getting some sort of disability for his service-connected loss of vision from the day he was released from the Army in 1969. The VA never gave out a damn thing until a veteran jumped through bureaucratic hoops. It is still that way today.

I started taking Steve to the Austin outpatient clinic because his "home" address was Smithville, about forty miles east of Austin. He sometimes stayed with his sister there. I helped him rent a post office box in Rockport so she could relay communications from the VA. The clinic in Austin was very well run, possibly because of the proximity to the State Capitol, and possibly because some bigwigs in government were veterans. Either way, Steve often showed up in Rockport and we hung out and occasionally got drunk or stoned together. Hey, if you want to help such people, you have to gain some sort of acceptance into their lifestyle. A rationalization, I know.

As Steve's health deteriorated and his drug and alcohol use gradually pulled him down, he increasingly turned to me for help. He finally stepped in front of a bus and was killed outside the Austin VA outpatient clinic. I had done what I could. He was incorrigible. I had personally driven him up for his last appointment and dropped him off, thinking his sister would come and pick him up. No such luck for Psycho Steve. As was the case for many of us, Steve sometimes had to wait an inordinately long time making follow-up appointments. I did not know how wide-spread that situation was until years later.

The tragic life and death of Steve was the most extreme example of the hardships some Vietnam vets experienced. There were two other veterans I helped during my ten years in

Rockport. One was Glen L., whose last name I omit for the sake of his family. He had served with the 101st Airborne and had definitely been involved in serious combat. Glen lived on a derelict sailboat in the marina. In the five years I counseled him and took him for appointments the boat never moved. I took him out several times on SIMPLY; but I found him to be uninteresting, vulgar, sometimes threatening, and mildly repellent. He was just an asshole. Never did a single thing in his degenerate life for anyone but himself. He had finagled some sort of disability out of the VA and got a check from Social Security for a phony back problem. He had a doctor at the Corpus Christi outpatient clinic and that's where I ferried him for appointments. He was rude at the reception desk, disrespectful toward the medical personnel, and yet somehow received pain pills and high blood pressure medication.

I hope it has improved by now, but in 2002 when I first took Glen to the Corpus Christi outpatient clinic, all the patients were given appointments at 0800. Every conversation at the reception desk was begun in Spanish. Everybody showed up and crowded at the door then got appointments at various times throughout the day. It reminded me of a bus station in Mexico. People crowded each other, elbow to elbow and waited for the ticket window to open, then jostled, shouted, and pushed their way to the front. There were screaming kids, sleeping grandparents, and frowning relatives jammed into the reception area. I could not stay long. I went for a walk, ate at a restaurant, strolled the beach, or sat at a city park talking with the homeless. Anything to not have to witness the spectacle of the Corpus Christi outpatient clinic. I must say that the VA has gone through a dramatic improvement in many ways since then...hopefully including Corpus Christi.

I probably took Glen over there five or six times in a three year period. Occasionally he had to go to the San Antonio VA Hospital, and the scene there was only marginally better, at least during that time period. It seemed all the clerks at every desk usually spoke Spanish. I did not mind this, being fluent and having generally enjoyed a good relationship with that culture. Glen, however, hated the "Mezkins" (his pronunciation) though, and when he approached a clerk sometimes asked arrogantly, "you speakee the English?" if they had been speaking Spanish to the previous patient. Like I said, an asshole. So he was treated in the manner in which he treated them. I must admit I lost track of Glen and heard he had died of alcohol toxicity or overdose on pain pills...probably both. Glen had understandable difficulty making appointments at times, and I can understand why.

Then there was "Yucatan Dan." Dan had been in the Army during the early Sixties – too soon to have gone to Vietnam. He had trained as a sniper and been a marksmanship instructor during his time in the Army. Dan was the opposite of Glen in every respect: intelligent, humorous, kind, and a lot of fun to hang out with. He had been some sort of engineer with NASA after the Army, was well-educated, and had sailed large sailboats across the Atlantic several times, having a Captain's license and a business delivering boats for the wealthy. We got along very well and shared some stories we seldom told anyone else. I told him of growing marijuana in Columbia and he told of once bringing a load of cocaine from Barranquia, on the north coast of Columbia to Ft. Lauderdale in the early 1990's. I joked that maybe I had used some of that product.

As nice as he was though, Dan also had a lot of trouble waiting for appointments at the VA in San Antonio. I took him up there from Rockport – 160 miles – many times and waited and waited for him to be seen by a doctor, or most often by a Physician's Assistant. He was well into his sixties and had serious medical problems with heart, liver, and spleen. He had more tolerance of the wait times that I did. I knew that a patient of his age with his problems would not have to wait so long at regular civilian hospitals. Dan died of untreated and unrecognized pancreatic cancer in 2008. He had given up on the VA and used Medicare and private insurance when he was waiting for an appointment for abdominal pain, vomiting, weight loss, and various severe symptoms. I became more angry over the lack of care from the VA than he did. We waited too long before seeking competent medical help. Then I encountered more evidence of apathy and incompetence.

The only time I had sought help at any VA facility was in 1992, when I had entered the Miami hospital for almost six months. During that stay, I received dental treatments for the missing molars from the explosion in 1969. Several crowns were inserted and a partial plate was produced for my missing upper teeth. The partial plate never fit well, and two of the crowns fell out within months. Ten years later in Rockport, a competent local dentist said he had never seen such shoddy work and the partial plate was composed of materials no longer in use. Upon hearing my story of how I lost the teeth, Dr. Jeremy Mills, DDS., manufactured upper and lower partial plates and somehow charged the VA for the work. I was unaware such a possibility existed. Evidence began to build up in my mind of incompetence at VA facilities in addition to long wait times for appointments.

In my excessive anger and impatience towards authorities in general and the Veteran's Affairs hospital system especially, I made the first of several serious mistakes. I made an appointment with the Patient Advocate, an Hispanic woman, at the San Antonio VA. When I mentioned long wait times she became immediately defensive and definitely hostile. Then I made the huge mistake of mentioning that I was thankful I spoke Spanish, since that seemed to be the primary language spoken at almost every desk at the Corpus Christi and San Antonio facilities. Whoa! That pissed her off. She went on an absolute rant over the fact that "we got here first...we're bilingual and you gringos aren't...etc." Yes, she used the derogatory term "gringo" to my face. I said that term led to "una lucha" (a fight) when I was growing up. That really pissed her off. I compounded and multiplied my errors by sending several letters implying she had used racial epithets and that "we White men" are sick and tired of being treated disrespectfully by minorities, and that we are the majority in this country and (biggest mistake of all) that I knew some pissed off "White" veterans who are "locked and loaded" for the coming race wars. Oh shit! That statement went further than I expected and was "cherry-picked" out of <u>one</u> letter I sent <u>one</u> time to the head director of the San Antonio VA hospital. I should have known. The Director was also Hispanic.

A few weeks later my home in Rockport was assaulted by an armed Federal Agent accompanied by two local deputy sheriffs. No knock. No warrant. They burst into my garage making a lot of noise because the makeshift double doors fitted poorly. I exited my house and asked casually, "what the hell, fellas?" I thought they had the wrong house. My non-threatening posture caused them to relax somewhat. They said they were investigating a threatening letter I had sent. I explained I was just protesting long wait times and that maybe the Hispanic Patient Advocate had over reacted. They did not search my person or my house, and seemed satisfied I posed no immediate danger. One of the deputies agreed that the wait times for appointments were too long because his brother was a veteran and had a similar complaint.

Later I got pissed off about the whole mess and wrote to the Inspector General of the whole VA system in Washington, D.C. Another big mistake! When I got no response, I wrote to several Congressional Representatives and generally made a nuisance of myself, drawing more suspicions and negative attention from authorities. I had stirred up a hornet's nest. The three words "locked and loaded" became the only aspect of my messages and letters anybody noticed and I was put in a special category within the entire VA system. I received the scary "psychiatric profile" tab in my chart which was the first thing anyone read in all future appointments in the whole system. That profile still exists today, eighteen years later and there is nothing I can ever do or say to eliminate it, despite the fact that I have been polite, non-threatening, congenial, and even humorous towards all VA employees ever since. Several later psychologists and at least one psychiatrist have unsuccessfully attempted to have it removed. There is definitely a "shit list" in the VA and God help you if you get on it.

For several reasons, I decided to leave Rockport. For instance: Wells Fargo held the mortgage on my house and had issued me a credit card with a limit of $20,000, most of which I had used repairing the house after several storms in 2008 and 2009. That wealthy banking institution had been receiving my disability check for about ten years. Then Wells Fargo, which did not need a government bail-out when many other banks did, raised the interest rate on my credit card from seven percent to eleven percent. I switched my VA check to be sent to another bank. I had always paid on time, always more than the minimum, and had never been late with the house payment or the credit card. The house was a mess with mold, a roof which still needed repairs, and other problems I could not afford. I decided to renege on the whole mess and walk away...to leave Rockport and maybe hit the road again and live on the fringe of society.

I contacted a lawyer who told me the credit card was an unsecured loan and Wells Fargo would never be able to recoup their losses if I skipped out. They could ruin my credit. They would foreclose on the house. They could sic various types of enforcers and collection agencies on me; but they could never obtain a grasp on either of my sources of income: VA disability and Social Security checks. I was "small potatoes" in the world of debtors.

There was $7000 left on the credit card, so I cashed it out and bought a beautiful, slightly used 2006 Triumph America motorcycle and moved to Temple Texas. Several veterans had told me the VA hospital in Temple was one of the best, and I would be closer to my Brother and Sister in Dallas. I sold, gave to Goodwill, or left a household of stuff and just drove off. I had already sold SIMPLY for $3500.

I intended to get one final prognosis on my general state of health and the status of my liver regarding the Hep C virus, then just live as long as possible free and clear of American society. Just ride this old horse until it drops! This was just after the first election of the half-white Muslim sympathizer, b. h. obama. (lack of capitalization deliberate!) Enough said.

I rented an apartment near the local VFW chapter and began volunteering there. I sought to be admitted as a volunteer at the Temple VA hospital and, to my surprise, was accepted. In the orientation program we were told that we were members of the hospital staff and would abide by all the rules and regulations of all the regular employees. We would recognize and greet all other personnel when we passed them in the hallways. We would wear a plainly visible name tag on neat, clean clothing. We would conduct ourselves with a friendly and helpful attitude in all our duties.

My job, which seemed minor to begin with but which I immediately realized was very helpful, was to pass out a packet of toiletries to patients who had been admitted the day before and had shown up with no expectation of staying. I was happy and felt useful when I showed up at a patient's room in the morning just when they were wondering how to brush their teeth and comb their hair. The kits were provided by various volunteer agencies and included soap, shampoo, toothbrush and toothpaste, and sometimes hair rinse and conditioner for female veterans. I very much enjoyed this volunteer work. It required from two to three hours a day. I got along with the other volunteers when we met before going out on our duties.

In Temple Texas, I got my first experience with a truly segregated city with regards to Black and White. There were two high schools, one Black and one White. The personnel in the hospital were predominately Black. The only Negroes (I use the world-wide accepted and genetically correct designation of their race) I had known had been in the Army and those soldiers had been MEN, just like every other man. When relating with my driver in Cu Chi, Private Tolbert, we got alone great, both being wise-ass trouble makers who did not fit in with regulations. We were friends. I respected big Edwards, my machine gunner when I was his Platoon Leader. I respected and liked him as much as any man I had ever met. My Father had been a jazz guitarist and idolized Louie Armstrong and the band leader and composer, Duke Ellington. My parents thought it was magnificent when the Negro entertainer and songstress, Pearl Bailey, was appointed as the United States Ambassador to the United Nations General Assembly. I was raised in a Jewish household and there are no people less racist or discriminatory than the Jews.

The Black people of Temple, Texas were a shock to me. Several of the (Black) ward clerks glared at me when I made my rounds to deliver the packets of toiletries. One clerk arrogantly asked me to show him what I was carrying in a small backpack, which held ten or twelve kits of items for the recently admitted patients. I greeted him every day with a friendly "good morning." He usually just bent to his work and said nothing. The vast majority of the predominately Black staff were polite and returned my greeting each morning with good will and respect. A few Black employees expressed contempt, ignored me, and did not say one word to me. This situation began to get on my nerves. I counseled myself toward tolerance. I rehearsed being first to be polite. I smiled and said "good morning" like a new mantra every single day. Some responses still ruffled my feathers.

One young man really got to me. He wheeled patients from their room to various other departments in the hospital. I passed him at least once every day. He not only failed to respond to my greeting, he refused to ever even <u>look</u> at me. This young "light-complected" Black man had one of the simplest jobs in the hospital. How hard could it be to take a patient in a wheelchair to another part of the building? I tried several tactics, sometimes accompanied with a humorous approach, to get him to at least acknowledge me as a human being. He would not look at me. He would say nothing to me. He wore his name tag upside down on his belt instead of visible on a ribbon around his neck so I could not easily see his name. We were clearly told how to wear our name tags. He was the only one who did not.

The day come when we were together in an elevator. I said, "excuse me. May I ask your name?" He replied with an exasperated sigh without looking at me, "William." "William what?" "Peak. William Peak," he said in an angry tone after a pause while the doors opened. He left without looking back. That did it. I was pissed. What the hell?

I went to speak to his supervisor, another Black man. He tolerated my explanation while glancing around the small room disinterestedly like he had better things to do. I became more than merely pissed off. I became determined. What if the situation were reversed? How would a Black man with any degree of self respect respond to such treatment? Why should I allow such a thing and not report this disrespectful and racist behavior? I tried to make an appointment with the Director of the whole hospital. He was never available so I made a proper appointment with the Human Resources Director. I met another disinterested Black man who barely listened to me and dismissed my story completely and did nothing about it. William Peak continued as before.

I discussed this situation with several of my veteran friends at the apartment complex where I lived. They all agreed that they had seen more or less the same attitude from many Black employees at that hospital. One friend told me he had been denied a job there and thought it was because he was White.

This all took place at a time when the phrase "women and minorities" was constantly attached to many news stories and commentaries on TV. A local bank advertised giving small business loans to "women and minorities." They may as well have advertised "White men need not apply." I became more and more pissed off. No amount of meditation, affirmations, or attempts at anger management techniques ameliorated the insult. That is what it was. That phrase was a direct insult to White men in America. Numerically speaking, the totality of "women and minorities" represented at least <u>seventy percent of the population of this country!</u> What the hell? White men were apparently the most disregarded, disrespected, and ignorantly universally blamed for all the complaints and maladies of the majority of people in the United States of America. I began to refer to this country as The Disunited States of Victims. Only White men could never claim to be victims of discrimination. Only White men had no spokesperson standing up for us. Every other separate group had its lobbyists, lawyers, and slogans of victimhood.

During my years of counseling, one piece of worthwhile advice I had received that seemed relevant was to just leave a situation that was leading to a stress reaction. If I was unable to process a scene toward internal acceptance, just leave. One final insult was the proverbial last straw that disrupted the whole caravan.

In addition to being a volunteer, I was also a patient at the Temple VA. I was in the blood lab being attended to by a young Black man who was going to draw several vials of blood. I had asked him to please not use the largest vein at the elbow since I had numerous veins that could be used and that largest vein had been damaged by a lab technician in the past. I have large veins due to a slender physique that has been extensively exercised. A young Black woman who was also a technician in the lab came over and said, "Whoa! Don' see vein like dat on a White boy ver' often." I did not respond. The man then deliberately jabbed the largest vein, penetrating through both walls of the vein into the tendon beneath. He glared at me arrogantly as he withdrew the needle a bit to draw blood. That was the final insult I would tolerate from the Temple VA hospital. I resolved to leave Temple and never again seek any medical help from the VA.

Having lived on both coasts of the US, both coasts of Florida, and the Gulf coast of Texas, I began to long for beaches, seagulls, and salt water. Galveston was a very interesting city with a diverse history and I had never been there, so I moved to that historic city. One bumper sticker I had seen read: Galveston Island – near Texas. That sounded good to me. Having continued to live very simply, my cash savings approached $10,000. Moving was no problem. Since I owned a motorcycle I thought it was important to sign in at the Galveston VA outpatient, just in case medical care became necessary. When my file was transferred I was in for a dark surprise.

The clerk opened my file, saw the "psychiatric profile" tab and called security immediately. The VA cop frisked me thoroughly before I was allowed to see any medical staff. What a shocker! I requested to see a mental health counselor and met Dr. Daryl Turner, one of the nicest, genuinely good men I had ever met. After hearing my story of why there was such a notice in my file, Dr. Turner understood and said he had heard the same story from many veterans complaining about long wait times and disrespect from Black employees, especially at Temple. He further related attending briefings and meetings at the Houston VA hospital and realizing he was the only White American man present out of a total of twenty personnel. Then he referred me to a social worker to see about removing that notice from my chart since I had never done anything remotely dangerous or threatening.

Ms. Yarlborogh, an experienced social worker, showed me a copy of one of several letters I had supposedly written. The letters were typewritten. I had written all my letters longhand, not having a typewriter or a printer for my computer. She said she would look into it. Nothing happened. I was still frisked by a polite, somewhat embarrassed cop every time I entered that Galveston outpatient clinic during the next three years. When I had to go to the Houston hospital for an appointment, I had to immediately report to the police then wear a name tag with "vistor" on it. Yes, someone was so uneducated they could not even spell "visitor" on a name tag. It was humiliating. I was a patient, not a "vistor." I was also frisked at the Houston hospital. They said they were "just following orders," stated with the same tone as the Nazis said that phrase at the Nuremberg trials in the late 1940's. Enough said.

A letter was forwarded to me in Galveston informing me to report for a re-exam of my primary disability of PTSD. Oh shit! Although Dr. Turner and my Psychiatrist, Dr. Nancy Rubio, both told me that in their combined twenty years of counseling veterans, they had never heard of anyone being reduced from 100 percent for PTSD after eighteen years of continuously maintaining that level of disability. I knew they were wrong. I was fucked. The exam was set in Temple, but since I had moved it was over a year later before the exam took place in Houston.

Having rented an apartment in an apparently gated complex, it was soon apparent that most of the residents were classified as "Section 8," meaning their rent was subsidized and they were probably all receiving welfare, food stamps, etc. My truck, an old Chevy S-10 with almost 200,00 miles on it was broken into several times during the first month I was there. I caught a Black woman deliberately leading her dog close to my motorcycle and allowing it to piss on my bike. I knew better than to confront her at that point. I walked out on a one-year lease after two months.

I modified my little Chevy to make a mini-camper in the bed and started camping out at the State Park. I traveled and camped out at a dozen State Parks during the year of waiting for my exam, occasionally returning to Galveston to check my mail at a P. O. Box. Being a disabled veteran I was allowed free day use at the Texas State Parks, where I could shower without checking in for a campsite. Most of them even had hot water. Nice. I always made a donation or bought a tee shirt if there was a store at the Park.

The VA system always sent a letter notifying a veteran of an upcoming appointment. This did not happen in my case. I was camping out in west Texas and just happened to be in a restaurant eating and recharging my phone on a Friday when someone from the Houston VA called to inform me to show up for a Psychiatric exam the following Monday. The notification letter showed up about a week later and was postmarked <u>after</u> the date of the exam. If I had missed that exam, the VA could have canceled all five of my service-connected physical disabilities and my rating for PTSD. I would have had to start the lengthy process all over again. True.

The exam consisted of a young psychologist, a 23 year old woman, asking me ten standard questions in ten minutes. Example: can you count backward by sevens from one hundred. Another one: I am going to give you three words to remember-dog, yellow, rose. Then five minutes later she asked if I could remember the three words. I did not pretend either question was difficult, thinking more profound questions would ensue. The famous eight questions to determine if a soldier had combat-related PTSD were: were you in ground combat; did you fire at the enemy; were you subjected to mortar or rocket fire; did you see your friends shot or killed; do you have dreams about the war; are there any current sounds or smells that cause you to remember the war; do you have disturbed sleeping patterns; were you a POW. Those were examples, not all of them precisely remembered. The only question I answered "no" to was if I had been a POW.

It was obvious from my scars and record that I had probably suffered Traumatic Brain Injury, had several instances of concussion from explosions nearby, and had a certain type of shrapnel wound referred to as "through and through" penetration where shrapnel had entered, passed through my body, then exited. There was nothing like these questions in the re-exam in

2013. And that was it. Ten minutes of standardized questions by a novice psychologist.

During four months of waiting for the decision I traveled and lived very simply, visiting State Parks all across Texas. When the expected news came it was no surprise. My disability for PTSD was reduced to 50%. My income dropped from over $2800 per month to $900. As usual in the VA system, one had to file an appeal which would require literally years to be resolved. Perhaps the Veterans' Affairs establishment hoped we would die off while waiting. Traveling back to Galveston, I worked at various low-paying construction jobs, surprising men half my age at my ability to keep up with them.

The Psychologist and Psychiatrist at the Galveston outpatient clinic were contrite at the news and admitted they had been wrong. That was no consolation to me. The appeal would take almost two years to be resolved. When I finally received a letter from the VA reversing their earlier decision, both counselors said they had never seen an admission as was clearly disclosed in the letter of admission of a mistake. I quote directly: "clear and unmistakable errors that are undebatable, so that reasonable minds could only conclude that the previous decision was fatally flawed at the time it was made." A check for reimbursement hit my bank account for $47,252. I had won the waiting game. Let this be a lesson for all others in a similar situation. **Do not give up!**

I bought a slightly used deluxe twenty-one-foot travel trailer and a two-year-old Chevrolet pickup to tow it with and moved to the Piney Woods of east Texas where I reside today. The plan to help other veterans is still active in my heart and my mind. I provide various levels of "Help Care" to several deserving older vets and will continue to do so. It is not just a job. It is my mission.

THE END – January 10, 2018

CPSIA information can be obtained
at www.ICGtesting.com
Printed in the USA
BVHW090732301021
620353BV00015B/434